THE UNIVERSITY OF LIVERP(

'DNE'   2

L.

- APR 2007

11am

Reclaiming the Streets

Power fortifies itself not just by what it destroys, but also by what it creates. Not just by what it takes, but by what it gives

Arundhati Roy

Reclaiming the Streets

Surveillance, social control and the city

Roy Coleman

WILLAN
PUBLISHING

Published by

Willan Publishing
Culmcott House
Mill Street, Uffculme
Cullompton, Devon
EX15 3AT, UK
Tel: +44(0)1884 840337
Fax: +44(0)1884 840251
e-mail: info@willanpublishing.co.uk
website: www.willanpublishing.co.uk

Published simultaneously in the USA and Canada by

Willan Publishing
c/o ISBS, 920 NE 58th Ave, Suite 300
Portland, Oregon 97213-3786, USA
Tel: +001(0)503 287 3093
Fax: +001(0)503 280 8832
e-mail: info@isbs.com
website: www.isbs.com

First published 2004

ISBN 1-84392-077-8 Hardback

British Library Cataloguing-in-Publication Data

A catalogue record for this book is available from the British Library

Typeset by GCS, Leighton Buzzard, Bedfordshire
Project managed by Deer Park Productions, Tavistock, Devon
Printed and bound by T.J. International Ltd, Trecerus Industrial Estate, Padstow, Cornwall

Contents

Acknowledgements   *ix*

1 Introduction: 'The friendly eye in the sky'   **1**
The new orthodoxy in the social control of the streets   4
Interpreting contemporary social control   6
Rationale and organisation of the book   8

**2 The disappearing state: social control, social order
and the state**   **13**
Liberal and functionalist theories of social control   15
Social reaction and neo-Marxist theories of social control   17
Neo-Foucauldian perspectives on social control   20
Social control and 'risk'   23
Governmentality: social control and power beyond the state   26
Conclusion   30

**3 Rediscovering the state: understanding camera
surveillance as a social ordering practice**   **33**
Theoretical prologue: the state in motion   35
Street camera surveillance and social ordering: investigating
    the social control agents within a neoliberal state   50
Conclusion   62

4 The neoliberal city and social control   **65**
Neoliberal states and spaces   67
Neoliberal order   71

Neoliberal discourse and social order in the contemporary
  British city 75
Street reclamation and remoralisation 79
Conclusion 82

5 **From the dockyards to the Disney store: the historical
  trajectory of social control in Liverpool** 87
Morality and policing social boundaries in the
  nineteenth century city 89
Political economy in Liverpool from the early
  nineteenth century to the 1980s 91
Civilising the streets: social control in Liverpool from
  the late eighteenth century to the 1930s 94
Policing and social control in Liverpool: 1945 to the 1980s 101
Social control of the streets in Liverpool from the 1980s 103
Recivilising the streets (again): a social control
  from the 1990s 107
Conclusion 114

6 **State, partnership and power: excavating neoliberal
  rule in the city** 117
Studying up the social and political hierarchy 118
Orchestrating partnership 119
'Policing' and partnership 121
Responsible partners and the responsibilisation process 127
Getting the message across: re-imaging and the local press 129
Leadership: who runs the city? 132
The politics of attraction 136
Spatialisation, city visions and street reclamation 141
Conclusion 149

7 **Reclaiming the streets: the techniques and norms of
  contemporary social control** 153
Street camera surveillance and renaissance in Liverpool 155
Targeting the cameras: the proper objects of power 172
A seamless web of control? Tensions within the neoliberal
  state 190
Conclusion 212

8 **Conclusion: visualising the neoliberal city** 218
Cameras and the landscape of risk 222
Cameras and the hidden landscape 226
Cameras and the unequal landscape 229

'The World in One City'?   233
Challenging the politics of vision?   236
Rethinking 'crime prevention' in the city   239

Appendix: interviewees   **245**

References   *246*
Index   *263*

Acknowledgements

I would like to say thank you to friends and family who have been supportive during the development and writing of this book. These people are Dave Whyte, Jonny Burnett, Gary Coleman, Helen Jones, Rachel Palmen, Pam Leng, Ben and Tina Favier, Pete Gill and Elizabeth and George Coleman. Thanks to Victoria Morgan for her proofreading, patience and 'outsider' input.

Kevin Stenson and Gordon Hughes have provided valuable comments upon the arguments in this book. Their input was appreciated.

Special thanks to Steve Tombs for reading various chapters and for his comradeship, comments and comma placement.

Lastly and most importantly, I want to thank my friend and colleague, Joe Sim, for his unwavering support, inspiration and critical insights at every stage during the writing of this book.

All errors belong to me.

This book is for my Mum, Dad and my Brother.

Chapter 1

Introduction: 'The friendly eye in the sky'

LIVERPOOL, England – it was just before 3 P.M. when the call came crackling over the walkie-talkie in the control center: four young males walking through the downtown shopping area, behaving suspiciously. 'There we go', the guard said, staring at a crystal clear picture of four youths as they swaggered down the street, stealing apples from street vendors, unaware they were being watched intently … The main concern of the guards on duty … was tracking the movements of known shoplifters, prostitutes and muggers. For 20 minutes the cameras followed the four young men. Several times, one of the men would enter a store, while the others stood outside as if standing watch. The guards in the control room watched carefully for any signs of stealing [and] on this afternoon radioed the police. Then as the young men rounded a corner, they ran into a waiting police officer. He took down their names and asked by radio if arrests warrants were outstanding on any of them. He seemed to give them a bit of a chewing out, and then sent them on their way. They trudged away from the downtown area, out of sight of the cameras, a bit less swagger in their step (*New York Times International* 11 March 1995: 'They're capturing suspects on candid camera').

The pulp-fiction narrative in the above quotation constructs a view of contemporary camera surveillance in Liverpool as an unproblematic surveyor of the public realm – targeting the wrongdoer, trapping and removing the villain and petty criminal so that 'people feel safer on downtown streets, even at night' (ibid.). All this, the article reports, facilitates wider changes in Liverpool - 'a gritty, industrial port city' that 'has worked hard to revive and clean up its downtown' into a 'gleaming new shopping center'. The article hints at, though never places as its central concern, the wider socioeconomic motivation for the camera network. This motivation is submerged under a common-sense fable propagated by proponents of street cameras that declares 'we know who the reprobates are and reprobates will be caught out'. The author of the article, like some criminologists, does not transgress the official discourse that depicts urban surveillance cameras as 'friendly eyes in the sky' and 'useful' crime reduction tools that may, or then again may not, 'work' in the prevention and detection of crime (see NACRO 2002). Purely technical questions of whether or how camera surveillance can 'work' do not have a place in this book. This is because such questions obscure a wider sociological investigation into the nature of social control, its relationship to state power and articulation and exercise by social forces at the heart of contemporary urban restructuring. In looking beyond 'crime prevention' and casting aside the 'what works' paradigm, this book examines a strategy of power that has as its target the social control of the streets. These forms of control that are organised around mass camera surveillance will be understood as political strategies that possess both technical *and* normative characteristics. As the latest trope in the pursuit of urban order, the 'role' of visual surveillance is understood to be more than a tool of crime prevention (Bannister *et al.* 1998; Norris and Armstrong 1999; Coleman 2003a) and instead is explored as both a symbol of political and economic power and a component in an ideological offensive to reclaim the streets in the name of a desired sociospatial order.

Not unexpectedly, media narratives such as the one in the opening quotation take the uses and targets of closed circuit television (CCTV) as uncomplicated and self-evident. Rarely do accounts of street surveillance question the targeting process and get behind the media-savvy imagery that obscures rather than facilitates an understanding of mass camera surveillance and the kind of society that it both reflects and is helping to reproduce. Moreover, the development of camera networks in the UK is taking place within an ideologically vociferous and politicised urban restructuring programme that is profoundly affecting the manner in which urban space is being thought through and experienced. Taking this cue, this book is about social control, the city and the state and how the inter-relationships between these domains contribute to the construction and reproduction of social order. It is the agents and agencies charged with articulating the means and ends of social control in the streets that are of concern here.

With the advent of mass camera surveillance it has become common to observe that the citizenry of the UK have become the most watched, catalogued and categorised people in the advanced world, and all with little public debate or opposition. Despite the lack of any democratic control of the visual surveillance net, there has been little critical research that understands CCTV within a broader appreciation of the social relations out of which it is growing and being consolidated. In other words, while many studies have focused narrowly on the intractable debates of whether 'CCTV affects crime', little has been written that questions 'why have CCTV at all'? This line of inquiry is particularly relevant given the growing acknowledgement that there 'is little substantive research evidence to suggest that CCTV works' (NACRO 2002: 6). Clearly, there is a need to analyse the political and cultural credence of CCTV and critically expose the social forces driving and shaping this technology for purposes and ends that cannot simply be taken as given from crime prevention rhetoric. Instead, this technology needs to be placed as part of a set of 'social ordering practices' (Lacey 1994) developed within particular social relations and prevailing philosophies and strategies of urban governance. This raises further questions concerning the relationship between surveillance, power and sociospatial control that are central to this book. Who defines the rationale and uses of surveillance cameras? What kinds of behaviours and activities does the use of cameras target and censure? What behaviours do the cameras ignore? Conversely, and of equal importance, what behaviours do cameras promote and legitimate? In asking these questions the book takes as its subject the changing nature of, and inter-relationships between, social control, the state and the cityscape.

In pursuing such questions, this book casts its gaze upwards to the powerful and to their perceptions of, and desires for, an 'orderly city'. Order maintenance in advanced capitalist cities is being profoundly refigured under a process of neoliberalisation, and camera networks play an uneven and sometimes contradictory role in the realisation of that order. 'Order' itself is not the result of chance or chaos – though these phenomena have a place – but is underpinned by powerful and idealised visions for urban public space that have been developing under a rightward political shift in the closing decades of the twentieth century and which seem only to have been intensified after the attacks in New York on 11 September 2001 (Mitchell 2003). In the following pages the focus is very much on the political processes shaping the uses of surveillance over and above a consideration of the procedural capability of cameras. It is the political-moral nature of social control that will be examined, as this allows a wider inquiry of 'the powerful' within the matrix of neoliberal statecraft and governing in the contemporary city.

The book explores how neoliberal statecraft is developing through the notion of 'partnership' and how such partnership forms are implicated in the development of social control practices deemed appropriate for the contemporary city centre. As a watchword of current neoliberal thinking, the form and functioning of 'partnership' rule are reconfiguring meanings and materialisations of 'public'/'private' and 'state'/'market' distinctions and in doing so are reconstituting the state form itself. The trajectory of these processes is shaped and filtered through particular politico-economic and sociocultural landscapes at the local level that highlight continuities and discontinuities between different locations (MacLeod 2002). Certainly, not all city regions across the globe are embracing camera networks in the same way and to the same extent as the UK. However, it is arguable that the powerful vernacular that underpins the camera network examined in this book emerges out of, and reinforces, a trans-local neoliberalisation process that is articulated by an increasingly powerful group of new primary definers who are shaping the urban political landscape, and whose project of urban reclamation and 'order in the streets' is redefining the meanings and uses attached to public spaces (Coleman and Sim 2000, 1998).

The new orthodoxy in the social control of the streets

The notion of 'reclaiming the streets' from the 'yobs', petty thieves, drunks, beggars and illicit traders assumes a strategic ideological position within the processes shaping the institutional terrain of urban governance (Coleman 2003b). These processes have themselves been taking place alongside an intensified politicisation of law and order, underway since the early 1980s, and are central to the rationales of both right and left political agendas which have been concerned to deregulate the market economies (Hay 1996) while increasing control and regulation in the social sphere (Gamble 1988; Elliott 1996). Since 1994 and the appearance of the first major open street or public CCTV systems, official discourses on camera surveillance continue to proffer the view that the technology provides policing agencies with an effective tool in the fight against crime and a harbour of public safety (Home Office 1994).[1] In Liverpool and elsewhere, cameras are depicted as neutral observers in the fight against crime and social incivility; a technical fix for an unease about urban disorder and degeneration. During the 1990s politicians, police, security industry pundits and media personnel all contributed to a largely uncritical discourse on the need for, and unproblematic effectiveness of, CCTV systems. From 1994 Liverpool city centre and surrounding areas have been wired up to a CCTV network with the aid of public and private financing. In 1998, the legislative framework of the Crime and Disorder Act provided the means for the extension and formalisation of the network. Launched in 1994, the privately monitored 20-camera city-centre system was extended in 2003 to 240 cameras through a £1.7 million injection of government money under the Crime Reduction Programme (Citysafe 2000). An approximate total of £5.2 million capital funding has been spent since June 1994 on street camera surveillance in Liverpool city centre. This does not include the cocktails of funding used to place cameras in schools, railway stations, on buses and in taxicabs in the city. With each street camera tagged at £15,000, the costs in terms of revenue funding for maintaining the system are not known but are met by the private sector and the city council. The long-term aim of this expansion is the integration of comparable CCTV systems – such as those installed on public transport – that can be linked to a master control room. Thus it is not only the city centre that can be monitored but also the outlying areas of Kensington, Old Swan and Dingle, as well as links provided to cameras in stores, public houses and nightclubs (*Daily Post* 22 August 2000: '£1.5m safety zone for city'). This latest surveillance expansion in the city centre incorporates 'revolutionary talking cameras' so the 'operators will be able to shout at would-be attackers to warn them they are being filmed' (*Liverpool Echo* 24 March 2001: 'Cameras set to cut crime').

In the UK, local-level developments concerning CCTV have been driven by successive government funding and accompanied by ministerial rhetoric referring to the problem of blighted streets and 'yob cultures' underpinned by a desire for disciplinary, back-to-basics style solutions. Under John Major's Conservative administration and then New Labour, CCTV has played a key role in crime control policy. Between 1994 and 1999, £38.5 million was dispensed from the Home Office with an estimated £51 million from the private sector to establish CCTV systems (*Hansard*, written answers 2 November 1999: col. 112). Under New Labour the 'roll-out' of social surveillance continued with the allocation of £170 million of Home Office funds to extend CCTV by 40,000 extra cameras in 1999 (Home Office 1999). Between 1992 and 2002 it is estimated that over a quarter of a billion pounds of mostly public money was spent on camera networks with upwards of three billion for the same period when maintenance costs are included (McCahill and Norris 2002). The competitive bidding process for camera money involves the building of local partnerships between 'responsible authorities' that have knowledge of local crime problems. This has promoted private sector expertise in the development and financing of camera schemes, crime prevention strategies and in the process of urban governance more generally (Coleman *et al.* 2002). As it stands today, the UK is the largest market for CCTV in Europe (Graham 2000: 45) and accounts for one-fifth of all CCTV cameras worldwide (*The Independent* 12 January 2004: 'Big brother Britain, 2004').

The centrality of CCTV to the mentality and thinking within governmental, corporate and media circles signals, 'not simply ... attempts to govern crime and criminals' but attempts to construct a form of 'government through crime' (Stenson 2001: 22). There is a need to deconstruct this governing process and explore the definitional trajectory relating to how particular behaviours and activities receive sustained attention and ideological significance. In other words, what *kinds* of crime and images of disorder are cities being governed through? In this context, the salience of CCTV images of street crime and other forms of disorderly conduct has come to the fore of a governing process that constructs and amplifies particular risk messages. The book explores the locally powerful articulation of risk, danger, harm and threat that, within a city attempting to reinvent itself, highlights a series of political processes signifying the identification and fear of 'the degenerate' in a 'regenerated' city centre.

Interpreting contemporary social control

> The material reproduction of urban society depends on the continual reproduction of space in a fairly concentrated geographical area ... The production of space depends ... on decisions about what should be visible and what should not; concepts of order and disorder; and a strategic interplay between aesthetics and function (Zukin 1996a: 44).

Although this book examines the materialisation of order in the city of Liverpool in the UK, it is not a book that intends to be merely a 'local study', but rather a study that utilises 'the local' in order to contribute to trans-local debates that concern the nature of entrepreneurial urbanism and its impact on the control and regulation of space in the advanced capitalist urban form. The practice of social control and the materialisation of order in the streets of Liverpool have been a recognisable feature of political and economic rule in the city since the beginning of the nineteenth century. The concept of social control has itself, to varying degrees, been associated with, and positioned as a key mechanism in, the development and rule of capitalist and post-industrial cities. It is in the cities where images and the organised filtration and pursuit of 'the dangerous', 'the criminal' and 'deviant' have been most acute within official and popular discourse. In general historical terms, therefore, concerns around the city as a governable entity have dovetailed with strategies of social control built upon discourses of 'fear' – of crime, violence and loss of a sense of 'place'. Furthermore, developments in control techniques and the discourses that underpin them traverse the rhetorical and material boundaries of inequality. In this book it is the relationship between control practices and the demarcation of space that is of concern and of how the policing of social boundaries plays its part in the political domination and material reproduction of the urban centre, understood in Zukin's terms as the 'strategic interplay between aesthetics and function' (ibid.). It is the governing agents in the urban centre and their material and ideological power that are explored here. The city 'visions' they espouse, and their preferred function and form for the urban landscape, set benchmarks for the identification and counteraction of those individuals, groups and behaviours perceived to hinder progress towards an 'orderly' urban centre. The linkages between discourses of crime, incivility and order on the one hand, and idealised visions for the city on the other, are not peculiar to the governance of today's cities and were crucial in the management and organisation of space in the nineteenth century city (Taylor 1999). Then, like now, debates about urban malaise have at the same time been debates about the 'quality' and 'experience' of the urban form, its utility and potential for disorder and criminality which are believed to hinder prevailing notions of urban 'advancement'.

In the light of these points, the advent of camera surveillance as a tool for street ordering poses problems in the interpretation of contemporary social control. Moreover, the study of social control is contested among criminologists and social scientists, who continue to articulate stark differences in their interpretation of the relations between social control, power, the state and social order. In examining the development of a local camera network, this book will seek to contribute to these interpretive debates in exploring the nature and direction of social control in the early part of the twenty-first century.

It is argued here that the development of street surveillance cameras in the UK shifts the terrain of social control from a post-liberal-welfare social control to one based on a free-market enterprise culture. As Sumner argues, contemporary social control reworks 'the dominant censures of the day' that enforce and 'reflect the antisocial interests of capital, patriarchy, and ethnicities' (2004: 28). According to McMahon

(1992: 205–6), 'the locus of social control in the penal sphere' is shifting 'beyond the ambit of criminal justice popularly conceived'. This is fostering new areas of intervention, novel strategies and technologies of control culminating in a form of social surveillance that engages with 'the pursuit and management of actual, and potential, petty violations' (ibid.: 206). From McMahon's observation, three inter-related processes are pivotal in the contextualisation of this book. First, new geographical areas have been opened up for monitoring and surveillance (the private malls, shopping complexes and 'publicly accessible' consumption zones of the urban centre); secondly, control strategies involve partnership building between public and private powers accompanied by a reconfiguration of responsibility for the identification and management of crime, deviance and social order; and, thirdly, in this process, new technologies of surveillance and control are utilised, notably the development of CCTV networks and hybrid layers of policing that surround them. The developments are not only technical in nature but have social origins and consequences. In essence, what kind of social order are these processes helping to reflect and reinforce?

Rationale and organisation of the book

In the following pages CCTV is explored as part of a more broadly conceived set of 'social ordering practices' (Lacey 1994) that involve the participation of locally authorised 'primary definers'. These are local credible experts and 'visionary' entrepreneurs, whose purposeful inroad into the realms 'crime and deviance management' is symptomatic of neoliberal statecraft.

Exploring and mapping partnership rule and the normative terms of that rule in Liverpool city centre force an understanding of the ideological and institutional restructuring of the local state. The input of business interests through public–private partnerships has carved out a political space for 'new primary definers' to articulate a preferred meaning of city centre space, and how it should be administered and utilised. Thus the role of CCTV is bound up with other questions relating to the meaning of partnership forms of rule in the city centre. More specifically, what is the *meaning* of 'order' – how is it signified and related to other spatialised discourses? Crucially, the book wishes to illuminate the 'proper objects of power' (Fiske 1993: 235) that neoliberal state servants articulate in the implementation and definition of a local politics of growth. In exploring the development of neoliberal statecraft it is possible to trace a reordering of power relations that weaves its way down to the streets and targets groups and behaviours that hinder a visionary entrepreneurialised landscape.

In recent years the analysis of social control, influenced by the 'governmentality' and 'risk' literature, has shifted emphasis in the direction of the 'rationalities' or 'mentalities' of control to develop what might be called a post-state understanding of social control. This literature leaves a number of issues unexplored and undeveloped in our understanding of the contemporary landscape of social control. It has assumed rather than demonstrated the absence of coercion as part of control practices. It has also ignored the continuing salience of censorious discourses that underpin practices such as mass camera surveillance and render them not merely technical but moral-political. Arguably, much of this work is based on abstract theorising that rarely has empirical studies as part of its canon and often fails to 'get underneath' official discourses and challenge their terms of reference. What Cohen (1979) identifies as 'social-control talk' is an important source for understanding the activity of 'social control agents' or the proclivities derivative of entrepreneurial rule that the book explores. However, a critical understanding of social control can be achieved by moving beyond assumptions found in official discourse and in casting a scrutinising gaze that ascends the social and political hierarchy. In 'studying up' and scrutinising the vernacular and actions of the powerful, the development of entrepreneurial rule and the camera network in Liverpool is explored by talking to those at the centre of decision-making as a means of rediscovering the reality of the state. Coupled with theoretical arguments, the use of interviews enables a critical exploration of the 'mentalities', material context and ideological formulations of those agents involved in the social ordering process. In order to achieve these aims the book is organised as follows.

Chapter 2 provides an overview of the theoretical issues surrounding the concept of social control with particular reference to the influential post-Foucauldian contributions. How have the relations between social control, power, state and social order been theorised within and between perspectives in social science? Within the post-Foucauldian literature a shift in understanding social control and social order hinges around a 'post-statist' or power beyond the state conceptualisation that has had an important bearing on an understanding of what drives contemporary control practices. These theorisations deem social control to be underpinned by an amoral and risk-bound rationale within a conceptualisation of power that is diffused and multiple. It is these theoretical assumptions that will be critically examined in the following chapters.

Chapter 3 challenges the assumption that the state is of declining importance as an object of inquiry when exploring social control practices in the city. The chapter sets out the theoretical framework and methodological issues pertinent to this book. In order to analyse CCTV in Liverpool, and to materialise its position within particular social relations, an argument is put forward for rethinking the relationships between the state, power and social order. The power of the state, and its scope for action, has never followed a static or fixed strategic path but has constituted a creative field of institutional arrangement and experimentation with the aim of managing and ordering social and spatial relations. Far from assuming the demise of the state, the chapter explores some of the conceptual tools necessary for understanding the transformation of the state and, in particular, how this is manifest within the public–private partnerships indicative of contemporary neoliberal rule. Indeed, it is a contention of the book that these partnership arrangements have rescaled the state form and reconfigured the power to define and enact local social ordering strategies within which street camera surveillance plays a central part. The book enters this state form and, in doing so, 'studies up' the social and political hierarchy to pose the question: *who are the powerful?* It is these new primary definers who inhabit and constitute a neoliberal statecraft that the book scrutinises in order to understand the social orientation of the visions and spatial discourses relating to city space and the development of surveillance practices.

In exploring surveillance practices in this way the book charts the rise of the 'entrepreneurial city' in the late twentieth century and into the twenty-first. What some have referred to as the neoliberalisation of space (Brenner and Theodore 2002) is explored in Chapter 4, along with the manner in which the discourses and practices of 'safety', 'security' and 'order' within the neoliberal city have gained a renewed intensity. In the UK a number of government 'urban regeneration' initiatives are reflecting these broad trends by setting in place various guidelines and legal mechanisms for urban partnerships to extend and formalise social control strategies that have as their object the rehabilitation of space. Drawing upon a range of literature, the chapter discusses the trajectory of a neoliberal 'logic' that can help in the interpretation of changes in both urban rule and sociospatial control.

Academic speculation that depicts 'clean breaks', 'shifts' and 'newness' regarding the tactics and targets of social control in city spaces can overemphasise historical discontinuity. Thus Chapter 5 provides an overview of social control and governance in Liverpool between 1800 and the 1990s in order to tease out the themes within, and the role of, discourses and narratives in urban politics relating to the regulation and control of the streets in Liverpool. Historically and in the contemporary setting it is precisely the control of city streets that commands political attention and action. In drawing attention to a particular city, the chapter concludes with a focus on the 'image problem' peculiar to Liverpool. The label of 'problem city' and the negative imagery associated with it became an issue in entrepreneurial city building and for city managers, marketing strategists and policing agencies involved in restructuring the city's political economy in the twenty-first century.

Following on from the previous chapter, Chapter 6 utilises interview material to discuss the development and trajectory of the neoliberal state in Liverpool city centre, and how the institutions of that state provide the arena within which the broader governing process and visions for the city are articulated. This is done in order to illuminate both the unevenness of neoliberalisation at the local level and the processes by which the locally powerful identify local problems to their rule as they attempt to craft a 'responsibilisation' strategy that seeks to enhance that rule. The formulation of strategic city visions, and the manner in which these visions are spatialised through the promotion of an idealised urban aesthetic, forms the political-normative backdrop to the process of contemporary street cleansing and the development of one of the UK's most expensive and sophisticated street camera networks.

In challenging the view of CCTV as merely a crime prevention technology, Chapter 7 places the camera network within this wider politics of space, as this is materially and ideologically rooted in the shifting lines of authority in the local state. Within this context, the ways in which the camera network is managed and targeted, and how the locally powerful and their security managers articulate this targeting are explored. *Who* is targeted and *why*, and under *what* conceptions of local social order does this targeting 'make sense'? The practice of social control rarely, if ever, unfolds in a seamless and entirely coherent manner. In recognition of this, Chapter 7 also highlights the unintended consequences, tensions and contradictions within the surveillance network of the neoliberal state, indicating how these tensions produce fractures but are also managed within and between locally powerful actors.

In conclusion, Chapter 8 revisits and draws together the central themes and arguments of the book in providing a discussion of the implications arising from the arguments contained with it. In particular a re-evaluation of the relations between surveillance, the state and the production of social order is put forward. The circuits of power that camera surveillance enables underpin a preference for a particular vision of order. The enabling and promotion of such a vision raises questions about the way city centres are governed, how spaces are controlled and for what purpose. Related to this are questions surrounding the symbiotic relationships forged between criminologists and the process of city building. The institutional interlinkage that is a feature of city building connects the academe to city regeneration projects in a manner that can compromise the role of intellectual scrutiny upon this process (see Coleman 2003b).

By the end of the book what should become clear is that we can no longer rely solely upon official pronouncements on CCTV or studies that evaluate the 'crime reducing' effectiveness of this technology. Such pronouncements do little in providing the necessary tools to understand the social meaning and political significance of camera surveillance and its role in the constitution of city space. Whether or not a democratisation of the surveillance practices discussed in this book is possible is left for debate elsewhere. What is of concern here are the processes by which camera surveillance is bound up with a particular political project of reclaiming city streets. Just recognising this is an important step for criminologists concerned to think beyond the official discourse of 'crime prevention' and to explore how practices subsumed under this label play a role in the symbolic and material organisation of space and the meaning of citizenship within it.

Notes

1. At the same time, these developments were coupled with rises in recorded crime and an increased public anxiety about becoming victims of crime. Such observations have dovetailed with a broad acknowledgement that policing and criminal justice agencies alone are limited in combating crime alongside an expansion in expectations of what the public and other agencies can contribute in this area (Garland 1996).

Chapter 2

The disappearing state: social control, social order and the state

> People really like to have CCTV cameras because the police and the people that live in the areas [*sic*] believe it brings greater security. In terms of providing people with a sense of security, this is a good investment (Lord Faulkner, *The Guardian* 29 July 2002).

In response to criticism that cameras do little to cut crime and anxiety about crime (see NACRO 2002), Home Office Minister, Lord Faulkner, gave what is the stock-in-trade rejoinder that fuels a doxa of political and media pronouncement on street cameras. Indeed, within the realms of 'state imaginary' (Neocleous 2003) a set of domain assumptions around street camera networks portray them as a necessary form of social control that protects the law-abiding from the criminal, the drunks, gangs of youths and/or those who are just a plain 'nuisance'. Reflected in press reportage that constructs the 'good' cameras that target 'them', – i.e. the disorderly (McCahill and Norris 2002) – official representations assume in general that street cameras are in the public interest and reflect a spontaneous and commonly held desire for 'good public order'.

What 'the public wants' in respect to camera surveillance is subject to dispute and confusion (Ditton 1998) and the official view of camera surveillance mirrors – albeit in a simplistic and skewed cynical sense – one of the earliest sociological accounts of social control found in the work of Emile Durkheim. His theorisation idealistically construed the position of the state in the development of social control and forms of punishment as unproblematically reflective of 'community' and popular sentiment. Durkheim argued that in 'healthy societies' social control and punishment would *not* transgress the spirit and morality of popular sentiment or the collective conscience. Whether Durkheim would view mass camera surveillance in urban centres today as an index of a 'healthy society' remains a moot point in that, within Durkheim's writing, there was an argument that allowed a role for the 'normal' expression of crime and forms of transgression as instigators of positive and healthy social change in non-authoritarian societies (Durkheim 1964: 68–72). However, as it is the central crime prevention practice in the contemporary cities of the UK, can the spread of camera surveillance be seen as simply responding to the public interest and a promoter of social solidarity and 'community empowerment'? On the other hand, does this form of social control point to evidence of an 'unhealthy society' that censures crime and deviance excessively, therefore underpinning governing institutions with a form of moral inflexibility and authoritarianism?

Theorists after Durkheim – particularly those of a neo-Marxist persuasion – developed the analysis of social control in a more critical direction and demonstrated that socio-legal, technical or state forms of control 'do not simply "express" ... [popular] sentiments – they also seek to transform and shape them in accordance with a particular vision of society' (Garland 1990: 54). This posits a view of social control, and by implication CCTV, that this book will develop: a social control that is, more often than not, tendentiously allied to particular social interests and, most importantly, allied to the powerful, *who are in a materially superior position to be able to promote particular political visions that underpin a desired and imagined social order.* By 'studying up' and scrutinising the powerful, this book seeks to excavate the *materialisation of order* as a contingent and processual endeavour, integral to the functioning of contemporary state power. In taking this position, a critical theoretical and methodological tract is mapped out that can (and should) enable social scientists to stand outside official discourses and those views of the world preferred by the powerful and from whom C. Wright Mills (1970: 214) urged us to remain independent.

The questions raised here point to the role of the state in terms of its theorisation and in terms of politically responding to state power. In thinking about these questions, the chapter traces the theories of social control from Durkheim to critical and neo-Marxist accounts to emerge in the late 1960s, followed by a discussion of more recent post-Foucauldian perspectives. These more recent perspectives on social control have established a new orthodoxy in theorising the relations between social control, state form and social order. This orthodoxy has its roots in poststructuralism, in particular, the thinking of Michel Foucault. The development of conceptual frameworks such as 'governmentality' and 'risk' have refocused the attention of scholars of social control to reconsider the nature of social order and the manifestation of power. This shift has a number of consequences for how we understand the trajectory of social control processes along with how challenges to these processes are formulated. In taking the state out of the equation, in viewing power as decentred, multiple and pluralised, and providing an overly technical-instrumental view of power, the neo-Foucauldian doxa has – by and large – moved away from a materialist analysis of order. These limitations are challenged in the course of subsequent chapters. Before setting out this challenge more clearly, there follows a discussion of the social control literature that has been most influential – particularly in the second half of the twentieth century – and has stirred critical thinking and debate as well as informed the analysis of social control developed in this book.

Liberal and functionalist theories of social control

Social control is a historically and politically informed concept tied to utopian and dystopian visions of social order and the city (Sumner 1997: 6–7). Thinking around social control since the early twentieth century has undergone many conceptual shifts, though one dynamic, central to this book, has remained relatively constant – and that is the fact that all theories of social control have attempted to understand the relations between social control, power and the constitution of social order. Early writings formulated the problem of social control within a broader political drive to secure a popular commitment to the prevailing social and moral order. The 'dizzying effects of rapid change' in the early twentieth century pointed to 'the apparent lack of an overweening moral force to guide people towards co-operative, peaceful and harmonious adaptations to this maelstrom of modernity' (Sumner 1997: 1–2). The new sociologies of social control were concerned with the breakdown of traditional communal ties and controls in the face of a laissez-faire and unregulated capitalism. The lack of regulation and order within complex industrial societies proved a central focus for a liberal sociology that viewed 'the powers of the state' as performing an effective role in reconciling or regulating conflicts between 'interest groups' within the framework of capitalism (Schwendinger and Schwendinger 1975: 129).

Armed with new conceptions about the nature and role of the state, community and the individual, and the relationships between them, the sociologies of social order developed the concept of social control. These developments underpinned liberal and functionalist perspectives that dominated the field of social control up until the 1960s. The work of

15

Durkheim was indicative in this respect, in its focus on the necessity of social solidarity through moral unity, and it provided an analytical context within which early trajectories of social control developed.

For Durkheim the great 'industrial centres' or cities represented the rapidity of social change and possibilities for destabilising social order. For him, the problem of modern industrial society was to be found in the weakening of earlier communal collective sentiments in the face of growing sectional solidarities associated with the complex division of labour under industrialisation. The complex and functionally differentiated inter-human relations found in the city were characteristic of organic solidarity and it is here that the 'anomic' character of modern societies is most apparent. The development of the modern city was thought to undermine traditional moral ties and segment them into less unified and isolated moral communities.

In the first half of the twentieth century, writers after Durkheim further stressed the relations between the city, disorganisation and social control. These concerns were developed in the work of the 'Chicago school' in the 1920s, where a sociological critique was pioneered to explore the prevailing social conditions in the expanding cities. The 'social ecology' approach to the understanding of cities, particularly in the work of Park, highlighted the notion of social control as 'the central fact and the central problem of society' (Park, 1921 cited in Sumner 1994: 45). The inevitable 'march of progress', changes in industrial organisation and movements in population were thought to correspond to shifts in 'the habits, sentiments and character of the urban population' (Park 1967a: 23). The processes of atomisation and individualism dissolved the moral order as it was spontaneously derived through the family and church (ibid.: 24). The problem of social control became pronounced as the growth of the city loosened traditional moral ties to produce both 'good and evil in human nature in excess' (ibid.: 46). The progressive aspect of city growth brought with it a downside in the form of 'social junk' as evidenced in poverty, vice and crime among those who 'have fallen out of line of industrial progress' (Park 1967b: 109). In this way, Park echoed nineteenth century concerns with the 'dangerous classes' when he wrote of the demoralised city zones, where the population tended 'to suppress characters which unite them with the normal types about them' (1967a: 45).

The work of Durkheim and Park postulated social control as a reaction to the fragmentation of morality and culture associated with modern urbanism. These writers presented a subtle criticism of laissez-faire policies that were seen to encourage economic, political and moral deregulation. The concept of social control after 1945, however, was developed in a qualitatively different way through the work of Talcott Parsons. Parsons stated that 'deviance if tolerated beyond certain limits will tend to change or disintegrate the [social] system' (1951: 206). Put simply, social control was necessary as a 'preventative' or 'forestalling' mechanism in order to remotivate 'the actor not to embark on processes of deviance' (ibid.: 298). The normative patterns of 'common culture' were 'more or less institutionalized' (ibid.: 250) and, following Durkheim, were also reflected in the integrative functions of law and other social control mechanisms (Cotterrell 1984: 88).

The liberal and functionalist proponents of social control argued for a moral and/or rational binding between the individual and the social. Indeed, without such bonds the idea of 'the social' would collapse. Such visions of social control expressed a desire for social harmony and consensus. Within the liberal and functional traditions, 'social control' has been depicted as a set of more or less co-ordinated practices that arise to reflect 'community values' and 'social norms' that are usually perceived as uncontested social entities. This view of social control most closely reflects the manner in which the locally powerful in Liverpool city centre represent contemporary social control practices such as CCTV – namely, as reflective of an idealised 'common good' and in the interests of 'the city and/or people as a whole' (see Chapter 7). Like liberal theorists of social control, those behind contemporary control processes are less concerned to investigate the forces underpinning social fragmentation and disintegration and more concerned to inculcate the means and ends of social control as blocks on deviance and the collapse of social order. The views of the locally powerful regarding their visions for social order and social control are discussed in Chapters 6 and 7.

Social reaction and neo-Marxist theories of social control

During the 1960s and in contrast to liberal and functionalist perspectives, social control came to be theorised as sectoral, serving particular powerful interests at the expense of the collective good. Liberal and functionalist accounts were questioned forcefully by social reaction theorists for their view of social control that 'started and finished with the lack of control-leads-to-crime causal sequence' (Hudson 1997: 454). Goffman (1961), Becker (1963), and Lemert (1967) challenged the orthodoxy of previous control theories in order to raise a different set of questions around the nature of social control. The focus switched from the deviant act itself to those moral entrepreneurs, rule makers and rule enforcers that operated inside and outside formal state institutions and served to create deviant categories as prerequisites in the processes of criminalisation (Becker 1963; Gusfield 1963). The power to label some acts as deviant and others as not necessitated a reconsideration of social control not as a neutral reactive force but as an active process that selectively defined deviance in line with the particular interests of controlling agents and institutions. The activities of control agents in influencing the criminalisation process, legislative change and patterns of enforcement need not necessarily reflect a consensus of interest among the wider population (Becker 1963). Within this perspective, social control intensified and amplified deviance through the organs of a wider 'control culture' that bestowed key roles for the media, and community 'leaders', as well as formal control agents in the generation of moral panics and the identification of societal folk-devils (Cohen 1972).

In recognising the advances made by social reaction theory in focusing on the activities of control agents, the emerging neo-Marxist analysis in the early 1970s sought to broaden the theorisation of social control and deviance in order to explain how 'particular historical periods, characterized by particular sets of social relationships and means of production, give rise to attempts by the economically and politically powerful to order society in particular ways' (Taylor *et al.* 1973: 220). Thus the activities of control agents needed to be situated within a broader recognition and critique of capitalist power and inequality along with an acknowledgment that the power to label 'is determined extraneously' (ibid.: 161). In situating the problem of social control within the reproductive processes of capitalist social relations, neo-Marxist theories incorporated a revisionist critique of control strategies that further challenged the progressive perspectives associated with liberal and functionalist accounts. For these writers the disciplinary regularities of the nineteenth century factory system served as a basis for the development of more widely situated forms of social control aimed at producing a disciplined existence upon the workforce through placing time and space constraints within the school, prison and other institutions.

Other neo-Marxist analysts within a structuralist tradition stressed the wider role of the state and law as lying at the centre of understanding control strategies in the twentieth century. Important in this respect was Poulantzas (1978) who drew attention to the monopoly of physical violence within the capitalist state and its role in keeping internal social order. This particular form of neo-Marxist analysis has sought to straddle the problems of consent and coercion in understanding the relationship between social control and the popular masses. Neo-Marxists have tended to stress the coercive aspects of social control (ibid.: 81). More accurately, the latter concept has been conceptually subordinated within Marxism to *state control*.

This form of analysis was not acceptable to all Marxists who sought a complex theorisation of the combinations 'of force and authority, of regulation and liberties, of coercive habit and legitimate consent' which had become dissolved in perspectives that caricatured the police, social workers, teachers, philanthropists and reformers as 'simply and solely the unconscious agents of state repression' (Hall and Scraton 1981: 470). The neo-Gramscian approach of Hall *et al.* (1978) offered a more sophisticated analysis of social control within a more general theorisation of the capitalist state. Consent does not arise spontaneously as in liberal theories; it is, on the contrary, something which is organised through powerful institutions charged with managing the social terrain. Such institutions of the state thus become important sites for an investigation of the organisation of social control and the form it may take.[1] Hall *et al.* (ibid.) developed this view of the state in terms of how it enlarges the cultural and social basis of its rule. For these authors the concept of social control served only a 'general descriptive' purpose and lacked historical specificity. Previous social control theories were thought to be limited in that they were not 'premised on a theory of the state ... of a particular phase of capitalist development' (ibid.: 195). The specific form of the state must be understood not only for its legal and coercive capacity but in its 'role of leadership, of direction, of education and tutelage – the sphere, not of domination by force, but by the "production of consent" ' (ibid.: 202). This led to forms of analysis of the ideological aspects of social and/or state control – of how popular consent for state coercion was produced and struggled over; of how the hegemony of ruling economic and political alliances was established through negotiation and compromise; and of how, ultimately, in times of economic crisis, the popular masses come to support the 'processes of criminalisation through which consensus is forced rather than forged' (Sim *et al.* 1987: 63). Shifts in the control apparatus of the state are underpinned by processes of criminalisation fuelled by recurring moral panics, law and order crusades, and a more intensive penalisation aimed at 'enemies within' – 'the underclass', criminals, the 'work-shy', illegal immigrants, militant feminists and those with alternative lifestyles. More repressive legal censures against such categories have been built upon and legitimated by a social authoritarianism that has fed a growing 'fear of crime' buttressed with a decline in social discipline. Thus state control, within the parameters of a 'critical criminology', has served to manage dissent within an established order rooted in the 'determining contexts' of class relations, patriarchy and neocolonialism (Scraton and Chadwick 1991).[2]

However, critical theories of social control that emerged from the 1960s were subsequently challenged from the late 1970s by perspectives with radically different questions and approaches to thinking about social control, social order and power. The 1980s witnessed a proliferation of poststructuralist and post-Marxist theories that attacked the theoretical tenets of the critical social science that emerged in the post war period, particularly for its focus on the relationship between class power and social control; its prioritisation of state activity; its universalistic explanatory framework; and the typically negative view conferred upon social control processes. It is to these theoretical developments that the next part of the chapter turns.

Neo-Foucauldian perspectives on social control

In his concern to construct a 'micro-physics of power', Foucault (1977) focused upon the 'technologies' of 'disciplinary power' that were developed as new rationalities for punishment in the prisons that emerged between 1760 and 1840. In studying this earlier particular period and beyond, Foucault set out to examine the shifts in the nature, rationale and techniques of punishment – from the public spectacles of torture and execution (monarchical punishment) to the techniques of 'soul training' towards the production of obedient individuals (carceral punishment).

Disciplinary power, aimed at training the 'soul' of criminals and delinquents, developed in the new prisons where human existence through space and time became subject to processes of classification, surveillance and routinisation. Underpinning these mechanisms of control was the exercise of a normalising judgement carried out by emergent professional groups armed with a new scientific knowledge developed within the disciplines of psychology and criminology. With the development of the prison, the professional gaze instilled a new form of disciplinary power under the principle of panopticism. This ensured a more intense, efficient and automatic functioning of power (ibid.: 206). Panopticism was built into the architecture of the prison, but was also primarily a 'political technology' that provided a laboratory to monitor, train and correct individual behaviour (ibid.: 203–5). Under a panoptic prison regime 'of conscious and permanent visibility', inmates were encouraged to regulate and discipline their own behaviour under conditions of constant, yet unverifiable, observation (ibid.: 201). Thus panoptic power functioned 'automatically':

> He who is subjected to a field of visibility, and who knows it, assumes responsibility for the constraints of power; he makes them play spontaneously upon himself; he inscribes in himself the power relation in which he simultaneously plays both roles; he becomes the principle of his own subjection (ibid.: 202–3).

For Foucault, disciplinary power displayed a tendency to become operative outside the prison walls as a new instrument of government that sought 'not to punish less, but to punish better', and with 'more universality and necessity; to insert the power to punish more deeply into the social body' (ibid.: 82). The spread of disciplinary power brought with it the possibility of 'the utopia of the perfectly governed city' (ibid.: 1977: 198), where the process of normalisation would proliferate and spread throughout carceral institutions. The theoretical underpinnings of panopticism and disciplinary power and their relevance for understanding camera surveillance in towns and cities have been picked up and developed by various writers (see, for example, Bannister, *et al.* 1998; Norris 2003).

More generally, the project of normalisation was thought to filter throughout the social body and create power-knowledge spirals that have as their object the creation of categories of 'delinquency', 'deviancy' and a host of other 'abnormalities' to be made 'knowable' and controlled. Thus the disciplines of the social sciences are implicated in control processes towards the management of entire human populations – what Foucault termed 'bio-power'. Both the sites and targets of social control are understood as varied and involve, for example, the identification and segregation of the sane from the insane, the criminal from the law-abiding and the sexually normal from the abnormal (Foucault 1977). For Foucault, control processes are bound up with the power to label, classify, segregate and rehabilitate towards the production of the correctly functioning and productive individual. The promise of panoptic power is thus the disciplined society – a knowable, regulated and controlled society with a new economy of efficiency:

> In each of its applications, [panopticism] makes it possible to perfect the operation of power. It does this in several ways: because it can reduce the number of those who exercise it, while increasing the number on whom it is exercised. Because it is possible to intervene at any moment and because the constant pressure acts

even before the offences, mistakes or crimes have been committed (ibid.: 206).

Foucault's writings suggested the existence of a set of complex relationships between social control, power and social order. His theorisation of these relationships differentiated him from liberal, functionalist and neo-Marxist perspectives. Foucault challenged the idea that social control develops in line with prevailing and established political and economic interests. At the very least, the relationship between control mechanisms and wider structures of power was rendered unclear. This in part was due to the way Foucault theorised power in modern societies: 'In short this power is exercised rather than possessed; it is not the "privilege", acquired or preserved, of the dominant class, but the overall effect of its strategic positions – an effect that is manifested and sometimes extended by the position of those who are dominated' (ibid.: 26–7).

Power is also conceived of as creative and not merely repressive and negative in its effects: 'power produces; it produces reality; it produces domains of objects and rituals of truth' (ibid.: 194). For Foucault, an analysis of social control and its disciplinary mechanisms must therefore direct attention to those local, regional and 'relatively autonomous' institutions in order to try to 'locate power at the extreme points of its exercise, where it is always less legal in character' (1984: 211). Furthermore, 'let us not, therefore, ask why certain people want to dominate, what they seek, what is their overall strategy' and instead 'attempt to study the myriad bodies which are constituted as peripheral subjects as a result of the effects of power' (ibid.: 212). This view radically altered how the state is positioned in theories of social control and its role in reproducing relations of domination. It is not that the state is irrelevant as a centre of power, but neither is it to be accorded a privileged location from where power and social control emanate.

A unitary and unifying concept of social control is, therefore, rejected with particular reference to the determinism identified in Marxist theories of the state (Lacombe 1996: 540). Within Foucault's writings, a strict separation can be identified between powerful interests in society and circulating forms of disciplinary control (Garland 1990). Indeed, the *interests* and *values* which may underpin social control practices (a central concern of all previous theories) are not the prime focus of analysis at all, in that 'The bourgeoisie could not care less about delinquents, about their punishment and rehabilitation, which economically have little importance, but it is concerned about the complex of mechanisms with which delinquency is controlled, pursued, punished and reformed etc' (Foucault 1984: 216).

It is precisely these mechanisms, diversely situated and decentred, that provide the focus for an 'ascending analysis of power, starting ... from its infinitesimal mechanisms, which each have their own history, their own trajectory, their own techniques and tactics' (ibid.: 213). The fragmentary and complex networks of social control with their 'methods of observation, techniques of registration, procedures of investigation and research, apparatus of control' are distinguished from a 'juridical edifice of sovereignty' (the state) and as such cannot be considered 'ideological constructs' that fulfil the requirements of a 'generalized bourgeoisie' (ibid.: 215–16).

Foucault was always at pains to point out the localised and autonomous forms of social control that lie *beyond* the state and which are targeted at a range of 'illegalities'. His work undermined the differences thought to exist between punitive and non-punitive institutions, as the spread of disciplinary power invests itself deeper into the social body in creating 'hundreds of tiny theatres of punishment' within the geography of the 'punitive city' (1977: 113).

These theoretical insights have been refined, developed and adapted by Foucault himself and various writers who have been influential within criminological theorising. It is to these 'post-Foucauldian' perspectives that the chapter will now turn.

Social control and 'risk'

Feeley and Simon (1992, 1994) crystallised the developments in risk-based social control. They identified an emerging scepticism towards liberal interventionist strategies of social control. Such strategies emphasised rehabilitation and the proportioning of responsibility, regarding 'making the guilty "pay for their crime" or changing them' (Feeley and Simon 1994: 173). For these writers, a 'new penology' was under development that was 'actuarial', and orientated through 'techniques identifying, classifying and managing groups assorted by dangerousness' (ibid.). The emphasis on the *management* of crime made this form of control different from disciplinary control:

Disciplinary practices focus on the distribution of a behaviour within a limited population ... this distribution is around a norm ... Actuarial techniques seek instead to maximize the efficiency of the population as it stands. Rather than seeking to change people ('normalize them', in Foucault's apt phrase) an actuarial regime seeks to manage them in place (Simon 1988 cited in Hudson 1996: 154).

23

The importation of risk assessment into the field of crime control has a resonance with neoclassical understandings of individual behaviour (Wilson 1975) and with neoliberal notions of choice and responsibility (Murray 1990). The management of the 'intractable crime problem' promises greater efficiency through risk assessment and loss prevention strategies.

The rise of actuarialism and risk-based technologies has raised a number of important issues in the conceptualisation and interpretation of social control practices. First, actuarialism is thought to be displacing the moral underpinnings of control and order with new technical modes of intervention that are both 'extra-judicial' (Defert 1991: 212) and concerned with the economics of probability (Ewald 1991). Shearing and Stenning (1996) argued that disciplinary techniques could assume various forms without necessarily being moral in orientation. The growth of private policing and mass private property is signalling a 'reconstruction in the social world' towards 'instrumental' ordering practices. The shift to preventive strategies has hinged around the 'language of profit and loss' which has, it is thought, replaced questions of right and wrong (ibid.: 416). This has led to a 'restructuring of our institutions for the maintenance of order and a substantial erosion by the private sector of the state's assumed monopoly over policing and, by implication, justice' (Shearing and Stenning 1985: 496). For these authors it has been the rise of large commercial complexes – such as Disneyland – that has undermined the unitary order of a sovereign state. The spread of disciplinary power, confirmed and driven by a new instrumentalism, has sought the maximisation of profit and brought with it 'not one conception of order but many' (ibid.: 417).

Secondly, as well as appearing to be uninterested in moral questions,[3] these new penal practices, based as they are within authoritative expert domains, contribute to an *appearance* of functioning outside politics. As will be explored in Chapter 7, these institutional relationships are not merely technical, but are underpinned by a normative set of relations that depict idealised representations of local social order. Indeed, the development of cost-effective risk control strategies has moved crime control to 'a de-politicized and hence uncontentious, scientific/technical realm' (Pitts 1992: 142).

Thirdly, the operation of an amorphous new penological venture has encouraged new sites of responsibility for crime control and questioned once again fixed distinctions between state and civil society, public and private spheres. In a range of work, Cohen (1979, 1983, 1985, 1987) critically developed Foucault's ideas around what became known as the 'dispersal of discipline thesis'. This thesis – picked up on and developed by risk theorists – focused on a move away from state control and intervention towards informal control; a move away from the impulse rigidly to classify and segregate the 'dangerous' towards de-professionalised and less remote forms of control; the gradual replacement of the closed institution with more benign forms of community controls; and a shift in the understanding and response to crime from rehabilitation to behavioural or risk-based forms of control. However, for Cohen (1985: 79) there was no fundamental break between 'old' and 'newer' practices: 'the most fundamental fact about what is going on in the new agencies is that it is much the same as what went on and is still going on in the old systems'. Thus the dispersal of social control into various sites – 'the community'; neighbourhood watch; private security patrols and the use of surveillance cameras to monitor public space – produced a number of developments of which Cohen warned would 'widen the net' of the formal system and bring about 'an increase in the total number of deviants getting into the system in first place'. This led to a 'thinning of the mesh' and increased 'the overall level of intervention, with old and new deviants being subject to levels of intervention (including traditional institutionalization) which they might not have previously received' (ibid.: 44). In the context of 'partnership' formation and the relationship between this process and CCTV networks, Cohen argued that a blurring of the 'old' boundaries between formal/informal and public/private forms of control was underway and this further amplifies the problem of disorder.

Within an exclusionary-based control, the stigmatisation and segregation of those deviants who cannot or will not be absorbed are intensified. The 'utopia of the visibly purified city' with suitable 'metaphors of banishment ... separation ... reservations and barriers' (ibid.: 230) serve to segregate the 'undesirable' and incapacitate the persistent criminal, thus reassuring the public 'that the state means business' (ibid.: 234).

A weakness within Cohen's work as with the wider risk literature, however, is that the state is left as unproblematic and its functioning and role are unexplored in relation to the developments related to new techniques of control. Whether notions of a 'risk society' are sustainable – with its sense of novelty and break with past practices and its amoral and decentred view of control – when applied to urban camera surveillance is debatable. These issues will be picked up in the last two chapters. However, the emphasis upon 'newness' and risk-based initiatives, as well as Foucault's earlier emphasis on micro-power, has informed the theoretical contours of an influential body of literature that has drawn upon Foucault's 'governmentality thesis'. In its application this work has challenged the analytical use of sociological concepts such as social control, the state and social order to understand strategies of 'governmental rule' in the contemporary setting. It is to a consideration of this literature that the chapter now turns.

Governmentality: social control and power beyond the state

In recent years a body of work has emerged under the banner of the 'history of the present' group (Barry *et al.* 1996) that has extended Foucault's notion of 'governmentality' and provided a broader consideration of his earlier concerns around the spread of disciplinary control throughout the social body. This work has by no means been homogeneous in its approach to social control. Indeed, it is more accurate to see it as a contested terrain around, for example, issues to do with the continuing role of sovereign and coercive techniques of rule (Stenson 1999) as well as a general neglect in this work of processes of political economy (see Stenson 2002).

Foucault's later writings laid some of the foundations for an approach to studying what he called governmentality. He argued that in order to understand how societies are governed it is necessary to move beyond an analytical focus on the state:

> The excessive value attributed to the problem of the state is expressed … [in] the form of analysis that exists in reducing the state to a certain number of functions … yet this reductionist vision of the relative importance of the state's role never the less invariably renders it absolutely as a target needing to be attacked and a privileged position needing to be occupied. But the state, no more probably today than at any other time in its history, does not have this unity, this individuality, this rigorous functionality, nor … this importance; maybe after all the state is no more than a composite reality and mythicised abstraction, whose importance is a lot more limited than many of us think. Maybe what is really important is our modernity – that is for the present – is not so much the etatisation of society, as the 'governmentalisation' of the state (Foucault 1991: 103).

For Foucault 'technologies of government' allowed the state to survive and, as mechanisms of rule do not emanate from 'a state', they need to be theorised as 'at once internal and external to the state' (ibid.: 103). Thus the focus on technologies of rule re-poses the problem of control as the problem of government – that is, 'finding answers to the question of what it is for an individual, and for a society or population of individuals, to be governed or governable' (Gordon 1991: 36). With these objectives in mind governmental rationalities can be investigated in terms of how they operate as strategies of power that not only constrain action but also 'act upon the possibilities of action of other people' (Foucault, cited in Hunt and Wickham 1994: 24). In broad terms, governmentality refers to the targeting of the population as an object of social scientific knowledge in both social and individual settings, and is orientated towards the maximisation of health, wealth, economic production and social stability. Governmentality operates through a triangle of power: 'sovereignty – discipline – government, which has as its primary target the population and its essential mechanism the apparatus of security' (Foucault 1991: 102). The rationalities and practices of rule towards shaping and regulating conduct represent a 'pluralisation of modern government' that is most apparent in forms of liberal and neoliberal rule. The 'pluralisation' of government contributes 'towards the relativisation of the notional boundary line between state and civil society':

> Among these processes might be numbered the initiating roles of private individuals and organizations in the exploring and defining of new governmental tasks (many aspects of social hygiene and medicine, social work, the collection of statistics, etc); the cross fertilizing interplay between different agencies and expertises, public and private alike (criminal anthropology and accident insurance; industrial sociology and psychotherapy); the propensity of public institutions of government to secrete within themselves their own multiple spaces of partly autonomous authority; the different forms of delegation represented by the 'quango' ... whose functioning as governing institutions rests on their positioning exterior to the state apparatus (Gordon 1991: 36).

Investigations into these forms of rule have developed a focus on how sovereign power is checked and consequently how rule through 'freedom' and 'liberty' can be encouraged beyond the state within a range of institutional settings. 'Freedom' is not viewed as an 'ideological fiction nor an existential feature of existence' but as a vehicle for government through procedures that attempt to enact a 'responsibilised liberty' (Barry et al. 1996: 8). In this sense neoliberal rule attempts to mobilise the individual citizen as 'player and partner', to maximise self-potential as a consumer who makes choices in the market. Self-regulation, 'care of the self' and individual training are the optimising technologies of rule within neoliberal government strategies (Gordon 1991). Rose and Miller (1992: 175) have developed this further, to argue that neoliberal

> government is intrinsically linked to the activities of expertise, whose role is not one of weaving an all-pervasive web of 'social control', but of enacting assorted attempts at the calculated administration of diverse aspects of conduct through countless, often competing, local tactics of education, persuasion, induce-ment, management, incitement, motivation and encouragement.

Miller and Rose (1990), Rose and Miller (1992) and Barry *et al*. (1996) have elaborated the governmentality thesis through the linked notions of 'power beyond the state', 'action at a distance' and the role of expertise in understanding neoliberal forms of political regulation. These writers have considered governmentality as being first of all a discursive activity: 'a kind of intellectual machinery or apparatus for rendering reality thinkable in such a way as it is amenable to political programming' (Miller and Rose 1990: 42). Forms of reasoning produce technologies of government which under 'advanced liberalism' include government by audit, marketisation, privatisation, quangoisation and the devolution of responsibility for the management of various risks – 'for health, wealth and happiness' – to non-state institutions and private individuals (Rose 1996: 54–7). Studies in this area have focused on the objects of governmentality – the city (Hunt 1996), welfare (Rose and Miller 1992), empire (Barry 1996), the school (Hunter 1996) – that in becoming knowable lend themselves more 'amenable to intervention and regulation' (Miller and Rose 1990: 5). Technologies of rule aimed at regulating the movement of goods, persons, the health of the population and criminality have become pluralised across a range of expert domains, and this has important implications for understanding political power and the possibilities for realising social order. Under neoliberal conditions, therefore, a state-centred model of power is inadequate where 'centres of government are multiple' (Rose and Miller 1992: 185). Furthermore:

> The technologies and devices that are assembled into the apparatus of a state have neither the functionality nor unity often ascribed to them. The 'power of the state' is a resultant not a cause, an outcome

of the composition and assembling of actors, flows, buildings, relations of authority into relatively durable associations mobilized, to a greater or lesser extent, towards the achievement of particular objectives by common means. This is not a matter of the domination of a 'network' by 'the state' but rather a matter of translation (Rose 1996: 42–3).

'Translation' refers to the process of linkage between 'loose and flexible' political programmes within specific localities whereby 'diversity becomes composed' and actors forge common interests, understandings and goals through flexible networks that establish commonality regarding the 'nature, character and causes of problems facing various individuals and groups' (Rose and Miller 1992: 184). Under neoliberal conditions, 'community' or the plurality of communities becomes the means of government in encouraging self-responsibilisation, choice and empowerment. Thus 'social control' is really to be understood as something exercised not on a fully social and inclusive terrain ('the death of the social'), but through diverse moral and/or lifestyle-based communities whose power of self-regulation can be nurtured through neoliberal rule. Furthermore, centres of government are multiple and 'seek to employ forms of expertise in order to govern society at a distance, without recourse to any forms of direct repression or intervention' (Barry *et al.* 1996: 14). The notion of 'distance' is viewed as 'real as well as metaphorical' (ibid.) and will be challenged in the course of this book.

The literature in this area has highlighted key problems for the study of regulation (government) and political cohesiveness in focusing on the emergence of alliances of authority that foster relations of expertise both within and beyond the state. It is not social control that is being dispersed here but rather political authority that seeks positively to enable, responsibilise and empower 'sectors and agencies distant from the centre, yet tied to it through a complex of alignments and translations' (ibid.: 12).

Within this work there are those who have explicitly rejected the analytical concept of ideology in favour of an analysis of the technical aspects of neoliberal rule (ibid.: 11).[4] The governmentality literature has thus forced a reconsideration of social control: its relationship to the exercise of power, the state and social order. Instead of being a leading social force, the state concept melts away into the social body and becomes no more than the combined effect of 'micro-powers'.

Conclusion

The analysis of contemporary social control has, following Foucault, developed around the concept of governmentality. This form of analysis has been influential in the attempt to understand forms of rule that appear to have complex relations to, or fall outside, forms of state power and activity. This chapter has outlined this analysis of 'government' that has drawn attention to the localised public and private coalitions that employ 'tactics rather than laws' and 'the use of laws themselves as tactics' (Foucault 1991: 95). In thinking about the development of mass camera surveillance in urban centres, aspects of this analysis will be drawn upon. In excavating the 'tactics' of control in city centre space the book rethinks the position of the local state: its institutional development, governing rationales, strategic direction and normative contours in terms of setting the boundaries for authoritative action. The state, in other words, organises local power flows and is, therefore, analysed as a *source* of power. Indeed, as a tactic of sociospatial control, CCTV is understood in later chapters as situated within the problematic of state formation in relation to urban entrepreneurialism and as a tactic that promotes, not the separation of morality from risk, but *a remoralisation of risk* indicative of a wider social ordering strategy and politics of censure. It is this wider strategy of control and its material and ideological manifestation that this book will explore. The trajectories of powerful risk categories that map out urban space are an aspect of state formation and can be understood in the context of an evolving entrepreneurial political urbanism. The agents and agencies of this latter form of governance are analysed in Liverpool in order to avoid a conceptualisation of risk that is non-ideological and avoid an analysis of governmentality that is dematerialised.

The theoretical contours and insights of the governmentality literature and the literature around risk will be further assessed in the next chapter. However, this will be done within the concerns of critical criminology discussed above; namely, a concern with the state is maintained throughout this book as a site for the organisation of power relations and the criminalisation process, and as an arena of negotiation and contradiction. Nevertheless, the state is not a static body in time or space and there is a need to rethink the state, notwithstanding the insights of earlier critical criminologists. The sites of state power and effectivity – its channels of articulation, consent and authoritarianism – have been changing since the 1980s and nowhere are these processes more intense than in the governance of the city and in the social control and regulation strategies being developed for city spaces. The key theoretical insights discussed above will be placed in the context of the emergence of partnerships developed between public and private bodies charged with urban rule generally and the instigation of control strategies and CCTV in particular. These developments are understood, conceptually speaking, as falling within an analysis of the state. Despite the Foucauldian-inspired scepticism that has contributed to taking the state out of the analysis, some writers have been less committed to the idea of a demise in the importance of the state. During the 1990s the proliferation of 'new' and localised crime prevention 'partnerships' built around CCTV schemes might not have amounted to a demise in state power but rather, following Adam Crawford, 'may be better understood as representing new, partial elements within the existing economic and political formation which co-exist alongside other (older) modes of administration and regulation' (1997: 233). The theoretical debates highlight the disagreements in understanding contemporary develop-ments in social control at the local level. A charge of 'too much emphasis on the state' has given way to an emphasis on 'the local', 'the micro' and a self-perpetuating and over-managerial conception of risk. In severing the relationship between social control and state formation, debates on social control render improbable a materialist understanding that is able to point to the social forces at work in such control practices and the points of generalisation regarding shifts in the practice of social control over time and between localities. In promoting these wider analytical concerns it is important to note that 'the state' has never assumed an outright monopoly on policing and social control (Johnson 1992), and those theories that assume state homogeneity and posit a definite break between 'state' and 'non-state' forms of control are limited in their marginalisation of the processual nature of both state formation and the development of social control practice. An understanding of technological change, as well as shifts in political forces and ideologies and their impact on strategies and the direction of social control, entails an understanding of what is meant by 'the state'. Thus the emergence and meaning of specific 'partnerships' and the local sociopolitical cityscapes through which they operate remain an important area of study for state theorists. The next chapter will make a series of theoretical arguments that challenge some of the assumptions of the Foucauldian-inspired social control literature and present instead a formulation for mapping and rethinking the state and social control in the city.

In according the state a central theoretical position and situating an understanding of state formation within changes in the social relations of the city, this book argues for a material analysis of social control and of the development of street camera networks. In order to grasp how order is materialised it is essential to be theoretically attentive to the ideological, normative and sovereign/territorial components of social control strategies as they are developed and transformed within the matrix of entrepreneurial urbanism and neoliberal state formation. It is therefore to a consideration of *how* the locally powerful can be analytically understood as the occupants and articulators of this state form, and of local social order, that the next chapter turns.

Notes

1 In illuminating this point, Chapter 3 will discuss the theoretical framework adopted in this book for thinking about the state, its form and role in shaping the contours of contemporary social control.

2 In contrast 'left realist' perspectives have challenged the 'idealism' within the above account – particularly in terms of the omnipresent authoritarian state. Left realists have stressed the reality of rising crime rates as a consequence of economic marginalisation affecting lower working-class communities (particularly in black areas) in the inner cities in the 1980s (Lea and Young 1984). The authors acknowledge penal severity as a feature of state responses towards the economically marginal. However, left realists have retained a notion of social control in what they have described as a progressive multi-agency strategy towards the creation of welfare interventions, community associations and a 'democratic' policing policy in the deprived areas of the city.

3 The 'apparent' amorality of these practices will be questioned with the material presented in Chapters 6 and 7 and in the Conclusion to the book.

4 More generally the governmentality thesis of Rose and Miller (1992: 177) has rejected the 'realist' traditions within sociology that have attempted to identify relations of causation, unearth 'real' interests behind political regulation or seek out ideological frameworks. Those analysts working in this area admit that studies in governmentality will not 'help us know if we should be "for" or "against" the present; such judgement should be left to other, perhaps more immediate, contexts and occasions' (Barry *et al.* 1996: 16).

Chapter 3

Rediscovering the state: understanding camera surveillance as a social ordering practice

Some commentators have ... confused a hollowing-out of the state form with a hollowing-out of state power (MacLeod and Goodwin 1999a: 522).

state management should be understood as completing some circuits of power and disrupting others (Ling 1998: 218).

To bring the state back into an inquiry of social control and begin scrutinising the powerful, this chapter sets out a theoretical and methodological rationale for analysing control trajectories that are infusing a neoliberal statecraft. In contrast to largely descriptive and technical understandings of neoliberalism discussed in the previous chapter, the concept is understood in this chapter as a political force that is as ideologically unified, as it is contradictory, in its role in recasting the politics of locality. In other words neoliberal rule is articulated in and though dominant social bodies and networks of state power. Neoliberal rule is understood as 'a class relation and a product of class struggle, an attempt to impose value discipline into society' (Eisenschitz and Gough 1998: 761). Thinking about neoliberal rule in this way aids an understanding of social control in the city as an outcome of political and moral struggle *within* the state form. What governmentality theorists call 'chains of enrolment' that are 'distant from the centre ["the state"], yet tied to it through a complex of alignments and translations' (Barry *et al.* 1996: 12) are understood here as state projects and forms of statecraft that indicate the prevalence of hierarchical relations that work in, through and on ideological relations in an attempt to impose order upon a given territory. 'Chains of enrolment' or the process of statecraft do not just happen but are formulated within, as they themselves reformulate, relations of power and domination.

The points are reinforced by empirical material presented in Chapters 6 and 7 that is organised around interview data accrued from state managers in Liverpool. This chapter seeks to reconstitute the state as a category for analysis and as the material manifestation of power relations. Researching the relations between social control, power and social order, it needs to be asked how these latter categories are socially defined and institutionally embedded. Therefore, the location of technologies and programmes of social control within 'the political' will necessitate an analysis of the latter as social relations (Pearce and Tombs 1998: 568). This position reinforces an argument made elsewhere in that 'studies in governmentality [should] occasionally stand back from the technical and engage with the political' (Ivison 1998: 562). Given this it is important to revisit the relations between social control, the state form, territorial power and normative conceptions of social order.

Revisiting these relations is important because it is not the 'technologies' of social control that possess the power to act, but rather the power to act is manifest within the social interests and forces that articulate control practices and render them meaningful. Turning attention to these social forces as they are organised through state institutions forces further scrutiny on how particular technologies and programmes are made to 'work' in a manner deemed to serve the broad purposes of a ruling social bloc – however contingent, contradictory and fragmented these interests might be. Thus, particular political programmes, technologies of social control such as CCTV and their predominance in materialising order within a locality will be reflected and reinforced within processes of state formation and the ideological representation of urban spaces.

In setting out these objects of inquiry the chapter is divided into two parts. The first part is divided into four sections, the first of which explores the relationship between state institutions and strategies of territorial control. The second section explores the state as a set of institutions charged with the responsibility for sovereign control over territory. The third explores contemporary state restructuring towards the rule of 'entrepreneurial' cities or regions. The fourth section develops an empirical basis for analysing the contemporary state and strategies of social control within it. These strategies will be understood as constituted by particular normative frameworks of power, which endow the state and social control with meaning and strategic direction. Following directly from this, the second part of the chapter sets out the approach adopted for studying the powerful whose location within the neoliberal structures of power remains neglected as a primary object of analysis. In entering the world of the locally powerful, the study opens up for scrutiny the processes that constituted a state in transition. This part of the chapter discusses how and why the line of inquiry adopted in this book sought to analyse the themes, politics and general anxieties that were brought together and articulated by powerful agents within the state form.

Theoretical prologue: the state in motion

In recent years 'surveillance studies' has emerged as an accompaniment to the social control literature. Theoretically, this work remains under-developed and has approached camera surveillance in a fairly predictable fashion in utilising, developing and critiquing the Foucauldian and neo-Foucauldian conceptual frameworks discussed in the previous chapter. Most notably, this has meant a focus on the panopticon as a tool to understand the rise of visual surveillance, its impact upon behaviour in public space, and the meaning, construction and varied perceptions of public space itself.[1] Other writers have rather uncritically and superficially applied 'risk' and 'new penology' frameworks to understand contemporary social control practices and surveillance generally. These approaches have been useful (McCahill 1998; Innes 2003), but their use has been largely descriptive and reinforces a trend of saying very little, if anything, of the kind of social relations out of which camera surveillance emerges and which it helps to reinforce. The same can be said of the much utilised governmentality literature with its notions of 'power beyond the state' (and, more implicitly, beyond ideology) and 'action at a distance' (Barry *et al.* 1996). This work is also weakened by a desire for political neutrality (Rigakos 1999). The literature on 'risk' and 'governmentality' has *overplayed* ideas of discontinuity and 'newness' in thinking about social control (Coleman 2004a). In their focus on the technical, they have *underplayed* the role of morality and censure in current official social control discourse along with a proper consideration of *who* is doing the talking. Without meaning to dismiss these studies en masse – as many have influenced my own work – they have failed to engage consistently and systematically with the political economy of surveillance and risk generally and CCTV in particular.

David Lyon (2003: 27) states that 'surveillance studies today is marked by an urgent quest for new explanatory concepts and theories' and, furthermore, 'the most fruitful and insightful ones are emerging from transdisciplinary work'. Taking this cue, the book and this chapter embark on an interdisciplinary path in order to understand CCTV within the social relations within which they inhabit, and in particular to conceptualise a view of power that provides a refocus on the state. Accepting the view that CCTV can be understood 'as a form of power with a number of dimensions' (Norris and Armstrong 1998a: 8), studies of CCTV have had very little to say about 'the powerful' who stand behind the camera networks. Who are the powerful within the landscape of urban order? How are they organised ideologically and institutionally? What is their role in driving and formulating contemporary statecraft? Crucially, and out of these processes, how do locally powerful actors articulate the trajectory of urban social control and construct risk, as well as the meaning of urban space itself?

With the aim of bringing the state back in and engaging with the political-economy of CCTV, the analysis in this chapter explores neoliberal statecraft as it processes, defines and negotiates sovereignty, social order and social control in the urban centre. The discourses and practices that give shape to this neoliberal state are indicative of a 'managerial state' form explored by Clarke and Newman (1997). Within neoliberal vernacular, foregrounding the discourses of 'business expertise', 'entrepreneurialism' and 'the third way' continues to reshape the rationale for state action and power and also, at the same time, mystifies – through a technical aura – the diktats of state power. This point is particularly important when exploring CCTV in Liverpool which, as an 'entrepreneurial' form of state rule, cannot be understood simply for its technical character, but rather through how it has been positioned within a highly political process of urban restructuring. Thus while the agents and agencies within the contemporary neoliberal state are 'getting on with "business as usual" ', this 'always [implies] some conception of a social settlement: a normative view of the social order' (ibid.: 159).

State and sovereignty

The literature in the previous chapter opened up a series of debates in thinking about social control and its relationship to state sovereignty. While important, this literature tends to separate social control from strategies of sovereignty, or territorial ordering, located within state processes. Garland, for example, argues that it is the contemporary 'state's task ... to augment and support ... multiple actors and informal processes' in a manner that disperses and pluralises social control, rather than engage in a project of 'establishing a sovereign state monopoly' (2001: 126). Contrary to this position, it is argued that 'the state' does *not* use or merely *support* other players (private authorities, etc.) and form partnerships with them; rather the state *exists* and is constituted through alliances and 'partnerships' that – however momentarily and with contradictory tendencies – define its boundaries and scope of action. Neither 'sovereignty' nor state power is on the decline, but these categories are *processual* and subject to rescaling. Careful assessment and nuance are needed when thinking about the capacity and power of the state, particularly at the local level.

However, other writers question the notion of any clean break that dispenses with state processes and issues of sovereignty, thought to be underpinning a 'new' penological venture. For example, Kevin Stenson (1997: 12) argues: 'while the recognition of a renewed emphasis on governing the local spheres is important, it is misleading and over-simplified to characterize this within a narrative which exaggerates a shift from the social to the local and communal'. He points to the coexistence of sovereign control over territory with devolution in responsibility for preventive and risk management strategies. This provides a more critical and material approach to understanding neoliberal forms of rule than that within the governmentality thesis and its reification of terms such as the 'freedom to act':

> The price paid for the entrepreneurial and individualist consumerist freedoms of the majority may be a growing reliance on the more punitive disciplinary and sovereign powers used to contain the recalcitrant and disaffected minorities. Whilst we may not want to embrace a full functionalist theory of the state, *it may be necessary to recognise some of the key strengths of ... the reconstituted state, in helping us to grasp the changing character of liberal rule* (ibid.: 13, emphasis added).

Similarly O'Malley argues against 'catastrophic theorisations' that may assume rather than demonstrate the existence of a 'mass risk consciousness' (2004: 185). For O'Malley, sovereign punitive power is compatible with 'new' actuarial techniques – they are 'mutually supportive' systems of power (1996: 198). The state is not simply relinquishing its claims to territorial dominance or moral authority, and indeed neoliberal attacks on collective and universal social provisions are couched within a highly developed political and moral rhetoric. These observations are, according to O'Malley, lost in much of the actuarial and governmentality literature:

> In such models there is no recognition of the increasing severity and scope of the sovereign dispositions that have accompanied the changes in the delivery of welfare [...] It is unsatisfactory to see actuarial forms of power as efficiently managing the population, and other forms (disciplinary and sovereign) merely as 'surviving' or 'persisting' in the face of a tide of actuarial power (ibid.: 197).

For others, governmentality theorists have remained silent on 'the endless forms of coercion deployed by [a] repressive state apparatus' against those who show dissent and resistance towards neoliberal forms of rule (Frankel 1987: 83).

Bringing sovereignty back in to the analysis, however, means that it must be thought of not just in terms of coercive power, but also in terms of the power to define and administer a given territory. Useful here has been what Latham (2000) calls 'social sovereignty' which historically has been the outcome of the interaction between state forces and economic forces working in contingent 'term setting' alliances, able to make claims for sovereignty over particular domains and spaces. The contemporary fracturing of sovereignty through a range of institutional sites and practices should not be mistaken for a disempowered state (ibid.: 1). In other words the analytical focus should move beyond zero-sum dualities between state and non-state actors to explore, instead, 'forms of cooperation and conflict between various agents in constructing and maintaining social sovereignties' (ibid.: 13). This important theoretical point will be illuminated in Chapters 6 and 7, which investigate how the powerful coalitions underpinning the surveillance network are engaged in setting the ideological and material limits for establishing and sustaining social sovereignty and ordered space in Liverpool city centre. In this sense, sovereignty may be achieved through the mobilisation of discourses pertaining to a contemporary demarcation of city spaces and their 'legitimate' uses. In mobilising such discourses, state actors can be understood as engaged in the designation of responsibility for sovereign control over territory. In other words, responsibilisation strategies – *the process* whereby *whom* and *what* are deemed 'responsible' actors and agencies – come to be defined and articulated within the field of power relations that constitute the state form. The power to responsibilise actors in the field of social control points to processes of ideological closure and censure – a point expanded in Chapter 6.

The state and 'responsibilisation'

Some writers have claimed that the contemporary neoliberal drive to responsibilise actors and agencies in the sphere of crime control has led to a situation characterised by 'government-at-a-distance' – 'distance', that is, from 'the state' in the drive to shape individual and institutional capacities and conduct. Apart from assuming a cohesive and readily identifiable boundedness to the state, this literature fails either to analyse what the state form *is* or *how* it is constituted, nor does it properly include normative questions within the analysis and ask, *who* and *what* is to be responsibilised, for what *purpose* and *aims*? How do new and relatively enduring forms and sites of power shape these processes?

Garland (1996, 2001) provides a detailed account of shifts within crime control, which remains sensitive to the changing character of central and local relations in interpreting emergent forms of control. His analysis begins with what he views as recognition among formal crime control agencies that crime has become a normal social fact. This recognition reorders the status of crime as an everyday risk – rather than a moral deviation that requires explanation – to be managed on a par with other 'unavoidable' risks such as road accidents and food safety. The rise of 'the new criminologies of everyday life', therefore, has sought to move the programmes for crime control away from a concern with the individual offender towards a concern for vulnerable victims and the environments that create opportunities for crime. Implied in these emergent discourses, and coupled with widespread disaffection with the capabilities of formal criminal justice agencies, is the recognition that the state is no longer primarily responsible for crime control (Garland 1996: 450–2). In attempting to 'adapt to failure' with rising crime rates and steady recidivism rates the crime control agencies of the state are faced with 'new problems of legitimacy and new problems of overload' (ibid.: 455). In this context, central government has sought 'to act upon crime not in a direct fashion through state agencies (police, courts, prisons, social work, etc.) but instead by acting indirectly, [through] seeking to activate action on the part of non-state agencies and organizations' (ibid.: 452). The proliferation of 'multi-agency' and 'partnership' initiatives towards crime prevention has been encouraged through schemes such as Safer Cities, the Crime and Disorder Act, funding criteria within the Single Regeneration Budget and CCTV initiatives. These have been characterised by Garland as 'responsibilization strategies', whereby the state is 'experimenting with ways of acting at a distance, of activating the governmental power of "private" agencies, of co-ordinating interests and setting up chains of co-operative action' which create new problems and difficulties as crime prevention and responsibility become diffused into ever more disparate parts of the social body (ibid.: 454). In this climate of 'responsibilisation' the state is not simply being 'hollowed out':

The state does not diminish or become merely a nightwatchman. On the contrary, it retains all its traditional functions – the state agencies have actually increased their size and output during the same period – and, in addition, take on a new set of co-ordinating and activating roles, which in time develop into new structures of support, funding, information exchange or co-operation. Where it works – and one should not underestimate the difficulties involved in making it work – the responsibilization strategy leaves the centralized state machine more powerful than before, with an expanded capacity for action and influence (ibid.).

This expanded capacity of the state is not to be confused with Cohen's (1985) 'net-widening' thesis in that what is occurring is a 'defining down' of deviance in the context of fiscal stringency. This means that minor offences are increasingly outside official interest and there is a growing reluctance to process and penalise minor offenders. This process is also about the scaling down of expectations in relation to what the state can do, but the process is contradictory in that state sovereignty over the problem of crime is simultaneously denied (hence the preference for responsibilisation strategies) and symbolically reasserted (the salience of law and order rhetoric, the evocation of 'folk-devils' and common enemies, and the contemporary rise in incarceration rates) (Garland 1996: 459–61). It will be argued in Chapter 6 that 'responsibilisation' is important – not for denying state sovereignty, but for restructuring it, along the lines denoted by Latham discussed above. Thus responsibility for the enactment of social control can be understood as a definitional process arising from particular relations of power prescribed within the development of the local state form. In negotiating the parameters of 'responsibilisation' the actors and actions involved in this process are negotiating strategies of power that are helping to forge 'new' risk categories in urban space alongside the development of urban subjectivities that buttress an idealised moral sensibility of the 'responsibilised urban citizen'. These dimensions of state power are returned to through the book and point to the processes of statecraft that underpin CCTV and neoliberal rule more generally.

State rescaling

The discussion so far has been predicated on the assumption that the state provides an arena for the organisation and implementation of control strategies in accordance with the circuits of power organised and articulated through the state form. In writing about surveillance and social control many present a false distinction between 'the public' and 'the private'. This has consequences for how power is theorised and understood as well as the formulation of challenges and resistance to that power. Writers have distinguished between state surveillance ('public') and surveillance beyond the state ('private') (Lyon 2001; Shearing 2001; Koskela 2003: 302), as well as suggested the total decentring, plurality and dispersion of surveillance practices (Shearing and Stenning 1996; Lyon 2001). On the one hand, these and other writers acknowledge that state power is not 'disappearing'. On the other hand, the state is left unanalysed by these writers and therefore its supposed 'power' and scope for action have been left assumed rather than explored. The point made here is that it is not a question of *either* studying 'state-public' power *or* 'non-state-private' power, but of how the state form itself traverses these distinctions.

Political geographers and other social scientists, more so than criminologists, have maintained an analytical scrutiny regarding the state, which has been understood as 'a rapidly moving target' (Hay 1996: 3). Some have grappled with the 'problem of the state' and how it can be theorised in relation to contemporary penal practices and control processes. In an analysis that attempts to understand legal pluralism within a range of contexts – 'popular' and informal justice, private government and 'semi-autonomous social fields' – De Sousa Santos (1992: 133) argues that the state has become a 'more problematic social actor':

> The analytical focus must therefore be on the state as contested terrain, a social field in which state and non-state, local and transnational social relations interact, merge and conflict in dynamic and even volatile combinations … To a certain extent this analytical strategy means 'bringing the state back' but, in a sense, the state is brought back to a 'place' where it has never been before. Under current conditions the centrality of the state lies in the way the state organizes its own de-centering, as in the case of the state sponsored back-to-the community policies. The state may thus reproduce itself and indeed expand itself in forms which, by their novelty appear as non-state, political forms.

The devolution of authority to 'extra-state' agencies, local crime prevention 'partnerships' and local security networks may be viewed as a 'heterogeneity of state action' that results in inconsistencies and disjunctures that make patterns of coherence more difficult to identify. This position needs development, not least in terms of identifying both the 'logic' of decentering (though Garland's analysis is useful here) and what it is that 'holds together the configuration of micro-states' (ibid.: 134). Weiss (1997) argues that although it has become less fashionable to theorise the state in an era of 'globalisation' (the official rhetoric of which assumes a powerless state) it has remained a key actor in building collaborative power arrangements – with other states, transnational institutions and private organisations – to meet new challenges to economic stability and social security:

> both domestic and regional coalitions imply that the state is not so much 'devolving' power – in a negative sum manner – to other power actors from whom it then maintains a passive distance. Rather, the state is constantly seeking power sharing arrangements which give it scope for remaining an active centre, hence being a 'catalytic' state (ibid.: 26).

These writers have highlighted the 'elasticity' of the state, which in turn has raised the problem of the nature of state boundaries and the authorisation of the power to act within a given territory and thereby manage and shape social relations. The 'state', as Jessop (1990: 366–7) reminds social theorists, is not a 'thing' that acts or exercises power, but rather its power and action are attributes of 'definite political forces in a specific conjuncture' where power is organised and activated by sets of politicians, officials and managers whose power of action defines the state's capacity for action and intervention in social relations. Rather than 'trying to define the core of the state', research would be best directed to analysing how state boundaries 'are established through specific practices within and outside of the state' (ibid.: 366). In the contemporary setting this argument points to the rescaling of the state in terms of its shifting institutional boundaries, institutional ensembles and scope for intervention. This has meant theorising state power as processual and analysing its boundaries as a product of historically variant spatial scales (within and between the local, regional, national and supranational). In other words, state power must be contingently analysed as 'sociospatial activity' that represents 'a series of context-specific – but actively constructed – processes' (MacLeod and Goodwin 1999a: 505). The urban and regional restructuring underway from the late 1980s across Western Europe has become the means by which state rescaling has been implemented in order 'to control and mediate, social relations among individuals, classes, class fractions and social groups in the context of the maelstrom of perpetual shifts in the global economy' (Swyngedouw 1996: 1502). 'Traditional' state forms (more particularly those constructed under an ideology of welfarism) are deemed inadequate to make possible the creation of 'competitive' and 'entrepreneurial' cities and regions. This is important for thinking about the means by which urban space is rendered 'orderly' for urban managers who articulate 'competitive' and 'entrepreneurial' philosophies (see Chapter 6). These processes can be placed as part of a broader accumulation strategy – which itself may never be fully or coherently realised. However, such accumulation strategies 'are always informed by particular models of the capitalist economy and its extra-economic preconditions and a particular understanding of the logic of capital' (Jessop 1990: 354). It is these 'extra-economic' preconditions (in particular the discursive representation and material ordering of city space) that are articulated through the neoliberal state form and set the context for the implementation of social control strategies in city centres.

Thinking about the state as a continuously rescaled set of institutions provides a corrective to theoretical traditions that have wrought fixed distinctions between 'state' and 'civil society'. Some theorists have based their analysis of state/society relations 'on the degree of domination, control or penetration of "civil society" by "the state" ' (Frankel 1987: 203). Such theoretical and conceptual distinctions have served to oversimplify social control processes through their failure 'to recognise that state institutions are not mere political-administrative apparatuses (that is, there is much more to states than the parties, bureaucrats, etc., who make laws), and will continue to be involved in many social relations normally defined as belonging to "civil society" ' (ibid.). This view echoes Antonio Gramsci's (1971: 259) expansive view of the state as an ethical set of activities and 'a multitude of other so-called private initiatives and activities' that constitute an 'apparatus of "hegemony" or civil society' (ibid.: 261). The contemporary forms of 'responsibilisation', 'enrolment chains' and 'empowerment' that have acted as 'distancing' techniques of advanced liberal rule (Barry *et al.* 1996: 11–12) are also political processes involved in the realignment of state power, state form and ideological representation. Thus the representative individuals whose 'expertise' and professional status are so important in instigating 'partnerships' and in activating 'power at a distance' can in fact be understood as 'new primary definers' (Schlesinger and Tumber 1994: 17–21) imbued with an institutional power and authority to act upon, and order, social relations (Coleman and Sim 2000). These new state functionaries and their ideological power are analysed in Chapter 6. Theoretically, the ascendance of this group and their role within a neoliberal state can be understood as 'constructor[s], organiser[s], permanent persuader[s] and not just simple orator[s]' (Gramsci 1971: 10). Such intellectuals act as spokespeople and, for Gramsci, provide leading social groups with a degree of 'homogeneity' and 'awareness of [their] own function' in organising, for example, 'the confidence of investors' in business, 'customers' for particular products and the articulation of a new legality and cultural sphere (ibid.: 5).

As participants in the building of a particular social bloc, itself always contradictory and discordant, the new primary definers can be understood as engaged in local political struggles designed to forge a 'hegemonic project' (Jessop 1990: 260) between the institutional components of the neoliberal state form. The building of a *responsible* economic, political, intellectual and moral leadership across the rescaled state may be possible to the extent that a 'representative regime' can be consolidated (ibid.: 345). Such a regime may be realised through the mobilisation of key territorial and functional agents, political parties, state managers and the organs of popular opinion, namely the local media.

It is these processes in state development that form the backdrop for thinking about the nature of social control in Liverpool city centre – its authorisation and normative articulation among key 'representational' players. This theoretical framework for understanding the neoliberal state foregrounds a discussion concerning the location of social control practices within this state form, along with a more precise outline of how these control practices are to be understood.

Researching the contemporary state: power and normative ordering

So far the chapter has outlined a set of arguments for thinking about the practice and materialisation of contemporary social control. Such practice is understood as organised and initiated through a state form that provides the arena for the actualisation of sovereignty over a given territory and the designation of responsibility for maintaining that sovereignty. In developing these inter-relationships this section will outline an approach to the state conceived of as a set of institutions geared towards the normative ordering of social relations.

Jessop (1990: 426) has argued that it is only through empirical analysis that the state can be understood and theorised. The state cannot be taken as given and an analysis must be directed towards those

> state practices and projects which define the boundaries of the state system and endow it with a degree of internal unity. The state does not exist as a fully constituted, internally coherent, organizationally pure and operationally closed system but is an emergent, contradictory, hybrid and relatively open system. Thus there can be no inherent substantive unity to the state qua institutional

ensemble: its (always relative) unity must be created within the state system itself through specific operational procedures, means of co-ordination and guiding purposes.

This is not an argument for an all-powerful, everywhere present and monolithic state but one that urges a careful analysis of changing state forms, fields of action and operations of power. Theoretical attention needs to be focused on the contingent strategic processes of intervention that endow unity and generate fractures within forms of 'partnership' that seek to align social interests, enact social control and bring about a relatively coherent social order. Therefore the focus should be upon

> The discourses which define the illusory community whose interests and social cohesion are to be managed by the stage [state] within the framework of a given historic bloc and hegemonic project. The latter provides political, intellectual and moral guidelines for the conduct of state policy. This may subsume an accumulation strategy but there is no necessary relationship between hegemonic projects and accumulation strategies (ibid.: 346).

Thus Jessop has offered a framework for understanding state forms and the exercise of state power that is neither reductionist, functional nor monolithic but relatively open and contingent. The work above suggests that in order to understand 'partnership' forms of rule in the field of social control it is necessary to place these alliances within the processual changes impacting on the effectivity of state power and the forms of action open to state actors and agencies to adapt to meet challenges in governance. This, as in the case in Liverpool, may mean 'traditional' state authorities such as police and elected officials working with the private sector; for example, through funding and managing street camera systems, the provision of uniformed patrols, and other investments in street cleanliness and crime prevention. The 'rise' of the private sector should not be exaggerated as something new, but rather seen as a the ongoing reconfiguration in the constitution of the state. Under a neoliberal market philosophy, Britain's city centres are facing challenges for local and national states that are attempting to construct a hegemony around strategies to regenerate local economies, while at the same time create orderly and 'safe' city spaces. This is leading to high investment levels by local businesses, police and political elites whose work within partnerships is forged around the attempt to unify responses to the 'common threat' of crime and deviance as perceived hindrances to urban regeneration (Taylor 1997).

Leading on from this, another aspect that is often missing from governmentality and new penology theories are the political processes that construct the problems that governmental risk strategies respond to and seek to remedy. In other words, what are the *political* and *moral* considerations that inform the work of 'partnerships' in the identification of problems and strategic responses towards a 'secure' city centre? To utilise Fiske's (1993: 235) phrase, who are the 'proper objects of power' that are targeted in the attempt to render the city centre secure? To return to these political and moral questions means acknowledging, yet moving beyond, the post-Foucauldian concerns with the 'efficient' deployment of technologies of control and re-entering questions regarding their legitimacy and general moral underpinning. As Garland (1990: 170–1) argues, the Foucauldian conception of power – and particularly the panopticon – is problematic in that it 'is strangely apolitical. It appears as a kind of empty structure, stripped of any agents, interests, or grounding, reduced to a bare technological scaffolding'.

Following this point, studies that fail to contextualise the power relations and or the concept of the panopticon within particular political interests and social relations are analytically weak from the start. In turning attention to the materialisation of partnerships in this book and their involvement in the regeneration and reconfiguration of social control, has in turn attuned the analysis both in terms of the technologies of control they employ and the interests and guiding purposes that are integral to their functioning. These alliances can be understood as the result of political and moral struggle, which will continue to be the substance of major conflict. The return to ideology, then, is not a reductionist argument per se, but is vital for investigating how ideas 'facilitate' social relations – 'how they come to be accepted as true, how they rationalize the strategies of groups and institutions … and … how they can lead to the establishment of particular mechanisms of … social control' (McLennan 1996: 60). The post-Foucauldian rejection of a state-centred analysis – rightly directed at reductionist and homogenising tendencies – and its replacement with a conception of multiple power centres has left itself open to the charge of depicting rationalities of power as 'free-floating, not anchored in relations of domination and subordination, exploitation, or indeed any conditioning material conditions' (Curtis 1995: 586). Thus, the role of neoliberal technologies of rule in ordering unequal social relations and preserving private wealth at the expense of collective social provision has been ignored in the governmentality literature (Coleman 2003a). Of particular concern for this book is how 'chains of enrolment' and 'responsibilisation strategies' are cemented – and themselves articulated – across authoritative institutions that constitute the neoliberal state. The building of 'a hegemony of vision' (Zukin 1996b: 223) across the rescaled state form is an important area of study in itself, not only because such visions facilitate the 'channelling of capital into the built environment' but also because they assist in 'producing, controlling and surveilling social and physical spaces' designed to construct 'a relative crisis-free and cohesive civic order' (Swyngedouw 1996: 1504). Indeed, the concept of ideology is useful here for its facilitating role in instituting and co-ordinating intra-state relations and informing the kind of entrepreneurial strategies of rule discussed in Chapter 5.

The above discussion provides a useful avenue for thinking about partnerships between powerful local interests and how these must be situated within their political and economic conditions of emergence. But what binds partnerships together? How do competing agencies identify constituent interests and come to work together in a strategy of rule? More importantly, this draws attention to how territoriality is constructed and construed through the *normative orders* that cut through the institutions charged with ordering and policing space. Social control needs to be theorised as a set of 'social ordering practices' within an extended notion of criminal justice in both its formal and informal settings, and within a range of sites that identify and respond to crime and deviance in 'a related but not entirely co-ordinated set of practices geared towards the construction and maintenance of social order' (Lacey 1994: 28). The conceptual frame of 'social ordering practices' is useful here; they do not operate within any one agency, and transgress the boundaries of formal criminal justice institutions and, in this sense, they are pertinent to the study of the social control strategies within the local partnerships that form part of the rescaled state. The concept can not only link diversely constituted criminal-controlling practices to strategies of social order – 'in a symbolic sense: with a society's sense of itself as a cohesive, viable, and ethical entity' – but can also point to the conflictual ideologies, norms and values that exist within and around criminal justice. This is important not only because it renders possible a critique of an ordering strategy 'on the basis of its own legitimating ideas as well as on the basis of values external to it' (ibid.: 29), but also in pointing to the precise social relations within which normative ordering occurs. The strength of this theoretical method over the post-Foucauldian perspectives is that it not only reintroduces the normative and value-laden aspects of control but it also, in line with a 'social analysis of penality', stands outside those terms of reference and official discourses that orientate, define and legitimate penal practices (Garland and Young 1983).

To return to the central thrust of this chapter, it is the neoliberal state where social control strategies are being devised and responsibilisation strategies tried and tested through the realignment of locally powerful actors and agencies. Thus an analysis of the complex relations of social control that operate within a particular locality will need to consider the emergent rationales of 'risk' based strategies of control alongside and inter-related with 'disciplinary' and 'sovereign' techniques. Furthermore, those who manage and make decisions within so-called 'multiple' and 'authoritative power centres' – their values, visions and interests – must be considered as an important object in the research process. Those who have argued within a 'dispersal of discipline' framework, as well as those who have stressed the dispersal of a risk management strategy have omitted these variables. Instead these approaches have prioritised a focus on the technical and practical aspects of control or rule, or in the case of the 'dispersal of discipline thesis' have assumed rather than investigated the 'correspondence of interests' (Hall and Scraton 1981: 474) that instils social ordering practices with meaning and purpose. In short what are missing are the wider power relations and social relations upon which partnerships ground their capacity to intervene and act, through the moral as well as the technical, and the frameworks within which partnerships construct the objects of their power. If risk is a sociopolitical construct and not merely an objective technical term (Douglas 1992; Sparks 1992; Adams 1995), then a social analysis must not take the term for granted and instead contextualise it – along with concepts such as 'security' and 'responsibility' – within the configuration of partnership agencies and underlying interests that operationalise these concepts as part of social ordering strategies. This broader framework would involve both a wider understanding of social relations of which 'social ordering practices' are a part, as well as making connections back to the early and expansive conceptions of social control – Durkheim and Park – that sought an integrative, non-coercive and civilising function in the drive for social order. In this sense linking the notions of 'social ordering' and the institutional ensemble of partnerships can help to make sense of an increasingly varied terrain of criminal justice, which McMahon (1992) identified in the introduction to this book. The focus on social ordering

> entails that criminal justice studies can contribute to our more general understanding of societies. It draws our attention to criminal justice as an index of how civilized a society is, and to general questions of how negative, repressive, or socially disintegrative criminal justice power has to be, and to what degree

if any it can have positive, socially integrative functions (Lacey 1994: 34).

Therefore, the catch-all category of social control that has meant all things to all theorists can potentially gain theoretical and analytical clarity in asking what is *social* about social control; whom does it control and for what purposes?

> The constituent elements of social control are always in need of specification in each and every instance; it is not a concept that speaks for itself with much volume or clarity. What is necessary if we want to continue using the category ... is a relational analysis of the forces that are clashing, an account of the circumstances and conditions that colour the prejudice of that clash, and a theory of the ideological and cultural mediation of those forces and circumstances through the categories of social censure (Sumner 1997: 142).

This chapter has presented a theoretical base within which to place Sumner's analytical request. Thinking about the contemporary meaning of urban regeneration, its institutional embodiment within a neoliberal state form and the circuits of power it has drawn upon will provide an appreciation of the wider social relations within which a mapping of the ideological contours of contemporary social control in the urban centre is possible. The prevalence of street camera surveillance technologies – and the politics of risk this is built upon – must be thought of as more than a piece of crime prevention technology. The technology mediates, and is mediated by, wider social relations and the 'risks' that street cameras reflect and reinforce cannot be understood outside these relations.

This chapter has provided a theoretical map to interpret these social relations as organised through state institutions that are concerned with the administration and ordering of physical space. In this sense the state can only be understood 'relationally' (Jessop 1990: 269) by analysis of the social forces that constitute it: 'The state as such has no power – it is merely an institutional ensemble; it has only a set of institutional capacities and liabilities which mediate that power; the power of the state is the power of the forces acting in and through the state' (ibid.: 269–70). As agents in the making of an entrepreneurial city, the locally powerful networks that constitute the local state are discussed in the next chapter and interview material gathered from them used extensively in Chapters 6 and 7. It is within these contemporary processes in urban rule that the trajectory of social control, and more particularly CCTV, will be placed.

In the next part of the chapter the methodological issues and questions arising from the theoretical discussion in this chapter are discussed.

Street camera surveillance and social ordering:
investigating the social control agents within a neoliberal state

> We need ... to have detailed studies of the 'locally powerful' to understand how powerful positions in the family or in the workplace or in the streets are sustained (Smart 1984: 151).

Like all criminological research the research process around camera surveillance takes place within in a politicised environment. According to Groombridge and Murji (1994: 283), visual surveillance is viewed in government circles as unproblematic and has also become 'big business' so that it 'now seems set to achieve the status of an article of faith in popular crime prevention discourse'. At times the debate around CCTV has been sharply polarised among researchers. Some writers have argued *for* CCTV as a necessary and straightforward policy response to increasing crime and incivility and as a tool in reviving the pubic realm (Home Office 1994; Brown 1995; Oc and Tiesdell 1997). This has encouraged a discourse of administration and efficiency. A concern with 'what works' continues to play a role in marginalising wider questions and arguments along with a deeper theoretical analysis concerned with the conditions of emergence regarding camera networks. On the other hand, those who have noted the problematic nature of research in this area and produced findings questioning the value of CCTV have 'often [been] portrayed as enemies of the public interest' (Davies 1996a: 328). Research in this latter vein has questioned CCTV for its detrimental impact upon civil liberties (Fyfe 1995; Davies 1996b; Fay 1998); its limited value regarding women's safety (Brown 1998); and for its role in encouraging private sector involvement in circumscribing the legitimate uses of urban public centres (Fyfe and Bannister 1996; Reeve 1998).

In broad terms, along with the expansion of camera networks has been the growth of a technical and pragmatic criminological knowledge based on a methodological approach informed by the mindset of public/ private security partnerships and their concern with efficient administration rather than a questioning of the domain assumptions and rationale that underpin this market/state nexus. In critically expanding the research process to include questions of social theory, a number of researchers have started to raise issues connecting the camera imperative to processes that point to a intensification in the exclusionary potential of contemporary social control (Norris and Armstrong 1998b); the privatisation of public space (Fyfe and Bannister 1996); and as indicative of an emerging 'new governmentality' concerned to manage 'the dangerous' (McCahill 1998). Despite raising issues concerning the social aspects of CCTV surveillance, work in this area remains remarkably undertheorised with reference to the wider shifts in state power that underpin the findings from these studies. Furthermore, too often a false and hasty distinction is drawn between public and private domains of power and expertise concerned with the management and control of urban spaces. Thus any historical continuities in the power to apply social censure to particular groups as ideological signifiers of urban decay are usually lost along with processes of state transformation. As noted already, there is a turn away from state theory in social science generally and criminology in particular. This turn is having serious implications for understanding the operation and trajectory of power in contemporary societies and the growth of city centre surveillance systems through which the power to punish is being transformed.

Scrutinising the powerful: 'studying up'

> sociology that 'studies up' often won't be seen as scientific – funds will be difficult to obtain, sampling frames non existent, access (unlike to the working class) well nigh impossible and so on. Indeed, the whole activity may not even be deemed worthy of the name of science. Legitimating seals of approval may well be withdrawn from a sociology that looks up and not down (Bell 1978: 29).

Most research within social science and indeed criminology is carried out on the powerless as opposed to the powerful (Bell 1978; Hughes 1996). Bell draws attention to the 'classic' problems of researching the 'locally powerful' that include gaining funding and access to relatively closed institutions (1978: 34–7). However, despite the problems involved in 'studying up', the powerful have been a figure and subject of research in criminology. Increasingly, there is a need for criminologists to 'study up' and fix their gaze upon state and corporate mechanisms so as to understand the actions and articulations of the powerful as well as challenge them (Tombs and Whyte 2003).

Much of the research that attempts to 'study up' can be grouped under the category of 'critical social research' (Harvey 1990). Harvey attempted to define broadly the parameters of this kind of research that cannot be honed down to a single perspective or discipline:

> At the heart of critical social research is the idea that knowledge is structured by existing sets of social relations. The aim of a critical methodology is to provide knowledge which engages the prevailing social structures. These social structures are seen by critical social researchers, in one way or another, as oppressive structures (ibid.: 2).

A defining characteristic of such research and what may distinguish it from 'non-critical' research is that the knowledge it can generate is seen as knowledge as critique (ibid.: 3).[2]

Within criminology a critical tradition has been sustained from the 1960s and has been dubbed a 'criminology from below' (Sim *et al.* 1987). Neo-Marxist frameworks, discussed in the previous chapter, developed this tradition to challenge the state in particular and associated official discourses, along with a deconstruction, as well as influence upon, social policy in general. In scrutinising key criminal justice agencies, issues of institutional racism, classism and sexism have been raised through, for example, neo-Marxist and feminist theoretical frameworks that have sought to widen an understanding of the workings of criminal justice as part of the workings of an unequal social order.[3]

With regard to this study, these broad analytical provisos make it evident that the study of the camera network in Liverpool is at the same time also a study of the locally powerful as they are organised through the 'partnership' forums of the neoliberal state. Crawford (1997) has attempted to trace the development of the partnership idea and its meaning for thinking about contemporary control practices. He argued that the discursive and practical 'appeal' to 'partnerships' in the field of crime control heralds a new era in the governance of crime and disorder (ibid.: 5):

> In contemporary appeals to …'partnerships', crime control is no longer conceived of as the sole duty of the professional police officer or other criminal justice agents. Rather, it is becoming more fragmented and dispersed throughout state institutions, private organisations, and the public. Responsibility for the crime problem, according to current governmental strategies, is now everyone's. It is shared property (ibid.: 25).

In line with arguments that depict a decline in state power, and hence the non-necessity of conceptualising the state, Crawford goes on:

> Simultaneously, there is a new found emphasis on informal mechanisms of social control … In sum, there appears to be a move towards a much broader conception of security and policing, which transcends the capacities and competencies of singular modern institutions (ibid.).

As argued earlier, the state does not represent a singular, monolithic institution but a set of practices and processes made up of social forces that constitute and define state activity. This book is not concerned therefore with a general analysis of the state, but of the processes and conditions of emergence that constitute neoliberal statecraft and define the scope of state power in urban centres. With regard to Liverpool, the nature of these processes and the techniques of power they mobilise are discussed in Chapter 6.

Camera networks as 'social-ordering practices'

As Crawford rightly argues, there is a 'pressing need for criminology to reconnect the "empirical" with the "normative" ' (1997: 2). In doing this it will be possible for researchers of criminal justice to create critical research spaces within which to ask questions of a wider and more 'value-laden' nature, that link the emergence of particular 'crime control' strategies with wider problems of governance and the nature and maintenance of social order. This concurs with the need to reconceive the study of criminal justice away from a narrow, technical and purely instrumental set of concerns (Lacey 1994). This means less stress on a typology of strictly bounded 'criminal justice' institutions and more of an emphasis upon criminal justice 'as a related but not entirely coordinated set of practices geared to the construction and maintenance of social order' (ibid.: 28). Viewing criminal justice as a 'social ordering practice' (ibid.) has methodological implications:

> approaching criminal justice as a social ordering practice dictates that we pay equal attention to its instrumental and symbolic functions. In other words, it suggests that we must attend to criminal justice practices themselves but also to the meanings they have for their participants, its subjects, their observers, *including their appeal to emotional and effective attitudes* (ibid.: 30, emphasis added).

Thus thinking about and approaching camera networks in this way means attempting to detect and interpret processes that cannot simply be read off from written official policy statements. Researchers concerned to critically interpret powerful strategies of governance in the field of contemporary social control will need to acknowledge more than the complex alliances and technological innovations that 'governmentality' theorists have reified (see Miller and Rose 1990; Rose 1996). Understanding the motivations and legitimating 'logics' behind the governance and control of 'crime' and 'disorder' will necessitate taking a methodological step beyond the formal organisation of techniques of rule to focus instead upon the powerful actors and their normative articulations that lie behind this rule.

Researching state agents: who are the powerful?

The research process was structured around the completion of 20 semi-structured interviews and regular attendance at a monthly security forum (Crime Alert) concerned with the management and targeting of the local camera network. This field research has been updated and supplemented by ongoing discussions with some of the key personnel and the monitoring of local conferences and media output. During the research a number of questions and issues continued to arise and reflect back on the research process. These issues ferment around identifying 'the powerful' and gaining access to their institutional domains and 'worldviews'.

According to Crewe (1974: 17) one problem with British 'elite studies' has been that they most commonly only recognise ' "obvious" elites made visible by their concrete social organisation'. Thus 'not all elites are embedded in tangible organisations with identifiable staffs, functions, buildings, etc'. This seems a particularly acute observation when considering neoliberal statecraft. Exactly what agents and agencies constitute this state? In the era of what Jessop (1997) calls the 'entrepreneurial city' with its new modes of governance, referred to variously as 'partnership' (Edwards 1997), 'local elite' (Taylor 1997) or as the 'networked state' (Collinge and Hall 1997), this question is pertinent. The mushroom growth of partnerships aimed towards the governance of a range of local issues has highlighted the problem of locating powerful individuals within often dense and informal alliances which are – in the case of the security network in the city centre – relatively closed off from public access and scrutiny, and involve complex lines of delegation between public and private authorities. This view enables a recognition of the changing material and ideological nature of 'the powerful' as those whose institutional status and informal connections make them key primary definers involved in defining and responding to local problems. The composition of a group of primary definers is not fixed and will change over time and vary between locations (Schlesinger and Tumber 1994: 19).

In the case of researching a local camera network, new sets of primary definers emerge as forces who engage in constructing powerful discourses that define and aid the response to problems of crime, deviance and disorder in the urban centre. These powerful groups and individuals have included not only established local actors such as the police and local authority but also the public and privately sponsored office of City Centre Manager, Urban Development Corporation representatives, developers, coalitions of local business and private security managers. The emergence of partnerships and their ideological cohesiveness that mobilises particular interests within local regeneration strategies are discussed in general terms in the next chapter and, in the context of Liverpool, Chapter 6.

Identifying key players and drawing the sample

As noted above the notion of partnership has been at the centre of a changed state in organisational and governmental strategies that reconfigure public and private interests in the processes of governing crime (Crawford 1997), initiating urban regeneration (Edwards 1997) and, as argued earlier in the chapter, in reconfiguring the state form itself. Although the notion has been given statutory status in the local governance of crime under the Crime and Disorder Act 1998 the development, idea and practice of 'partnership' have been indicative of the establishment of informal and what Edwards (ibid.: 829) terms 'expedient alliances' between public and private interests. It is the nature of these alliances and the meanings attributed by key personnel to them that are of concern here. The meanings attributed to 'partnership', and the role of partnership in shaping idealised visions of the city centre, are important to ascertain for a deeper understanding of social control practices (such as CCTV) in the city centre.

The imprecise institutional boundaries, relative invisibility and operational flexibility implied in the processes of 'partnership' formation in the city centre meant that a precise sample 'hit list' of research subjects was not available at the outset of the research. The research identified three inter-related target groups as pools from which to interview and collect information. First, public and private agencies concerned with regeneration in the city. These agencies are neoliberal in their conception and derivative of 'Third Way' speak. They include 'visionary' management and marketing agencies concerned with a range of issues such as 'quality of life' indices and land reclamation. Secondly, public and private policing agencies. Thirdly, the business and retail sector. These target groupings had considerable overlap in terms of their linkage within various formal and informal partnership forums. For example, subjects from each target group were members of the Liverpool City Centre Partnership (LCCP and now called Liverpool Vision), the Government Office for Merseyside and the Stores' Committee, discussed in Chapter 7. The first and third target groups establish the forums within which public and private police work together. These agencies, Crime Alert and Town Watch, underpin the CCTV system and are discussed fully in Chapter 7. In establishing these bodies the agents of regeneration are able directly to influence the rationale for the working practices of agents working within Crime Alert and Town Watch. In other words, the 'higher level' strategic visions for an orderly city centre have a connection with lower-level social ordering on the ground. To reiterate: these target sample groups do not have hard and static boundaries. For example, a senior Merseyside police officer and interviewee – employed inside the Government Office in the Urban Regeneration Section – acts as a locally recognised spokesperson on, and architect of, local regeneration as much as policing. In recognising the fluidity and interconnectedness of the target groups, the sampling strategy employed here coheres with the theoretical approach outlined earlier in the chapter.

The neoliberal state is understood as organised both upon an institutional flexibility *and* a normative dimension concerning the social ordering of a given territory. This 'flexibility' is relative within the working dynamics of partnerships so it is important to enter these networks and interview those locally powerful orchestrators of local social order. The second target group (i.e. those who staff the new security and policing bodies) are not involved in the process of strategic thinking regarding Liverpool's regeneration, but they are agents employed and redeployed as part of 'regeneration thinking' (discussed in Chapter 7) and within forums whose origins can only be explained as arising out of local higher-level strategic decision-making.

This is not to say that the activities of lower-level social-ordering agents are determined mechanically (in any instance) by the locally powerful who are higher up the chain of command. Recognising the political origins of these bodies does not foreclose a research strategy that seeks to enter the world of lower-level social ordering agents to ascertain their views on what it is they think they are doing and for what purpose.

Thus the meanings that these lower-level social ordering agents brought to their work were important to investigate for two reasons: first, in order to identify levels of coherence with, and departures from, the locally powerful visions for order that led to the establishment of front-line security networks on the ground in the city centre; and, secondly, to avoid a reductionist and non-contingent analysis – as the meanings attached by those working on the ground in the security network need to be demonstrated empirically and not assumed.

Initial inroads into this arena were made with more obvious subjects made publicly visible by their prominence in local media reports. These key players are the City Centre Manager (indicative of town centre management schemes up and down the UK), the Chair of the Stores' Committee and the Government Office for Merseyside. From these initial contacts other contacts followed after informal requests for eligible interviewees. Thus a strategy of 'network' or 'snowball' sampling proved useful. Network sampling has often been used for identifying people and agencies suitable for study when no obvious list exists from which to select subjects. This method of sampling can apply when 'the target sample members are involved in some kind of network with others who share the same characteristic of interest' (Arber 1993: 74).

Further means of accessing the world of the locally powerful involve the researcher collecting data from regular attendance at meetings and the recording of information through field notes as well as gathering official publications, pamphlets and press releases emanating from the subject population. These are strategies for framing an understanding of the locally powerful and the workings of the neoliberal state.

Inside the neoliberal state: approaching subjects and access

Jupp (1989: 19) referred to the problem of access in criminological research in noting 'many of the institutions of criminal justice are truly closed, particularly to those not doing officially sponsored research'. For Jupp, the power of gatekeepers will vary between formal powers of exclusion and the denial of access to particular sources of information. Either way the problem of access and the role of gatekeepers can have crucial constraining effects on the research process concerning the type of research that gets done and the nature of research questions themselves (ibid.). Problems regarding the gaining of access into organisations are reported by Bryman (1988). Bryman (ibid.: 14–16) summarises a number of strategies, not without their problems, to secure access to powerful organisations. These include the promise of feedback to the organisation, engendering interest in the research in institutional representatives, and a strategy of top-level/managerial permission and access. Cultivating interest among the subject population was a strategy adopted in this research and involved scanning local media and partnership brochures and newsletters to get a flavour of what concerns key players have and the language they employ in speaking about the city, alongside their visions for the city and associated notions of 'safety' and 'security' therein. These are important to digest in order to become familiar with the powerful vernacular of urban regeneration and to comprehend the ideological mindset of partnership players. The power to shape the urban form and forge an 'urban identity' through the imagery of 'regeneration' – 'a powerful and particularly encompassing metaphor' (Furbey 1999: 420) – sets the context for grasping the means and ends of social control strategies in the 'reconstituted' urban centre. The signifiers of regeneration can be accrued from urban managers, for example, in 'talking up' the city as a 'forward looking' entrepreneurial city – economically competitive, 'politically stable' and as a 'security conscious' place. These powerful promotional discourses provide the researcher with both a linguistic map with which to forage the 'common sense' of the locally powerful and a linguistic glossary to assist in the process of approaching subjects. This was useful when structuring a letter to potential interviewees as well as in structuring the interview itself and avoided the researcher approaching subjects 'blind', as someone appearing to be potentially 'irrelevant' to the concerns of regeneration agencies. From this initial process of gauging an impression of subject interests a standard letter was drawn up for distribution. Thus all agencies who took part were initially contacted by letter addressed to senior management or director level requesting a formal interview that covered three key areas: 1) perceptions of security and insecurity in the city centre; 2) level of involvement in security and policing initiatives and rationale for being involved with them; and 3) general views expressed upon the meaning of a 'secure', 'orderly' and 'regenerated' city centre.

Access to the locally powerful takes the researcher into a world that the public would not normally have access to. However, no major obstructions occurred to gaining entry. Thus, representatives from the police, private security, local government, local business and city developers participated in the research by way of formal access to meetings and in granting interviews. A number of points can be made regarding this relative ease of access. Hughes (1996: 67) notes a shift in the 1990s towards 'a grudging "perestroika" ' regarding criminal justice research that has brought a more open system of access for researchers.

This in part is being fuelled by the rise of auditing in criminal justice, which has fostered concerns for the legitimacy of criminal justice practices. More specifically, explaining the relative ease of access concerning this research must in part be explained by the fact that the educational institution within which the research is based is also a key player at corporate level in the partnership forums concerned with regenerating the city centre. The university logo is highly visible in sponsored forms of political management in the city and appears in many regeneration and partnership brochures. Liverpool John Moores University is a key representative within LCCP, a major regeneration agency, through which the university is involved in bringing derelict land and buildings back into use as well as part-sponsoring city centre projects. Other academics within the university are involved in partnership work, acting as research advisers in the implementation of security and policing initiatives in the city, as for example in the City Safe initiative, discussed in Chapter 5. The status of the university as a recognised ideological player is illustrated by the appointment of its ex-Vice Chancellor to the position of Chairman of the Liverpool Culture Company (a body concerned with the city's Capital of Culture Campaign for 2008). Scrutinising the power of neoliberal state forms can be difficult for researchers given the entrepreneurial pursuit of external research funding that has been consolidated with the involvement of universities within urban growth machines. As two commentators have indicated: 'As all institutions of higher education seek to forge ever more symbiotic relations with local and regional, public and private sector interests it is pertinent to wonder to what extent debate in certain media will be circumscribed by these evolving dependencies' (Hall and Hubbard 1998: 318).

These wider symbiotic relations form the backdrop within which the research fieldwork could be carried out. Ongoing and intense debates, reflected through local media and local conferences, concerning the strategic direction and governance of the city centre, have been a catalyst for the research, and this researcher often felt that he was being welcomed into these circles as both someone coming from an institution recognised as a 'partnership player' and as an academic who may be 'useful' in some way. For example, one interviewee spoke of the problems of instigating partnerships and managing them towards 'security minded' regeneration initiatives. His concern, and assumption, was that I was 'on board' with these issues:

Winning hearts and minds can't be done in a day; it's a cultural thing. You coming in here is part of the trust. Your paper and research will be read by people and there may be some fairly powerful messages in it – so the truth needs to come out. It will be interesting ... to see how other organisations perceive this – whether they align or not with what I have said. The difficulty with this [regeneration process] is that we have to tell it convincingly and that's difficult (1: Superintendent Merseyside Police, Government Office for Merseyside).[4]

Indeed, openness and candour, particularly from the private sector, mark the responses of partnership players during interviews. For this group 'red-tape' and bureaucracy – associated with formally accountable political decision-making arenas – are a non-issue in terms of impeding their views.

The confidence of the new primary definers was a reflection of their enhanced political power and clout in the city centre, unrestricted by what they described as 'old style' politics. In this sense, as Chapter 7 discusses, CCTV is expressive of that confidence for its role in reclaiming, both physically and discursively, city centre space.

Attendance of meetings and field notes

Access was also granted to the monthly meetings of Crime Alert based in a suite of a major city centre retailer. These meetings provided a forum for private security and police to collate information and discuss strategies for the coming month. In sitting in on these meetings (eight were attended, each lasting a maximum of one hour) in the role as the researcher, I was given the opportunity to observe the course of the meetings and talk informally to security and policing personnel (each meeting was attended by between 25 and 35 people) as well as to establish further lines of contact. After introducing myself to the meeting at my first attendance I established a pattern at further meetings whereby I would sit at the back to observe and take notes. In this context the role of the researcher cohered with what Gold (1969: 35–6) referred to as 'participant-as-observer'. As in other researcher roles adopted in the field, the role of participant-as-observer can bring with it problems, in this case, 'the field worker is often defined by informants as more of a colleague than he [sic] feels capable of being' (ibid.: 36). This problem can compromise self-conceptions and role conceptions and manifest for this researcher during one meeting of Crime Alert. Here, I was asked by the chairperson if I would 'update the group' on my research, and in particular, whether I could 'shed any light' on the 'problem' they were discussing, namely identifying and keeping homeless people out of the stores. I answered that I was still interviewing and that no firm findings had emerged as yet. In my field notes I recorded that I was taken aback by this and felt uncomfortable in being asked to contribute 'positively' to a 'problem', the terms of reference of which I did not agree with. My answer was couched in a way that allowed my researcher 'role' to act as protection (ibid.: 31). This helped to balance the tensions between the irreconcilable perceptions that, on the one hand, I identified my research role as one that was not in collaboration with the social ordering agents but, on the other hand, that subjects within this agency identified the researcher as 'colleague' and 'collaborator' in aspects of their work.[5]

Collecting official documents and attending relevant local conferences

The development of the 'entrepreneurial city' has brought with it the production of many materials and texts which themselves can be understood as contemporary 'state discourses' (Jessop 1990: 347–50). As noted above, prior to and during the interview process time was taken to procure a range of literature emanating from the subject population and relevant to their management visions of the city centre. These included promotional materials, marketing documents and conference reports pertaining to Liverpool city centre. It was important to collect this material in order to familiarise myself with regeneration vernacular and to enhance my own 'cultural capital' and 'credibility' when interviewing locally powerful actors (Arksey and Knight 1999: 123). Furthermore, the attendance of local conferences (which I was encouraged to attend by several interviewees) provided further cultural capital and supplemented my understanding of the trajectory of locally powerful rule in the city centre. These conferences were organised by and for local regeneration and state managers and provided an insight into the discourses pertaining to 'regeneration', the tensions between players arising from this, and the linkages these players made between 'order', 'regeneration' and processes of social control.

Interviewing the powerful

Other studies have suggested that powerful individuals may have an interest in being duplicitous with what they say in interviews, protecting both institutional and personal credibility and status from public scrutiny. The powerful in this study seemed interested neither in guarding comments nor in being concerned with confidentiality. As one interviewee states: 'My views are well known on this, as are others. It's not a popularity contest, so it does not matter to me whether I am named or not' (Chairman, Stores' Committee). For one interviewee, 'openness' was welcomed but it was the perceptions of other powerful players that mattered: 'I hope you realise I am being amazingly frank with you. It's quite a relief to do it' (Home Office Adviser, Government Office for Merseyside). This same interviewee expressed concern about being 'misquoted' and 'misunderstood'. For him confidentiality was important in that he did not want 'open wrangling' between himself and other partnership players.

The use of in-depth, semi-structured interviewing allows freedom and flexibility in the interview process towards the discovery of meaning consistent with the social processes the research seeks to investigate. Therefore, in-depth research interviews provide a tool to ascertain the meanings of 'regeneration', 'order' and 'safety' that were held among key partners. Material from the interviews form the basis of the discussion in Chapters 6 and 7 that explore the meanings attributed to 'orderly space' that impinge upon the politics of space, or the process of 'spatialisation' (Ryan 1994: 40) in Liverpool city centre. As Ryan argues: 'Assumptions and judgements about space become part of the taken-for-grantedness of everyday life. How spaces and places become commonly defined for what they are is rooted in discourses and practices deeply structured in prevailing relations of power' (ibid.).

Conclusion

CCTV cannot be understood in isolation from the processes of spatialisation that surround it. Furthermore, it must be positioned in relation to other policing and security initiatives found within the locality and as part of a combined effort towards the enactment of a social ordering strategy. Exploring such a strategy enables a wider social understanding of the development of a camera surveillance network within the political, ideological and economic imperatives that inform the strategies of powerful coalitions and partnerships engaged in a process of 'regeneration' in the city centre. The arguments in this book are based on a local case study but this should not be mistaken for an understanding of the local as self-contained, nor for a view of local developments that are necessarily discontinuous and disconnected from other 'localities' and extra-local social processes.

Neoliberalism is itself a hegemonic global discourse (Wacquant 1999) that displays continuities and discontinuities at different 'local', regional, national and international scales. However, in noting the importance of 'the local' the argument here is not one of closure, in terms of a contribution to wider empirical or theoretical debate that has emerged around the nature of contemporary social control. Neo-Foucauldian approaches to social control discussed in Chapter 2 stressed the micro techniques of power. These studies have been, at best, contingent and, at worst – in the call for attention to the 'local' and 'particular' – so particularistic 'that we can never know when any particular is particular enough' (McLennan 1996: 70). 'Ultimately', Ward (2000: 171) has argued, 'concrete empirical observations must be supplemented by, and integrated in, theoretical developments'. Thus in setting out the research aims, and the research findings in Chapters 6 and 7, the book will contribute to contemporary debates into the nature of social control and its relationship to power and social order. In this sense, as Bryman (1988: 18) has argued, 'case studies are indeed capable of generality if understood in theoretical rather than statistical terms'. Given these points it is recognised that a study of a local security network is also a study of 'the locally powerful' as organised through the public and private partnerships and alliances that constitute the local state.

This chapter has presented the theoretical and methodological rationale that underpins the research strategy for scrutinising the locally powerful and in doing so trace the development and meaning of a local street camera network. The process of 'studying up' towards the new primary definers challenges an approach to social control that has viewed the latter as an apolitical set of practices. The ideological aspects of these strategies, within which the rationale for developing a CCTV network is formulated, are themselves made a subject of the research in order to identify and illuminate the underlying features of local social order as envisaged by the locally powerful. An examination of the locally powerful enables an understanding of CCTV not merely as a piece of crime prevention technology but as a key mechanism in a broader social ordering strategy. In taking this position, the 'common sense' surrounding mass camera surveillance can be subject to greater scrutiny. In studying up, then, the book engages in a deconstruction of neoliberal vernacular: how it shapes visions for order and argues for the necessity of street surveillance. Before returning to the case study of Liverpool the next chapter explores the nature of neoliberalism in contemporary cities. The imposition of neoliberal strategies of rule in North American and British cities is fermenting politically charged forms of spatial restructuring. A form of 'entrepreneurial urbanism' is shaping not only the frontiers of the state but also a vision of social control as an expression of this state's power.

Notes

1   More generally, Garland (1990: 170–1) made the point in the last chapter that the Foucauldian conception of power is problematic in that it is 'strangely apolitical'.
2   Furthermore, in contrast to an administrative research agenda, which may attempt to facilitate existing practices, a critical agenda mobilises research findings to push for more substantial change to criminal justice practices either in a reformist or even abolitionist sense.
3   An overview of some of this work is contained within Sim *et al.* (1987: 7–39) and in Scraton and Chadwick (1991).
4   Each research interview source will be referenced in the text that shows occupational title and/or institution of an interviewee. A full list of all those interviewed is provided in the Appendix.
5   Verbatim quotes accrued from field notes are used in later chapters. Field notes were therefore important in helping 'keep track of the analysis by documenting thinking processes and capturing the ideas that elevate the descriptions of empirical events to a theoretical level' (Howell 1994: 99).

Chapter 4

The neoliberal city and social control

> The universal and ineluctable consequence of this crusade to secure the city is the destruction of accessible public space … The privatisation of the architectural public realm, moreover, is shadowed by parallel restructuring of electronic space, as heavily policed, pay-access information orders; elite data-bases and subscription cable services appropriate parts of the invisible agora. Both processes, of course, mirror the deregulation of the economy and the recession of non-market entitlements (Davis 1990: 226).

Mike Davis (ibid.) depicts a possible future urban scenario in his analysis of Los Angeles as the 'bad edge of postmodernity'. Following the publication of this book as series of debates centred around whether Los Angeles could stand as a model for the development of 'fortress cities, brutally divided between fortified cells of affluent society and places of terror where the police battle the criminalized poor': a place where 'the market provision of security generates its own paranoid demand' (ibid.: 224). In many respects the scenario painted in Davis's book reminds us of nineteenth-century city building that fashioned its own 'demands for security' against the perceived contagion of 'the dangerous classes'. In the contemporary setting, Davis depicts the convergence of public and private police, property developers, planners and politicians in the creation of highly demarcated space, complete with 'pseudo-public space' and a certain political sophistication and refinement in the processes of securitisaton, segregation and ghettoisation. Implicitly, Davis's book raises questions about what states *are* and what they are *doing* in urban centres. Changes in the state form and its effectivity in the governance of urban areas cannot be separated from questions relating to the development of a 'new order' in the urban realm and the social control processes that accompany it.

Urban scholars and criminologists alike have drawn attention to the processes involved in securing city spaces in terms of the powerful coalitions involved as well as the consequences this may have for the construction and legitimate uses of city public space (Sorkin 1992; Goss 1996; Mitchell 2003; Coleman 2003a). In the UK and USA since the early 1980s the 'partnership' approach to urban governance and economic management became consolidated through the manifestation of the discourses of the New Right. Over 20 years, these discourses have constructed a particular story of global socioeconomic restructuring (Tombs and Whyte 2003) and furthered the hegemony of a neoliberal strategy of marketisation, self-responsibilisation and entrepreneurialism. In the present-day setting, concerns with crime and disorder are increasingly linked to economic decline in city centres that, along with the growth of 'out of town' shopping, is thought to bring a detrimental impact upon investment and lifestyle within cities. In responding to these and other signs of urban degeneration, partnerships are investing heavily in a vernacular of 'safety' aimed at particular audiences. Tied to this vernacular is a parallel emphasis on a remodelled social control and security doxa that taken together amount to a tactics of 'risk suppression', which is 'restructuring policing and with that, the way we use space' (Sheptycki 1997: 312).

After arguing for the importance of the state and a research strategy that scrutinises the powerful in the previous chapter, the current chapter provides a general overview of 'neoliberal cities' today and how the constitution of their governance through contemporary statecraft is shaping the nature of order in the streets. Neoliberal rule, however, is more than the sum of its governmental technologies. This form of rule is forging a 'politics of image' concerning city spaces that relays a set of normative ordering strategies concerned to re-moralise space in a manner that prescribes its broader social meanings and uses. Neoliberal statecraft in the city encompasses a physical reclamation and a moral recovery of space for the propertied and 'respectable'. As shall be seen in the next chapter, the notion of 'reclamation' has been a component in the governance of cities since the mid-nineteenth century and in Liverpool has maintained an organising core in debates around 'public space' in the city today.

Neoliberal states and spaces

More generally, in the UK throughout the 1980s and into the 1990s, the 'partnership' approach to urban governance and economic management became consolidated through the impact of global economic restructuring and the political and ideological strategies of the 'new right'. Within the context of national and international competition for investment, the governance of cities has included the forging of new alliances and collaborative arrangements between public and private agencies. In their analysis of American cities Logan and Molotch (1987) depict the city as a 'growth machine' which is re-ordering inequalities within and between cities. Within such a growth machine 'local actors link parochial settings with cosmopolitan interests, making places safe for development ... The growth ethic pervades virtually all aspects of local life, including the political system, the agenda for economic development, and even cultural organisations' (ibid.: 13). The local politics of growth is, therefore, leading to a redefinition of the rationale for local governing with the consequence of building and consolidating commanding alliances between locally powerful interests that take on an important role in this process:

> This convergence of private sector (typically business and property) interests and the public sector has inevitably undermined working class constituencies, and resulted in a heightened control of the polity by new bourgeoisie and property interests, almost exclusively consisting of businessmen (Hall and Hubbard 1996: 155).

Therefore, in response to the increased potential for global market flows (Picciotto 1996) there has 'been a mushroom growth of local state institutions which are not part of (or only loosely related to) elected local governments' (Cochrane 1993: 121). Such developments have involved the application of management techniques that appear to offer developmental growth as a 'value-free' and technical solution to urban problems claimed in the interests of all (Hall and Hubbard 1996: 156). In fact, these developments are serving to reflect and reinforce *new and more established* sets of power relations.

The drive towards an 'enterprise culture' (Deakin and Edwards 1993) inaugurated in the early 1980s, it was assumed, would bring lasting economic, social and environmental regeneration with the central involvement of the private sector in decision-making (Harding and

Garside 1995: 167).[1] These shifts have been encouraged by central government and European funding regimes (the Single Regeneration Budget, City Challenge, European Objective One Funding), which have encouraged competition between urban areas. Local-level recognition of competition for grant funding and national and international investment are leading to the creation of Regional Development Agencies (based on the Thatcherite model of Urban Development Corporations) and are leading changes in the local state as it engages with place management. Savage *et al*. (2003: 182) argue that these processes are developing 'a plethora of state institutions with different spatial scopes' whose work is reconfiguring local public participation in local government.

Urban government characterised through partnerships – initially orchestrated through ad hoc alliances between local/city government, property and business groups, utility groups, universities and local media – has thrown up new problems of urban leadership and consent in relation to local populations (Judd and Parkinson 1990). The power of partnerships to act is not of necessity dependent on the electoral process but through strategic alliances, informal decision-making and proximity to legal and statutory authority as well as the ability to engage with criteria laid down in funding regimes. Partnerships are the means by which local statecraft is becoming reconfigured in constituting a process that is deemed essential in promoting successful and orderly urban regeneration.

The work of partnerships towards local economic development has intensified the commodification of the city and its reinvention towards the hegemonic construction of place and local identity. As Harvey argues:

> The active production of places with special qualities becomes an important stake in spatial competitions between localities, cities, regions, nations. Corporatist forms of governance can flourish in such spaces, and themselves take on entrepreneurial roles in the production of favourable business climates and other special qualities (1990: 295).

Further to this process, cities 'forge a distinctive image ... to create an atmosphere of place and tradition that will act as a lure to both capital and people "of the right sort" ' (ibid.). The marketing of place has thus intensified processes bound up with attempts to lever investment and provide the basis for positive re-imaging through the selling of an area's economic 'benefits' in terms of infrastructure and labour force, the selling of cultural products, tourist attractions, the general quality of life (including crime and safety) and a range of consumption and leisure facilities (Madsen 1992). These marketing discourses will be discussed in relation to Liverpool in Chapter 6. As well as attempting to make the city more attractive to potential investors, this 'manipulation of image' has played 'a role in "social control" logic, convincing local peoples as to the benevolence of entrepreneurial strategies' and in providing a framework for the construction and maintenance of partnerships (Hall and Hubbard 1996: 162). The work of partnerships has been to build symbolic support and appropriate material resources to pursue selective aims.[2]

In thinking about this state form, it would be wrong to conceive of these developments as the wholesale replacement of the 'State' by the 'Market'. As the previous chapter argued, the state should be understood not as static thing but as field of power relations, encouraging some modes of action and cutting off others. For Savage *et al.* (2003: 197, emphasis in original), the state remains central in local regeneration strategies 'as *organiser* of new forms of investment, market regulation, new forms of control and policing and as *disorganiser* of old forms of welfare and social collectivity'.

Instead of marginalising an analysis of the state, as in much neo-Foucauldian literature, this discussion aims to bring it back in. The multifarious processes of state restructuring are conceived of as part of a neoliberal project of rule that 'represents a complex, multifaceted project of socio-spatial transformation – it contains not only a utopian vision of a fully commodified form of social life, but also a concrete program of institutional modifications through which the unfettered rule of capital is to be promoted' (Brenner and Theodore 2002: 363). The impact of neoliberalism on the urban spatial form can be characterised as a process of 'creative destruction'. As well as being *destructive* of forms of welfare provision, regulation of financial and monetary speculation, forms of targeted public funding and certain rights and social entitlements, neoliberalism has produced 'moments of creation', including; the building of free-trade zones, privatised spaces for high-earner consumption, the unleashing of zero tolerance initiatives and targeted surveillance, and the development of powerful and insidious discourses aiming to re-image cities within a vernacular of 'renaissance' (ibid.: 363–72). An important component in the armory of these neoliberal strategies has been the creation and uses of Business Improvement Districts (BIDS), much in evidence in the USA and now on the agenda in the UK. In return for paying annual subscriptions, commercial property owners are able to fund a private body charged with managing city centres. Within BID partnerships 'street cleanliness' becomes a catch-all category under which problems of marketing, environmental improvements and 'street safety' become conflated. BIDS are publicly unaccountable bodies set up to police and monitor the 'debris' of neoliberal urban visions – litter, graffiti, the homeless and prohibited street trading. Far from being value free, it is a politics of investment that defines the techniques of this strategy of rule (Savage *et al.* 2003: 182).

Thus the contemporary meaning and trajectory of social control can be understood through exploring the alliances bringing together factional interests towards the construction and procedural maintenance of social order within the 'entrepreneurial city'. As will be discussed in Chapter 6, central to the regeneration process in Liverpool is the attempt to re-image 'place' and regulate a series of negative images of the city. Essentially the problem of place management (the selection of 'desirable' images and the dissemination of information about 'place') is the problem of representing and maintaining order within the locality. The problems of defining an orderly urban fabric, in a broad sense, and instigating management strategies for its maintenance, are discussed in Chapters 6 and 7 respectively.

Thus far the chapter has discussed how the work of urban regeneration partnerships is bound up with changes in state capacity and rationale for the governing of a given territory. In promoting the economic growth of the city the new primary definers or place entrepreneurs – often represented in provincial media as 'local heroes' (Lowe 1993 cited in Short and Kim 1999: 120) – are contributing to long-term shifts in urban governance, namely around the marginalisation of welfarist objectives in favour of competitiveness and growth, the speeding up of placed-based competition for public and private investment, and the development at the local level of a business-political bloc increasingly visible and proactive in the process of strategic urban management. The promotional strategies of local state managers are setting in train and entrenching a series of taken-for-granted assumptions as to the 'proper' rationale and procedures for urban governance. These processes are made in an appeal to affluent, professional and white-collar sectors, while marginalising 'older' (and by definition less relevant) constituencies within the poorer blue-collar sectors. The marketing of cities has been targeted at business firms, corporate and divisional headquarters, investment capital, tourists, cultural establishments, and established and potential residents in order 'to replace either vague or negative images' previously held by the various targets of city marketers (Halcomb 1993: 133).

In conclusion to this section, the political processes discussed here point to a reconfiguring of the locally powerful through a neoliberal statecraft that is introducing, and attempting to normalise, rationalities for rule that cultivate new subjectivities in support of that rule. In moving away from welfarist forms of local decision-making and introducing entrepreneurial techniques of rule, the democratic deficit in partnership activities is arguably consolidating a new authoritarian state form. A danger in the concentration of public funds, state capital and social capital within a small locally powerful network, who have shaped the urban fabric in their own image, is identified by Swyngedouw:

> The 'hollowed out' state is characterised ... with a decidedly undemocratic and double authoritarian touch, both at the supra-national and local (urban/regional) level. In short, the production of post-Fordist spaces is paralleled by disturbing political transformations and a redefined citizenship (1996: 1503).

A discussion of these political transformations is useful for con-textualising later chapters. However it is worth noting that they tend to gloss over the peculiarities and contingencies involved in marketing particular places with their distinct socioeconomic contexts, political complexions, cultural forms and other issues that fall under the broad category of 'quality of life'. Nevertheless, the composition of state managers may in some respects be shifting under neoliberal conditions of urban rule, but those groups and individuals targeted as problematic for that rule are remaining broadly the same. This point is explored in Chapter 7, and underpins the lack of a deeper historical narrative of social control within theorisations of risk.

Neoliberal order

> Amidst its multiplicity of expressions, every city is to some degree a panoptican, a collection of surveillance modes designed to impose and maintain a particular model of conduct and disciplined adherence on its inhabitants ... The spatial concentration of power for social production and reproduction was what the first cities were primarily for. It has remained central to urban life ever

since, even as new functions were added. Such commanding geographical presence differentiates the urban from the rural, adherents from the not yet adherent, polites (citizens) from idiots (hicks, rubes, the uncivilised) ... the major transformations of modern society, especially the growing role of the centralised state in maintaining surveillance and adherence via national citizenship and institutionalised identity politics, should not obscure the continuing power at the city and the citadel (Soja 1996: 235).

In a very generalised sense many writers have highlighted an increasing concern with social control and order in the spaces of 'the new city'. Soja points to historical continuities regarding the spatialisation of power, those 'invisible processes of normalisation' that engage city and state in the attempt to maintain contemporary forms of representative democracy (ibid.). Soja (1995) utilises the notion of the 'postmodern city'[3] to interlink several processes of change and continuity affecting the urban form as identified by urban researchers. The first process of restructuring he identifies is the shift from a Fordist to a post-Fordist urban economy based on flexible production and accumulation strategies. Another geography of restructuring has condensed the above processes in developing new forms of social fragmentation, segregation and inequality. For Soja this has had both positive and negative impacts in that new alliances across class, cultural and political domains have emerged along with 'new landscapes of despair, interethnic conflict, crime and violence' (ibid.: 133). Furthermore Soja argued: 'Perhaps the greatest challenge facing the post-modern city is how to build on the former while keeping the latter under control' (ibid.). Urban restructuring, as an outcome of the above, is instigating 'Kaleidoscopic complexities' within cities which is rendering them 'increasingly ungovernable' under the fragmenting rubric of 'traditional' local government. The result, following Davis (1990), is the coming to prominence of the 'carceral city' – heavily enclaved and policed using spatial surveillance and military technologies (Soja 1995: 133–4). Another important process here is the 'most postmodern' of urban restructuring and it '... involves the intrusion and growing power of an urban hyperreality, of simulations and simulacra (defined as exact copies of originals that do not exist), into the material reality and ideological imagery of urban life' (ibid.: 135). For Soja this development represents a form of behavioural, cultural and ideological restructuring that affects urbanism as a way of life. What can be gleaned from this analysis is that hegemonic images, the preferred connotation and marketing of cities are becoming integral components within a developing system of social control that is being normalised into the contemporary urban landscape.

In another account Sorkin (1992) offers a dystopian description of the 'the new American city' and puts forward three characteristics that distinguish this emergent city that form the basis for 'models for urban development throughout the world' (ibid.: xv). The first characteristic driven by globalised capital, electronic production techniques and mass culture, is repetitively universalising city spaces into the predictable, 'familiar' and 'known'. Secondly, the new city can be characterised as increasingly concerned with security, both technological and physical, leading to new forms of urban segregation and distinction among city inhabitants. Thirdly, the new city increasingly assumes the character of a 'theme park' as reflected in its architecture and imaging which in turn reflect 'a spuriously appropriated past that substitutes for a more exigent and examined present' (ibid.: xiv).[4]

The material and symbolic reinvention of the contemporary city introduces new urban forms into the built environment. These forms are characterised as representing a shift from the modernist city of industrial production to the postmodernist city of a new consumerism (Zukin 1992). The enclosed spaces of the neoliberal urbanism – shopping malls, heritage and cultural centres, science parks and conference centres – are concentrating the spatial practices of consumption, leisure and entertainment for local inhabitants, tourists and business. These urban forms including 'flagship' developments, such as the Albert Dock in Liverpool and London's Docklands, are often cited as evidence of a shift towards the privatisation of public space, which is thought to be having an impact on how these spaces are regulated, ordered and policed (Bianchini 1990; Davis 1990; Sorkin 1992). The spaces represented by urban plazas are a site in which American downtowns have been privately developed (through Business Improvement Districts), funded and policed towards the creation of 'exclusionary environments' providing protected and comfortable spaces for the target group pursued by developers.

In thinking about the rationale for and expansion of these consumerist spaces, Goss (1993) argues that partnerships between designers, planners and developers are constructing total consumption environments that have their roots in shopping malls but are increasingly important in the architectural landscaping of city centres. He argues that a complex social control logic runs through the reconstruction process:

> developers have sought to assuage the collective guilt over conspicuous consumption by designing into the retail built

environment the means for the fantasised dissociation from the act of shopping … designers manufacture the illusion that something else other than mere shopping is going on, while also mediating the materialist relations of mass consumption and disguises the identity and rootedness of the shopping centre in the contemporary capitalist social order. The product is effectively a *pseudoplace* which works through spatial strategies of dissemblance and duplicity (ibid.: 19).

These spaces work towards social differentiation through the use of 'class based cues' (ibid.). Applying this analysis in Liverpool, for example, the construction of heritage sites, 'high art' and public sculpture is placed alongside, and within, 'normal' consumption spaces in the attempt to collapse any distinction between art, history and commodities. The contemporary built environment can be understood as 'as a system of signification that gives symbolic expression to the cultural values of consumer capitalism' (ibid.). The creation of idealised environments – 'spontaneous', 'spectacular' and naturalised – are themselves ideological representations of the city that underpin contemporary urban management strategies that attempt to foster a particular experiential mode or urban ambience. These broad strategies of urban rule through ideological and idealised representations of the city, its design and image management are illuminated in Chapter 6. Such ideological representations as articulated by the locally powerful reinforce a particular set of social relations that set the spatial context within which practices of social control are developed.

The attempt to order space – make it predictable, sanitised and secure – is, for one writer, bound up with the process of 'boundary erection', constructed through individual and institutional conceptions of abjection and hostility towards 'difference' (Sibley 1995). The idea that surveillance practices in public space repress 'difference' has been put forward by several writers. For Sibley, boundaries of separation are reflected within the built environment and are also moral boundaries (ibid.: 39–43) underpinned by a fear of the 'other' and constructed along class, gender, ethnic, sexual, age and disability lines. The urges to purify and dominate space are, given the politics of space identified in this chapter, relatively 'unnoticed' features within 'the spatial separations of city centre development' (ibid.: xiv).

The above writers have highlighted an increase in concerns with social control and order in the contemporary city that are part of the restructuring process of urban centres. Goss (1996) has issued caution in analysing these city spaces as being recent advances in privatisation and overdetermined by capitalist economics that 'collapses the dialectic of social control into a totalizing mechanism' (ibid.: 240). For him these spaces are 'contradictory' and 'organised by capital and state in public-private partnerships for instrumental effect' (ibid.). Indeed, the broad, even 'global', trends outlined above may not apply uniformly in particular localities and social contexts, but they do provide important pointers for the purposes of this book. The chapter now turns to a general contextual discussion of the contemporary British city in terms of the debates that have informed a restructuring of social control in the British urban setting.

Neoliberal discourse and social order in the contemporary British city

The application of CCTV in the cities of the UK intensified during the mid-1990s at a time when recorded crime continued to rise from the postwar period, with notifiable offences up from 2.4 million in 1979 to 5.5 million in 1992. By 1995, 5.1 million crimes were recorded by the police (a fall of 2.4% on the previous year), though crimes of violence increased by 5% on 1994 and robbery by 14%. Police clear-up rates have declined from 41% in 1979 to 26% in 1995. Furthermore, there has been increasingly intensive public and official scrutiny of police effectiveness. In 1996 an Audit Commission report indicated that 80% of the public were unhappy with the level of foot patrols (*The Times* 29 February 1996: 'Why police force of 2,500 has only 125 on the beat'). In their defence the Association of Chief Police Officers argued that although crime had doubled since 1980 and 999 calls had risen by 133%, police manpower had only increased by 8% (ibid.). This led to an acknowledgement that policing and criminal justice agencies alone are limited in terms of combating crime with a consequent expansion of expectation in what the public and other agencies can contribute in this area. The growth of the private security industry has been particularly evident. Figures show that from 1970 its turnover had grown from £55 million to £1.2 billion in 1990. During the 1990s, estimates of the numbers of private security personnel began to show that they outnumbered the police by as much as 12,000 employees (*The Independent on Sunday* 11 June 1995: 'Private lives').[5] The increasing politicisation of law and order since 1979 can be placed alongside a rise in public concern around safety and security that, according to the 1994 British Crime Survey, is manifest in public anxiety about becoming victims of crime over and above worries to do with job insecurity and illness. Alongside this the 1995 British Social Attitudes Survey reported that the majority of those surveyed believed that the court system was too lenient on criminals, that increased public support existed for police surveillance measures, that concern for civil liberties was declining and that the fear of crime was rising, particularly amongst the young and women (*The Guardian* 22 November 1995: 'Hard times for the libertarian').

It is within this context of academic and political concerns around increases in recorded crime, police ineffectiveness and heightened public anxiety that 'The material and symbolic significance of "crime" and "fear of crime" in different conurbations is increasingly linked with other issues to do with "urban fortunes", as understood locally in past, present and future terms' (Taylor 1996: 332). These concerns point to a perception that the city centre is an increasingly insecure place both economically and socially, for business and consumers alike, and this is acknowledged within successive central government programmes which have sought to target potential victims, vulnerable environments and all those who are capable of exercising responsibility for reducing criminal opportunity (Hough *et al.* 1980). In the UK a neoliberal vernacular has taken centre stage in constructing and responding to these problems in a language that promotes ideas of 'responsibility', 'empowerment' and 'community'. Under the Action for Cities initiative launched in 1988 a range of problems were identified in Britain's cities and targeted under this new initiative which sought to improve investment and enterprise; tackle dereliction and improve development; improve transport; develop the arts; and make city areas safe and attractive places to live and work in. From this initiative the Safer Cities Projects emerged, which by 1998 operated in 55 cities and towns. This programme represented the Home Office's centrepiece crime prevention initiative and has had three main aims – 'to reduce crime', 'to lessen the fear of crime' and 'to create safer cities where economic enterprise and community life can flourish' (Home Office 1991: 2). The programme provided Home Office support through central co-ordination, advice, expertise and the funding of partnerships at the local level. The funds made available are also used as a levering device to attract other local funds, particularly from the business community, for the purposes of crime prevention. Though control over the process is firmly located within the central government domain, it is managed locally by non-profit-making organisations such as the National Association for the Care and Resettlement of Offenders and Crime Concern. The latter body was established in 1988 by central government to encourage private sector funding and involvement in crime prevention through acting as an 'independent' consultant to local partnerships and encouraging 'good practice'. Central government also established the Crime Prevention Agency in 1995 to co-ordinate national objectives by bringing together the Home Office, police, business leaders, Crime Concern and academics (*The Guardian* 23 November 1995: '10,000 spy cameras for high streets').[6]

Alongside these developments has been the increasing deployment of surveillance cameras in non-residential environments as a central component of current 'crime prevention' thinking and practice. In Britain during the 1990s, the drive to secure urban space became big business with the market for CCTV doubling since 1989 to an annual spending of £300 million. The British Security Industry Association (BSIA) trumpeted an observation that CCTV was becoming an acceptable and 'permanent fixture' on the streets of Britain and that on a 'typical day' each one of us is viewed by eight different surveillance cameras (BSIA 1997: 23). Indeed, more recent estimates claim there is now one camera for every fourteen people in the UK (*The Independent* 12 January 2004: 'Big brother Britain, 2004'). Under John Major's Conservative administration, CCTV took a central role in government thinking around crime prevention and, as the Introduction to this book observed, this thinking was maintained and intensified under New Labour. In encouraging this growth the Conservatives removed the need for planning permission to install CCTV systems (Home Office 1994: 17–18). Furthermore, as the Home Office publication *Crime Prevention News* (Home Office April–June 1996) made clear, CCTV was to be placed as a central component of the Conservative law and order strategy. John Major's desire 'to make every street safe' underpinned the intention to generate 10,000 extra cameras by making £15 million available in a 'CCTV Challenge Competition' (Home Office 1995). The bidding document made funding available only to those schemes that could demonstrate a 'partnership' approach; were 'broadly representative of the community'; had the support of local police; could clearly identify a 'crime problem'; and could secure private sector funding to maintain a CCTV scheme (ibid.: 1–2).[7]

In Britain, the police and the Home Office are actively encouraging private industry to invest millions in crime prevention including the sponsoring of police cars and the establishment of surveillance cameras. This has been necessary, argued the Police Federation, in a climate where crime costs £1,000 a second and £31 billion a year (*The Guardian* 19 May 1997: 'Firms urged to fund crime fight').

Thus CCTV emerges when a political shift is occurring that prioritises a language of 'partnerships' and emphasises a 'shared responsibility' for crime prevention that amounts to wider 'responsibilisation strategies'.

This discourse is exemplified under the Crime and Disorder Act (CDA) 1998, aimed to reduce public concern around issues of crime, disorder and nuisance. The Act aimed to formalise and co-ordinate, with central government guidance, the work of local crime prevention partnerships. The Act depicts local crime prevention through the language of 'community safety' and can be seen as an attempt 'to solve the problem of "who owns the community safety problem?" ' (Audit Commission 1999: 20). The CDA allows a certain level of continuity regarding local discretion for the identification and solution of local problems. Home Office guidance has stressed 'maximum flexibility for local freedom': 'the Act does not prescribe in any detail what the agenda for the local partnership should be, nor what structures will be needed to deliver the agenda' (Home Office 1998: Foreword).

However, the Act imposes a legal duty on the police and local authorities to work with other 'responsible authorities' in order to conduct three-yearly crime and disorder audits as a means for setting strategic priorities. In line with this, computer technology known as geographical information systems (GIS) is being developed in order to map high-risk areas or crime 'hotspots'. The formalisation of business involvement in strategic partnerships is being pushed by the Act. Local Chambers of Commerce and privately sponsored town centre management consortia should be incorporated into local strategic partnerships, not merely as 'a source of funds' but as educators in the skills of 'project management and technical know-how'. Local crime and disorder strategies must therefore seek the active participation of the business sector that has 'a legitimate expectation that the strategy will address issues of concern to them' (ibid.: s. 2.33).

Interpreting these developments in the shift to 'community' based crime prevention has left questions for scholars in the field. The re-invigoration of appeals to community has sat alongside the 'democratic deficit' following the curbing of local authority power by central government during the 1980s (Hughes 1998: 147). As Hughes suggests, 'the "unfinished business" around appeals to the ideologically volatile vision of community' (ibid.: 129) has left the concept more open and contestable than some have argued. Evoking 'community' may serve 'countervailing forces ... on the wider social fabric/body politic' in terms of provoking 'the possibility of "unsettlements" of the state's dominant agenda on crime control' (ibid.: 128). However, the possibility of 'unsettlements' of dominant crime control (and social control) agendas will come up against powerful official discourses proliferated by well organised local elites towards setting the parameters around what is and what is not relevant to the strategy of 'partnership' (Atkinson 1999). These discourses shape the meaning of regeneration and partnership strategy in Liverpool city centre as we shall see in Chapter 6.

Street reclamation and remoralisation

The initiatives currently occupying the governance of cities in the UK (and the in USA) are concerned with a particular construction and production of the 'public realm'. This process is not only active at the discursive level, but is tied into a vigorous appropriation strategy enacted through locally powerful coalitions, whereby physical space is occupied and taken. Such an appropriation strategy is subjecting space to curfews and restrictions, as well as a form of rule based on coercion. The partnership approach that is built around these strategies – and characterised by the CDA – cannot be divorced from the 'growth machine' that underpins local development. For Taylor (1997), the partnership approach is indicative of a defensive collective movement. This point was underscored bey van Swaaningen (1997: 175), who characterised so-called 'risk' orientated crime and safety initiatives as defined through the targeting of 'nuisances' that have mirrored the urban social defence practices of the 1880s.

In the contemporary setting, a study by Beck and Willis (1995) is used to justify the reclamation strategies currently being employed. It reports that town and city centres are facing decline because consumers are increasingly expressing a preference for out-of-town shopping and enclosed malls which offer the reassuring presence of private security and surveillance cameras. The public survey conducted for their study identified a number of 'nuisances' that the public perceive as obstacles to consumption in the city centre:

> The term nuisance is widely used as convenient shorthand for members of the public being upset in any way whilst shopping. This may include shoppers being subject to behaviour which causes them distress, or it may involve the unwelcome or un-wanted presence of certain persons in the shopping environment. It may be manifest through unpleasant or offensive gangs of threaten-ing youths; children hanging around in town centres and shopping centres; people selling things on the street; and distress caused by prostitutes, vagrants, beggars, drunks or buskers (ibid.: 31).

Such a wide range of 'incivilities' were 'seen in themselves, irrespective of their actions, as contaminating the environment' (ibid.). Predictably, the survey advocates the greater use of surveillance cameras and uniformed security to reassure the consuming public. The research concludes that retailers and town centre managers will have to be prepared to fund 'safer shopping' strategies as part of the drive to maintain profitability in the city centre.

The fusion of regeneration strategies with 'crime prevention' and a wider order maintenance is exemplified in the growth of city and town centre management techniques that have broadly aimed to promote an improvement in the quality of the environment of the city centre. Such management techniques are indicative of the entrepreneurial forms of rule discussed previously. The concept of town centre management (TCM) originates from the recognition by local authorities and business interests that the economic viability of a town centre is on the decline and draws upon the model of the commercial management of large out-of-town shopping complexes. The pooling of resources from both public and private sources has been used to establish the office of town centre manager, a position usually filled by seconded business personnel from one of the major retail chains. The impetus therefore has been towards the enhancement of the commercial viability, through publicity and partner mobilisation, of the city or town centre. Studies indicate that in attracting investment and consumption to particular locations, TCM prioritises the targeting of non-consumptive activities through environmental improvements and CCTV that aims to discourage begging, roaming youths and unlicensed street vending (Reeve 1998).[8] The management of safer city centres has become a growing academic specialism that has broadly encouraged the implementation of a range of situational measures open to city centre managers as a means towards greater civility and a reduction in criminal opportunity (Oc and Tiesdell 1997). In encouraging the remoralisation process, these authors state that although opportunity-reducing measures are crucial to safer city centres, they will not prevent crime and must be placed alongside measures to encourage moral responsibility:

> What is therefore also needed is the curbing of social incivilities by better personal behaviour and conduct within the space of the city centre. Rather than a culture of excuses for poor behaviour in public places, what is required is a culture of expectations for more civility (ibid.: 238).

This political and academic clamour for the remoralisation of the spaces of city centres is most usually couched in a 'Third Way' friendly language of individual responsibility and anti-social behaviour. Discourses of civility and civic responsibility punctuated the views of the locally powerful in Liverpool and form part of their visions for an orderly city centre. Appealing to notions of 'civility' and 'quality of life' is a highly skewed process that attempts to build a popular legitimacy for neoliberal statecraft and city building. As shall be seen in later chapters, in defining these notions a problem arises with the increasing divergence of control tasks between powerful public and private authorities that is opening up 'the development of crime prevention projects which are not necessarily directed at "crime" in the legal sense of the word'. This is sedimenting a process of bringing 'people under penal control under whom no legal suspicion is established' (van Swaaningen 1997: 196). The developments discussed here are understood as a merging of 'crime control/prevention' with a broader notion of 'quality of life' that is reflective of a process to re-image and construct a particular city's 'place' in the regional, national and international urban hierarchy. At the local level, this has been accompanied by a move towards 'public order', 'zero tolerance' or 'quality of life' policing that has been aimed at groups 'perceived to degrade the urban aesthetic and make life difficult for the "law abiding"' (Stenson 2000: 216). It has been argued that targeting the homeless, drunks and vandals has been underpinned by a widespread fear of the ungovernable and a tolerance of social exclusion that leads to 'acceptance of harsh methods of controlling and disciplining the poor and the deviant' (Currie 1997: 136). Indeed, as we shall see later, unattractive and irksome reminders of social inequality are being airbrushed out of the imaginary representations and material realities of city life.

As noted earlier, 'quality of life' forms a thread in regeneration discourse and acts as a key discursive device utilised across partnerships in the construction of place-marketing initiatives for the purposes of attracting inward investment. The concern with 'quality of life' increasingly incorporates local crime indexes and those local, national and international reputations and identities that particular places are perceived to engender. Thus partnerships between local business, police, local government, developers and local media are becoming increasingly geared towards the management of local problems and threats deemed to destabilise a local risk calculus increasingly used as an important source of information in investment decisions.[9] This recognition of the salience of 'crime' among local elites and its importance in the competitive re-positioning of cities have been reflected in central government initiatives such as Safer Cities, which since its demise as a discretely funded programme has seen funds transferred to the Single Regeneration Budget (1994). This transfer makes 'the control of crime' a central component of urban regeneration rhetoric and policy, making 'crime prevention' an element that must be competitively bid for alongside, and as part of, any successful regeneration strategy. Thus the identification of a 'crime problem' becomes a key strategy in gaining scarce central resources. This is reinforced by legislative and official guidance documents that stress a linkage between crime and disorder and 'successful' regeneration. The CDA and Local Strategic Partnerships (2000) provide examples of attempts to co-ordinate this line of governance in what is officially recognised as 'joined up', 'responsible' government. 'Joined up' government takes shape under a neoliberal ideology of managerialism and intensifies a process of subordinating social policy to sustaining economic competitiveness and fighting 'crime and disorder' (Crowther 2000: 151). Managers and proponents of mass camera surveillance, in shaping how the technology is ideologically represented and used, have further reinforced the link between 'orderly' urban space and urban renaissance. Attempts to 'join up' experiments in neoliberal rule and co-ordinate agents and agencies in the neoliberal state are at the heart of a 'Third Way' politics, a central aim of which is the restoration of sovereign or state control over the 'socially excluded', 'hard to reach groups' or, as we used to say, the poor. The identification, social censure and management-in-space of incongruous urban groups will be explored later alongside the strategic visionary ideals for urban space that underpin neoliberal order.

Conclusion

The chapter has indicated how scholars have begun to explore economic, political and policy processes that underpin the building of the contemporary city. Understood as a landscape of power, these kinds of cities – underpinned by an ideology of entrepreneurialism – have given rise to social control strategies that reflect and engage with wider programmes of urban regeneration, re-invention, re-positioning and re-imaging. The landscaped city is therefore not accidental or the result of an ad hoc venture. In other words: 'Landscape … naturalises in material form the values of the powerful marking out moral geographies that exclude and exile feared social groups' (Gold and Revill 2003: 36–7).

These general trends and process are displaying remarkable similarities within advanced capitalist cityscapes (Wacquant 1999). This does not equate, however, with a homogenised governing process or symmetry regarding the meaning and form attributed to city spaces. The points raised here have not explicitly focused on the important dynamics of resistance and tensions related to neoliberal rule but have attempted instead to map out a neoliberal 'logic' in the process of sociospatial ordering. Neoliberal rationales 'unfold in place-specific forms and combinations' (Brenner and Theordore 2002: 368) and engage with particular inherited institutional politics and cultural histories. The visions of the locally powerful and the moral geographies that underpin the landscape of power in Liverpool are explored here in later chapters, when looking at the redrawing of state boundaries and scope for action in the city. In excavating current forms of statecraft it can be seen how the technologies of government and control may have changed from the nineteenth-century city, but it is a matter of empirical debate as to what extent the categories of 'crime', 'disorder' and 'incivility' have fluctuated in their meaning and in their relationship to the processes of ordering and marginalising in the city. The social reproduction of such categories and their role in the building of a landscape of power cannot be underestimated.

The development of the neoliberal state and its impact upon the trajectory of social ordering bring together both technical and moral dimensions. It would be incorrect therefore to take the 'entrepreneurial state' and its 'responsibilised', efficient, risk avoidance strategy at face value. Van Swaaningen (1997: 90) warns of the dangers in losing a normative framework that would help make sense of the contemporary 'politics of prevention': 'It is crucial to reveal the gut reaction populism on which this politics is actually based, and to place criminal justice politics in a socio-economic framework.' In the age of the rule of 'partnership', this 'populism' is as likely to be articulated by so-called 'risk-based' private actors as it is by public authorities charged with territorial censure and control in the landscaped city. Furthermore, the pairing of 'risk avoidance' through 'partnership' in the contemporary urban setting forces a consideration of wider local material conditions from which 'risk' develops a normative dimension. Remoralising city spaces may support, contradict or be indifferent to a local growth strategy. But any discursive re-taking of city streets by locally powerful coalitions work to the extent that they accommodate the wider visions for order now at work in entrepreneurial cities.

The co-ordination of neoliberal rule may be uneven and contradictory at the local level but, as this chapter has argued, its impact on social control practices *cannot* be interpreted within a framework that rejects thinking about the state and substitutes this with a framework that promotes a simple plurality of power. The notion of 'partnership' does not signal a universally empowering free-for-all, real or metaphorical. The kind of statecraft now at work in many advanced capitalist cities is reworking and reinforcing dimensions of power in a normative sense. A focus is necessary on the normative dimensions of power in order to ascertain the trajectory of neoliberal statecraft itself, and how authoritative appeals to leadership in civil society from within this state form are articulated. Gramsci made this point when arguing against 'organic' distinctions between state and civil society. He argued for a view of the state (not as a 'thing') but as a crafted and re-crafted site that privileges particular political rationalities and programmes of rule. Any such distinctions between state and civil society are 'methodological' and furthermore:

> since in actual reality civil society and state are one and the same, it must be made clear that laissez-faire too is a form of state 'regulation', introduced and maintained by legislative and coercive means. It is a deliberate policy, conscious of its own ends, and not the spontaneous, automatic expression of economic facts. Con- sequently, laissez-faire liberalism is a political programme, designed to change – in so far as it is victorious – a state's leading personnel, and to change the economic programme itself – in other words the distribution of the national income (Gramsci 1971: 160).

The re-marketisation of the city through a neoliberal ethos is changing what states *are* in cities, and *how* they organise circuits of power and intervene, reflect or reinforce – discursively and materially – the local landscape of inequality. The political processes that manage this landscape are underpinned by discourses of fear that identify threats to a desired and visionary notion of the 'city as a whole' and exclude it from the shares in a global marketplace.

The following chapters explore the processes involved in reshaping the urban form in Liverpool and how problems thought to hinder the emergence of a 'new' urbanity are identified, articulated and responded to. In exploring the boundaries and scope of local state action, the research process is directed upwards towards a local state's leading personnel, to identify the themes discussed in this chapter regarding the trajectory and meaning of 'partnership' power. In exploring these social relations, the context will be set for investigating social control in Liverpool city centre in Chapter 7. Next, the book turns to a focus upon the historical inter-relationship between prevailing economic, political and social relations in the city of Liverpool and the processes of social control that have emerged along with these relations.

Notes

1   The increased role of the private sector in urban decision-making and economic growth should not be exaggerated (Harvey 1985), but has been influential in the ability of cities not merely to respond to market forces but to act as 'very much a part of global restructuring, and a pernicious part' (Lovering 1997: 79).

2   These developments in governing the city have been criticised for prioritising a market and property-led agenda and for the exclusion of other interests and in failing to empower the poorer members of the community (Bassett 1996). Edwards (1997) questioned whether partnerships with their discursive armoury of 'community empowerment' and 'trickle-down' wealth creation would offer any solution at all for urban regeneration in terms of addressing poverty and job creation.

3   These broad observations have echoed a concern with security and social control identified by a range of writers within the contemporary 'postmodern' metropolis. The category of the 'postmodern' used variously by many writers has been applied to capture some of the developments affecting the city and the urban experience. Although 'no clear understanding separates modern from post-modern cities', Zukin argued that through the lens of postmodernism 'we sense a difference in how we organise what we see; how the visual consumption of space and time is both speeded up and abstracted from the logic of industrial production, forcing a dissolution of traditional spatial identities and their reconstitution along new lines' (1992: 221).

4   For Sorkin (1992), these developments have begun to undermine traditional notions of public space as represented for him through freedom of human interaction and political debate. Sorkin called for a more 'authentic urbanity' and claimed that 'the effort to reclaim the city is the struggle for democracy itself' (ibid.: xv).

5   The Association of Chief Police Officers was eager to point out that this rise in private and unregulated security provision was set to continue if cuts in police manpower budgets were not reversed (*The Guardian* 25 January 1995: 'Police chiefs fear cuts will increase use of security firms'). By 2000 the private security industry had grown to be worth £4 billion (*The Observer* 23 April [2000]). At the same time, police detection rates have continued to fall to an all-time low of 24% (*The Guardian* 12 July 2002: 'Abrupt end to six-year fall in crime').

6   The work of this agency was maintained under New Labour's Crime Reduction Programme in 1998.

85

7 The criteria to receive funding laid down in this document have remained unchanged under New Labour's funding arrangements for CCTV through the Crime Reduction Programme.

8 The development of TCM has been a feature of Liverpool's regeneration. Personnel working within such bodies were interviewed for this book, the data from which are discussed in Chapter 6 and Chapter 7.

9 The processes involved in defining the police role and their positioning in local investment strategies will be highlighted in Chapter 7 with regard to Liverpool.

Chapter 5

From the dockyards to the Disney Store: the historical trajectory of social control in Liverpool

Liverpool's trades union leaders of 1991 crowing atop piles of stinking rubbish like cockerels on dung heaps, its welfare mentality growing upon the destruction of wealth producing jobs … poverty and crime nourished on the thin gruel of welfare, the whole mess financed by borrowing whose costs choke any tentative industry or commerce, was the world's image and the terrible reality of Britain in the 1970s (Tebbit 1991: 23).

Morphocity is now undergoing a cultural and contextual revolution. The city is reinventing itself and tuning in with the requirements of modern learning curves. Morphocity is now informed by a new and different set of values: openness, meritocracy, social diversity, plurality of skills, youth culture, transparency, vision, change, experimentation and cosmopolitanism (Humphreys and MacDonald 1995: 50).

The two qualitatively different quotations above point to the nuances between historical representations of place. These highlight the centrality of struggles over image, identity and reputation concerning the city of Liverpool and its population. The quotation from Norman Tebbit encapsulated for many political and media commentators what appeared to be 'wrong' with Liverpool during the 1970s and into the 1980s: a political, economic and cultural backwater, a disorderly city at odds with the cutting edge of neoliberal discourse and practice, and the maker of its own demise. Such representations of the city are not self-contained and emerge out of popular myth as much as concrete political and economic struggle. In contrast the notion of 'morphocity' emerges from a document that speaks of the 'new' Liverpool, a city in renaissance: forward looking, replete with the latest technologies of urban management and reminiscent of a general trend in the advanced capitalist city, characterised as 'playful space', full of 'spontaneity' and 'creativity' (Christopherson 1994: 409). The contemporary 'renaissance' in Liverpool encapsulates these two contrasting positions. The drive to re-image the city is, for local state managers, highlighting a clear contrast (and indeed a contest) between dystopian and utopian discourses of 'place' that is perceived to affect the city and its ability to claim its share in a 'global marketplace'.

Representations of the city traverse the problem of order – its ideological signification and material realisation. Contemporary powerful discourses relating to place are attempts to reverse negative perceptions and images in a manner that navigates a strategy for order. Such a strategy, as is the case in Liverpool, can have complex and unintended outcomes (see Chapter 7). Within the matrix of locally powerful vernacular, what is striking today is the tension between the desire to 'talk up' a place and, in contradistinction, an urge to pathologise aspects of the same place. These contradictory discourses have a particular focus on the streets of the city. Activities within, as well as the 'look' and 'feel' of, the streets are celebrated at the same time as other aspects of street life are pathologised. Within renaissance vernacular, the streets are *idealised* as ordered and yet *represented* as disordered. These contradictions within official discourse mirror the material contradictions within neoliberal city building. Locally powerful representations of place, identify the objects of power in a manner that renders such objects manageable and suitable targets of regulation and control.

As the previous chapter showed, the centrality of mechanisms geared towards effective social control in the regenerated city is displaying both 'global' and 'local' characteristics in the marketisation of security provision (Sheptycki 1997; MacLeod 2002):

> Underlying these developments is the discourse of insecurity and the practices of risk suppression … The distribution of risks depends on the segregation of suspect populations (which will be differently defined in different locales but which will, in any case, be those without access to the economic and political levers of power) (Sheptycki 1997: 312).

In Liverpool, 'image' – particularly the production of negative imagery – has played a strong role in the city's development in relation to the management and control of the economically and politically marginalised. The distribution of risk in Liverpool underpins a pathography of the streets that, as an aspect of capitalist urban rule, identifies and targets 'suspect communities' and prescribes the legitimate uses of what is ostensibly public space. It is the local expression of social control in the city that this chapter focuses on with a reminder that discourses that construct urban violence, 'dysfunctional' activities and pathologies play a part in organising the locally powerful and in establishing the course of local state action. What follows is an overview of social control and policing in Liverpool that takes into account historical themes and issues that broadly illuminate the rationale underpinning social control strategies, policing and their targeting. In drawing attention to these historical processes the chapter begins to forge an appreciation of continuities in the formulation and targeting of social control in the city. Those writers that stress the 'newness' and strategic novelty of contemporary social control practices – concerning, *who* is targeted, and by what *means* – often lack a deeper historical reading of social control and its role in the materialisation of order at street level. As part of their rule over a given territory locally powerful coalitions mobilise, to varying degrees and levels of success, discourses that attempt to construct the meaning of place. Included here is a trans-local language of pathology that has been an aspect of capitalist urban development. The intensity of this pathography has varied at different historical moments and between different places but is, in the contemporary setting, reinvigorating a moral geography of public space that constructs identities and reputations of those members of the urban population who are deemed to hinder, or whose mere presence calls into question, a strategy of order and rule.

Morality and policing social boundaries in the nineteenth century city

The official and bourgeois depiction of the disorderly nineteenth century industrial city spurred debates of the time around urban dystopias and the perceived need for the development of a variety of social control measures. During the 1840s a discourse of 'moral environmentalism' targeted the urban poor and was enacted through the studies and observations of early modern philanthropists, medical experts and state servants (Mort 1987). Such moralistic models found various incantations in later sociological theorising such as those found in the Chicago School. Prior to that, the domains of 'expertise' in the early and mid-nineteenth century helped to construct certain places and particular groups as 'dangerous' and as 'other' – outside the civilising norms encapsulated within bourgeois thought. In this sense 'nineteenth century discourses on the metropolis created an urban topography in which the slum, the sewer, the poor and the prostitute were effectively separated from the suburb'. Furthermore, 'this separation enabled the social reformer, as part of a process of validation of the bourgeois imagery, to survey and classify its *own antithesis*' (Marriott 1999: 83, emphasis in original). The complex structure of Victorian morality underpinned programmes of intervention aimed at the 'Dickensian city-scape of dirty, crowded and disorganised clusters of urban villages ... where the "Great Unwashed" lived in chaotic alleys, courts and hovels just off the grand thoroughfares' (Walkowitz 1992: 119). Victorian reformers sought to classify and counter the perceived contagion of the 'rough' elements and places within the industrial working class. The multiple threats this group posed were perceived in terms of contagion across a range of fronts, most notably health and sanitation, the growth of 'dangerous' political ideas, the immorality found in the lifestyle of the causal poor and the 'rampant criminality' of those on the margins of economic life (Pearson 1975; Stedman-Jones 1981; Walkawitz 1992).

Underpinning urban reform programmes in the nineteenth century city were the class and gender-related polarities that constructed virtue/vice, cleanliness/filth, morality/depravity, civilisation/animality (Mort 1987: 41). These discursive frameworks and their role in the promotion of social order displayed explanatory tensions between environmentalism and individual morality in understanding the condition of 'the poor'. The role of the emergent state of this time, in dealing with identified problem groups and behaviours, also displayed tensions between criminalisation and/or education as the appropriate response (ibid.). The notion of the 'dangerous classes' was central to discussions of crime, criminality and criminalisation, and was linked to the discourses and practices regarding what the city is and ought to be. The perception of threats to these visions or urban ideals was bound up with the contestations between powerful interest groups and professions that sought to control, regulate or influence urban life generally and the urban poor in particular.

As Cohen (1985: 205) puts it, 'We are haunted by the old idea that the city stands for something'. The catch-all symbolism of the 'dangerous classes' therefore posed, and continues to pose, a threat to powerful visionary discourses pertaining to an orderly city. Such visions of order in the nineteenth century city related to the emergent class, gender and racial hierarchies associated with Victorian morality, which hegemonically constructed ideas of 'respectability' to serve as models of behaviour towards thrift, work, discipline and sex and sexuality (Mort 1987; Walkowitz 1992). Such sentiment fuelled the 'great fear' of a 'bastardized race' within a 'class degraded by misery whose vices [stood] like an invincible obstacle to the generous intentions that wish to combat it' (Foucault 1977: 275–6). 'Respectable' fears and concerns in the context of Liverpool are explored below. These concerns for the viability of a political, sociocultural and economic vision of city life are not a nineteenth century discursive throwback, but continue to be articulated today by the 'new' architects of urban renaissance, armed with an 'expertise' cloaked in a 'new' morality and underpinned by a language of risk.

Political economy in Liverpool from the early nineteenth century to the 1980s

> There is no city in the world, not even London itself, in which so many foreign governments find it necessary to maintain consular for the safeguarding of the interests of their exiled subjects. It should, however, be noted that this amazingly polyglot and cosmopolitan population, consisting of races which are backward in many ways, and maintaining itself largely by unskilled labour, vastly increases the difficulty of securing and maintaining the decencies of life (Muir 1907: 305–6).

The political economy of Liverpool in the nineteenth century was established around the largest and most complex dock system in Western Europe that, along with the city's identification as a commerce centre, placed Liverpool as the second city of industrial Britain and of the British Empire. It is not often recognised that the prosperity and growth of the city were built on slavery, with over 40% of all slaves traded from Africa by European countries, and transported using Liverpool-based ships (Gifford *et al.* 1989: 25). Indeed, without the slave trade Liverpool's economic prosperity would not have been possible (Williams 1964: 63).

The town of Liverpool contained around 1,000 inhabitants in 1670 and 7,000 in 1710. Between 1811 and 1861 the population growth in the city multiplied five times with 22% of the local population in 1851 being migrants from Ireland (Morris and Rodger 1993: 2–3). The population was largely transient. In 1872 the Chief Constable John Greig estimated that at any one time the city possessed a shifting population of about 20,000 (Lane 1987: 34). Local manufacturing had a minor role in economic development that relied on the Liverpool port, which by 1857 was responsible for approximately half of Britain's exports and one third of its imports (Merseyside Socialist Research Group (MSRG) 1980: 28). In the 1860s, the local Chamber of Commerce presented with pride an image of Liverpool that was based not on the industrial factory system but upon the 'gentlemanly' pursuit of commerce. The dominant mercantile class accrued its wealth and profits through overseas trade on the back of a vast, and significantly immigrant, casualised labour force divided by work opportunities, culture and race (Brogden 1982: 46). Up until the mid-nineteenth century Liverpool was dominated politically, economically and culturally by 'the old families' who were organised through 'three or four handed partnerships' that combined the business interests of merchanting, ship owning and insurance whose considerable influence in the governance of the city was maintained through involvement in sitting on various committees that promoted 'civic duty' and improvements in the local 'quality of life' (Lane 1987: 53–82).

By the early twentieth century, family firms and partnerships had been absorbed into larger corporations that progressively became detached from Liverpool. Of necessity, these enterprises looked beyond the city for their continued prosperity though evidence of their economic and cultural hegemony can be seen in the spectacle of Georgian and Regency architecture that remains in and around the city today. Liverpool produced more wealthy families in the nineteenth century than any other English city and this wealth became closely connected to local politics through the Liberal and Tory Parties and various philanthropic organisations that procured for the local elite 'some intelligence of the *other* Liverpool' – the poor, destitute and otherwise casualised labourers (ibid.: 131, emphasis added). Up until the mid-nineteenth century, Liverpool was a town 'in which the public good was equated with commerce' and accordingly the water supply and refuge collection were left to private enterprise, while no responsibility for building regulation and sewerage was bestowed upon the Liverpool Corporation (Power 1992: 35). Merchants dominated the town council up until municipal reform around 1835 – 'what it lacked in accountability Liverpool more than made up for in its single minded devotion to furthering commerce' (ibid.: 25).

The 'second industrial revolution' by-passed Liverpool, whose economic structure drifted away from national trends and the majority of whose labour force stood outside permanent and stable work. By the 1920s, 37% of Liverpool workers were involved in production as compared to the national average of 67% (Belcham 1992: 3). After the First World War, the docks had started to decline though over half of

Liverpool's working population were involved in shipping, dock-work or in related transportation. For male workers in the city there had always been limited opportunities for employment outside the port. Women's exclusion from this arena meant that if they worked outside the home they were mostly employed as domestic servants for the merchant and professional classes. Between 1921 and 1931, around 30 women in every 100 were engaged in servant-based occupations at a time when such work was steadily in decline as the wealthy moved out of the city centre area (MSRG 1980: 31).

In conjunction with these processes the trajectory of the political economy of Liverpool during the nineteenth and twentieth centuries 'ensured a classic lumpen-proletariat, low skilled and outside the disciplines of industry and the predictable security of a weekly wage packet' (Brogden 1991: 3). Casualisation and a low-skill economic base underpinned this residuum. The composition of the working class in the nineteenth and early twentieth centuries was divided organisationally and culturally on sectarian and racial grounds. The Tory Party controlled the city council and governed the city for most of the nineteenth century and the first half of the twentieth century in a manner that reinforced these divisions through the appeal to 'religious-cum-national stereotypes' (Waller 1981: 18). Sectarianism divided the working class and helped ensure that radical alternative politics did not develop in the city during the period (Taplin 1994: 19).[1] It was not until the Liverpool General Transport Strike of 1911 that the waterfront unions grew in numbers and influence. However, before and after the First World War the contraction of British capital was increasingly evident in the decline of export-based industries that had a particularly devastating impact on the docks and related industries in Liverpool. The shift to manufacturing and service-based industries in the 1920s brought some growth in Liverpool's traditional commercial and financial sector along with increases in seasonal work through the employment of shop assistants (MSRG 1980: 33). By 1929, a relative boom year, the number of Merseyside people living below the official poverty line stood at around 30% with another 14% just above this. During the 1920s and 1930s the male unemployment rate on Merseyside remained higher than the national average and stood above 20% (ibid.: 32). The over-reliance on the docks and the predominantly unskilled and casual workforce left Liverpool in a particularly vulnerable situation in the depression years, and this was recognised in the special powers granted through Parliament in the Liverpool Corporation Act of 1936 and sustained in the Merseyside Plan in 1944, which enabled the local authority to buy up land on the city's outskirts in order to build factories, relocate the population and offer incentives for inward investment (Meegan 1989). It was not until the 1960s that large-scale manufacturing moved to the region in the form of multinational ventures by the likes of Ford, General Motors and Standard Oil. The impact of this restructuring was negligible in that traditional industries continued to decline and unemployment remained higher than the national average. The 'growth years' only really served to stave off even greater catastrophe for the region as a whole, and Liverpool in particular, as increasingly local economic fortunes relied upon decisions made outside the area and on national and international market conditions. Between 1961 and 1971, the Merseyside Region – dubbed 'the Bermuda triangle of British capitalism' (MSRG 1980: 9) – lost 76,000, jobs while a further 40,000 manufacturing jobs were lost between 1979 and 1984. Employment in the docks fell gradually from the late 1940s to the 1970s. By the mid-1990s the Mersey Docks and Harbour Company employed just 900 workers.

Civilising the streets: social control in Liverpool from the late eighteenth century to the 1930s

> No town ... contains so difficult a population as that of Liverpool (Chief Inspector of Reformatories 1898 cited in Waller 1981: 170).

> the stress of sheer necessity bore hard on a crowded cosmopolitan port – Liverpool had to have a more effective police force than practically anywhere else (Midwinter 1971: 66).

The local *Liverpool Mercury* newspaper in 1851 trumpeted the fact that 'the centre of the town of Liverpool is becoming more and more a place of business only' (18 July 1851: 'The population of Liverpool'). This was placed in sharp contrast to the vast unenfranchised groups who lived in cellars around the dock areas. The popular concerns of the masses did not affect the hegemony of the mercantile aristocracy. Indeed, they were usually ignored up until the mid-nineteenth century:

> The division between the political concerns of the Liverpool masses and the elite was never more evident than during the 1840s. The social control of the elite, achieved by their monopoly of political and economic power, was seldom challenged. At one level the masses could be contained by coercion; the mobilisation of volunteers and militia was not uncommon in Liverpool but electorally the various mechanisms of patronage were generally sufficient to ensure order (Collins 1994: 67).

Writing of the masses, in his early and influential *A History of Liverpool*, Ramsey Muir contrasted the great wealth of the city evident by the late eighteenth century with a distinctly 'uncivilised' drunken and riotous history swelled by Irish and Welsh immigration (Muir 1907: 273). The population stood at 54,000 in 1790 (Marriner 1982: 70) with 6,780 living four to a cellar room (Muir 1907: 272). Muir argued that the misery of this 'wretched population' was intensified by the 'extraordinary number of licensed houses which the slackness of the magistrates had allowed to grow up' (ibid.: 273). In many respects Muir's history established a political-moral precedent that can be traced up until today within official formulations around the relationship between 'the masses', social control and the city centre of Liverpool. He characterised a sizeable proportion of the city's population around the turn of the eighteenth century as 'A population so degraded and so drunk sodden ... inevitably turbulent and unruly. The streets of Liverpool were constantly the scenes of riots and open fights, especially in the days of the press-gang; at night they were unsafe. For there was no adequate police' (ibid.).

In 1811, the Town Council reorganised the police in appointing 21 constables and seven head constables to patrol the seven boroughs of the city. The wealthy residents of Toxteth Park financed their own force to patrol the line between their estates and parks and the city centre (ibid.: 274). By the 1840s, the 'other', poorer Liverpool consisted of a shifting mass of migrants, both under- and unemployed, who formed a casual residuum segregated from the respectable working class and artisans who had gained new housing which conformed to public health standards. This residuum came to occupy the living space in the waterfront. Although the old families had begun to desert these areas they where still the space that the machinations of 'commerce and industry ... occupied by day' (Lane 1987: 87). The hovels and alleyways of the dockland area grew into a city within a city and contained a quarter of a million people by 1901 (ibid.). For the police this area was known as the Scotland Division and contained, in the words of one chief constable, 'the failures'. He went on to state that this was largely an:

> Irish population, with the reckless, violent disposition of that people, and with the unfortunate taste of preferring whiskey, which makes them dangerous, to beer, which would make them sleepy. There were many absolute ruffians amongst them, brought up in poverty, without education or religious influence, wearied with the struggle of life, with a hatred of society, and none of the surroundings which might wean them from drink, and vice, and violence. There were streets in the Scotland Division that were

unsafe for respectable persons to enter, and where even the Police could not carry out their duty without patrolling in couples (Nott-Bower 1926: 148).

Squalor and disease were endemic. The city was the first in Britain to appoint a medical officer under the Liverpool Sanitary Act in 1847, that also gave powers to the local Health Committee to evict around 30,000 people from illegally occupied street cellars. The removal of people on to the streets put greater strain on the poor at a time when alternative accommodation was extremely scarce (Midwinter 1971: 97). Coupled with these concerns were the 390,000 Irish who arrived in the city in 1846 and 1847 that led to 'such turbulence that 20,000 townsmen had to be sworn in as special constables, and 2,000 regular troops camped at Everton' (Muir 1907: 305). Within this context one local historian commented:

> After London, Liverpool was the saddest example of industrialism and urbanisation creating a choking, swirling maelstrom of humanity, with which came an intensification and a reorientation of crime. As dockland expanded, theft and prostitution tightened their grip, often with thief and whore working in evil concert … Property was sacrosanct. It was the mundane, day-by-day theft that troubled shopkeepers, merchants, and owner-occupiers of Liverpool (Midwinter 1971: 56–7).

Writers on this period refer to the alarm with which 'respectable' citizens viewed the streets of Liverpool that were perceived to be filled with a range of pathological pursuits and immoral activities which threatened to overwhelm the ideological construction of the city as a centre of civic and commercial propriety. It was widely perceived that the great commercial wealth 'had not brought civilization in its train' and instead had let fester 'a sordid and degrading misery, stunted and brutalised' (Muir 1907: 270). The sheer scale of this growing problem of urban ungovernability meant that

> Reckless seafarers from all over the globe, together with thousands of thieves, prostitutes, vagabonds and juvenile delinquents crowded into the dockland areas and those insanitary parts of the town nearest them. Here, numerous receivers of stolen property, brothel keepers and managers of beer houses and beer taps earned a steady income. In 1836, for example, more than 1,000 known male thieves lived in the town, whilst 500 others 'stole at intervals'. Some

600 more operated at the docks and upwards of 12,000 children, less than 15 years of age, worked as thieves for adults (Cockcroft 1991: 4).

In the light of these concerns 'something drastic had to be done to protect Liverpool's law abiding citizens' (ibid.), hence the establishment of the Liverpool City Police force in 1836. For Brogden (1982), the formation of the modern police in the city has to be placed alongside the mode of production as it had developed up to this point. The volatility in the mode of production and the casualised labour process that flowed from it underpinned the growth of a huge 'illegal' secondary economy that operated to serve the casual poor in the streets and included street traders, gaming houses, pubs and brothels. This created a 'peculiar problem of control for the merchant class' (ibid.: 46). Thus what spurred the formation of the Liverpool City Police in 1836 was neither 'mob eruption' as Midwinter (1971: 57) saw it, nor the desire 'to suppress the manifestations of direct economic conflict' (Brogden 1982: 52). For Brogden (1991: 87), the emergence of the new police extended and reformulated older practices established by the Corporation, Town and Dock Watches. The New Police gained a substantive legal remit and acted under a series of directions from a newly formed Watch Committee (that swayed between Liberal and Tory domination) that, taken together, granted the police considerable autonomy in enacting 'social control of the streets' as 'the major historically derived police function' in the city (ibid.: 88). Furthermore:

> The New Police were used directly to demarcate the territories of the dominant classes in the city – the merchants, the shopkeepers, and the new professional and white-collar strata – from the territories of the poor. The preponderance of requests (some 90%) and subsequent commands – were for the control of the streets, and associated recreational contexts (Brogden 1982: 62).

Between 1836 and 1910 the policing mandate was for the most part uncontroversial and the aim of police action remained fairly constant: 'to divide off, to map out, the lower class areas' (ibid.: 52). Thus:

> The subjects of police work – 'disorderly boys', 'children trundling hoops', 'rough characters', 'prostitutes', 'hawkers', 'Arab children', and adults playing 'pitch and toss' – were penalised as the source of mercantile discomfort (ibid.: 63).

Communications from merchants, shopkeepers and other businesses to the Watch Committee between 1836 and 1872 show that demands for police deployment were targeted overwhelmingly at 'disorderly street behaviour' followed by 'sabbatical disorder', 'traffic obstructions', 'street traders', 'thieving', 'brothels and prostitutes', 'gambling and street games' and 'public houses' (ibid.: 65). Such police practices became routinised and amounted to 'moving on' and street cleansing which meant that officers operated 'as a kind of uniformed garbage-men' where 'arrests, other than for minor misdemeanours were rare' (Brogden 1991: 1). Towards the end of the nineteenth century, the Liverpool Police's sense of moral purpose was strengthened due to its closer working contact with other public and private agencies in developing various local campaigns against beer houses in the 1870s and vice in the early twentieth century. In particular, officers aligned with the courts and purist organisations (notably the National Vigilance Association) in working towards closing down brothels, prosecuting under obscenity laws and investigating abduction cases. In 1874, the most popular meeting places of the lower orders – public houses, beer houses and off-licences – outnumbered all grocery, chemist, furniture and stationery shops in Liverpool. This numerical imbalance outraged local temperance groups and members of the Vigilance Committee (Waller 1981: 23). During the 1870s a number of elite partnerships emerged to promote moral hygiene in the form of temperance movements that underpinned social reform in the city and attempted to tackle the perceived relationship between drink and crime, and, more particularly, drink and prostitution. Such movements aimed to improve the condition of the poor in setting up sports clubs, domestic science classes and friendly societies. Exemplifying these trends, the Police Court and Prison Gate Mission was established in 1879 and was the first of its kind in the country to be followed by the establishment of the Women's Shelter in 1887. These early experiments in social control, which sought to remould working class morality, assumed 'that poor people would cease to frequent public houses or join street corner gangs if they were provided with alternative recreational facilities or had contact with well intentioned middle class citizens' (ibid.). However, the predominant response on behalf of local elites remained one of brisk street cleaning carried out by the police.[2]

In 1890 the purists, who saw criminal law as a key tool for improving public morals, gained much political influence in siding with Liberals in Liverpool to overturn successfully the Tory administration who were deemed too sympathetic to publicans and brewers (Mort 1987: 135). The attempt to drive vice and prostitution off the streets also demonstrated conflict between local businesses and moral organisations. Thus cleaning the streets of such 'unsavoury' and 'immoral' practices associated with vice was not supported by a consensus of opinion among local elites in that such practices sustained the secondary economy which was integral to the balance of class forces in the city. As Brogden (1982: 69) argued: 'The mode of production, especially the dependence of the merchants on seamen, created the demand for prostitution, and the profits from prostitution promoted the well-being of small-scale capitalists in the city.'[3]

The strategy described above regarding the policing towards Liverpool's poorest and most dispossessed communities had particular resonance with the city's black population who have been identified as constituting a particularly 'dangerous' section of the population. Liverpool's black population, concentrated around the south docks and in Toxteth, has been continually discriminated against and subordinated by local government, police and media (Fryer 1984; Gifford *et al.* 1989; Murphy 1995). The endemic institutional racism in the city, fuelled by competition over increasingly scarce employment in the docks, spilled on to the streets – most notably in 1919 and 1948. The black population attempted to defend itself from organised racist violence which the police, at best, ignored but more usually aggravated by 'swamping' black areas and raiding meeting places and arresting suspects (Fryer 1984: 298–303; Murphy 1995: 60). During the 1920s, the police even became involved 'in the agitation for repatriation of "undesirable" racial groups' in the city (Murphy 1995: 62). Institutional, organised and individual racism were downplayed by the media who instead 'explained' the disturbances by painting a threatening picture of 'animalistic' black men harassing respectable white women on the streets or, as the case in 1948, referring to black people as 'welfare scroungers' (ibid.: 43–52, 126–7).

During the interwar period, the police in Liverpool underwent dramatic changes as a consequence of the police strike in 1919 over pay, promotional structures and the government's failure to recognise the National Union of Police Officers. Over half the Liverpool and Birkenhead Police and three quarters of those in Bootle went on strike and were subsequently dismissed to be replaced by a well paid 'scab' force constituted of ex-servicemen and a majority of new recruits brought in from the regions of Scotland (MSRG 1992: 92). Police violence against the organised working class during the Liverpool Transport Strike in 1911 and towards unemployed demonstrators in the city in 1921 demonstrated the existence of more general fears on behalf of elites as to the rise in working-class militancy. In the 1920s and 1930s, the police continued to play a key role in maintaining order in the city so that 'Outside working class areas, in commercial or suburban districts, police powers could be used freely against those who obviously did not belong there, to impose a kind of unofficial curfew on the working class' (ibid.: 93). The attempt to maintain orderly city space was carried out on a number of fronts. First, a form of bourgeois morality was imposed upon women in public space, particularly those thought to be prostitutes (that is, women alone on the streets and without the company of men). Police harassment focused particularly on the increasing number of women thought to be frequenting public houses and thus blurring the boundaries between 'respectable' and 'tainted' womanhood. Flower sellers also became the target of police action and were sometimes prosecuted for prostitution rather than obstruction (ibid.: 94–5). Secondly, other policing priorities gauged from chief constables reports of the time focused on raiding and harassing gay meeting places and the clubs frequented by black people. Again, fears of inter-racial sexual contact seemed to underpin police concerns here as the Chief Constable noted of one meeting place in 1935:

> The club was frequented by white, coloured and half-caste men and women. Nightly this place was the scene of excessive drinking, foul language, filthy conduct and dancing during which the greatest indecencies took place. Between and during the dancing indecent conduct between men and women was openly indulged in. The sanitary arrangements in this club were of the most primitive character (cited in ibid.: 96).

Thirdly, youth were targeted. During the 1930s there was an increase in charges being brought against young people, despite the Children and Young Persons Act 1933 (Pearson 1983: 46–7). One magistrate in Liverpool in 1935 pointed to a 'new' danger in the city when he complained of 'The startling rise in the number of cases of hooliganism and assaults on the police in Liverpool ... Today the youth of the city is out of hand. Every night the police come into contact with lawless youth' (cited in MSRG 1992: 88). In Liverpool, during the 1930s, the 'problem' of youth on the streets and rises in recorded juvenile delinquency can be contextualised within the climate of casualism particularly affecting young people so that by 1934 there were 13,000 unemployed 14–20-year-olds in the city (ibid.: 24).

Finally, there was the targeting of those groups who posed a threat to public order. During the 1930s the police developed a number of novel tactics – such as the baton charge and driving sidecar motorcycles into crowds – for dealing with demonstrations, including the hunger marches and local strikes. The intensification of public order policing towards the social control of the streets in the interwar years served to demarcate and marginalise further the poorest sections of the population from the city's commercial and political structures:

> In 1928 ... the police deprived over 3500 people of their liberty, albeit temporarily, for drunkenness; over 600 for 'street obstructions and nuisance'; almost 600 for offences concerned with prostitution and further criminalised over 700 people for gaming and betting and 400 for begging, both being crimes without victims (ibid.: 105).

Policing and social control in Liverpool: 1945 to the 1980s

So far the discussion has focused upon how the proper objects of power in Liverpool were identified in the city's streets. The battery of legal powers that the police possessed was brought to bear in regulating the economic, cultural and leisure pursuits of the lower orders. The old Watch Committees provided the vehicle by which the mercantile class could insure the containment and regulation of the 'criminalised poor' in and around the city with very little conflict recorded between committee members and chief constables (Brogden 1982). With the slow decline in port trade, from the 1930s, came the decline of the political class in Liverpool. With the increasing importance of the multinationals to the British economy in the 1960s, both local and central state strategies increasingly embraced extra-national economic interests. At the local level these changes in economic dependencies, underpinned by a succession of fiscal crises, manifested themselves in the rise of corporate managerialism in an attempt to exercise greater control over council finance, local services and the local workforce (Cockburn 1977). In terms of policing, the upshot of these broad developments in urban management was the enhanced autonomy of chief constables within the new arrangements for local police governance under the Police Act 1964. The authority and independence of the chief police officer were thus enhanced by 'his corporate management status' and in his or her local 'specialist knowledge of the threat to social order', thereby leaving the local Police Authority – now composed of the elevated ranks of small business owners and self-employed professionals – with control of policing resources for local strategies (Brogden 1982: 91).

According to one commentator the development of the Liverpool police in the postwar period marked a continuation of efficiency, despite insufficient manpower, towards curbing the established problems of crime and disorder in the city – juvenile delinquency, drunkenness, prostitution and maintaining the public peace (Cockcroft 1991: 8–30). During the Second World War, indictable crimes committed by juveniles in the city increased by 25% and continued at a high level after the war. The police pioneered the Juvenile Liaison Scheme in 1949 which, along with the established practice of cautioning youths in the city, was designed to work closely with welfare agencies in order to 'learn of potential delinquents at an early stage and take immediate action to prevent them developing criminal tendencies' (Chief Constable Charles Martin cited in Gordon 1987: 124). After the establishment of the scheme it was perceived as a success by the proprietors in the city, in particular 'managers of the larger city stores – formerly plagued by swarms of children seeking a chance to steal, reported a great drop in such incidents' (Cockcroft 1991: 13). By 1965, almost half the total recorded crime in Liverpool related to petty theft and in 1966 the reported value of stolen property exceeded £1 million – a new 'record' in the city's history. In contrast, local press reports painted a picture of increasing violent crime and supported police-led campaigns for a 'war on crime' (ibid.: 81). In 1964, the Liverpool City Police were among the first to experiment with camera surveillance: under 'Operation Commando', a mobile camera was active in the city centre (alongside 54 plain-clothes officers) in order to halt 'attacks on ... persons and property' (Liverpool Chief Constable 1965 cited in Williams 2002: 3).[4]

According to Brogden (1982: 88), the Police Authority consistently bowed to police requests supported by crime statistics for increasing resources so that, by the middle of the 1970s, Merseyside police had the highest recorded crime rate, the greatest number of employees and highest costs per capita than any other force in Britain excluding Northern Ireland. Between 1974 and 1981, Merseyside police had grown by 27% (compared to a national average of 15%) and the yearly budget exceeded £80 million (*Liverpool Echo* 1 April 1981: 'It's teamwork we need to beat crime').

Social control of the streets in Liverpool from the 1980s

For Brogden (1982: 241), the effects of the mercantile economy in the post-1945 period left a 'sizeable' proportion of the city's population excluded from the local economy and political structures so that 'policing that residual strata, and opposition to that form of control had always been a major manifestation of that continuing exclusion'. Most notably – though not exclusively – the black community in Toxteth Liverpool 8 continued to be on the receiving end of particularly tough policing methods. As one community representative from Toxteth noted: 'The black community is fed up of being hounded. No-one is safe on the streets after 10pm. One gang we know has given the police an ultimatum to lay off within two weeks or they fight back. It could lead to civil war in the city' (Simey 1971 cited in Scraton 1985: 72). Subsequent chief constables' reports the police, on the other hand, referred to the increasing rates of violent crime and 'inter-gang' wars that posed difficulties in policing the area and which had led to a number of confrontations between police and residents (Oxford 1981: 6). In July 1981, Toxteth along with 19 other areas in the Merseyside district, witnessed several major confrontations between the public and police (ibid.). The confrontations in Toxteth were particularly ferocious and a total of 781 police officers were injured with 1,070 recorded crimes and 705 arrests (Kettle and Hodges 1982: 162).[5]

Lord Scarman himself noted that relations between Merseyside Police, the Police Authority and sections of the local population were in a state of crisis (Scraton 1985: 80). In response, a special police unit known as the 'Toxteth Section' was set up in 1982 to police the 11,000 people in Toxteth that amounted to a curious mix of hard and soft policing in the locality. Margaret Simey, Chair of the Police Committee, saw this in terms of a continuation in hard-line and racially abusive policing in the Toxteth area, adding that:

We have this utter folly of an official policy of softly, softly backed up by a strong arm. The people do admire the local police for their courage ... we talk about 'our Don' [i.e. community policemen]. But the minute there is trouble they are sent out of the neigh-bourhood, and what we regard as trained thugs are brought in to impose control (cited in Gifford *et al.* 1989: 165).

During the 1980s, the crisis of legitimacy in the force intensified through further disturbances in 1985 after which the Police Authority was accused of being 'anti-police' for challenging police tactics in policing the streets (*Daily Post* 16 October 1985: 'Fury over "no-go" Toxteth'). Nearly 10 years after the initial 1981 disorders the Gifford Inquiry recommended the 'eradication of racist policing on Merseyside' (Gifford *et al.* 1989: 190).

If the police institution seemed to be fighting a losing battle – particularly after the mass street disorders in Toxteth in 1981 and 1985 – it could justify its policing practice by reference to the 'peculiar characteristics' of the policed in the city. Quoting from Ramsay Muir's *A History of Liverpool*, the then Chief Constable Kenneth Oxford stated that 'it is a matter of historical fact that Liverpool has been beset by problems of violence and disorder throughout the centuries' (1981: 3). Such representations formed part of Oxford's evidence to the Scarman Inquiry where he referred to what he perceived to be the historical threads that formed the 'aggressive nature' and 'belligerent attitude' of the 'true Liverpudlian'. Such criminogenic tendencies as constructed by the Chief Constable have always 'found expression in violent disturbances similar to, though perhaps in minuscule, to recent outbreaks in Toxteth' (ibid.: 4). Oxford argued that waves of immigration into the city up to the mid-twentieth century had 'brought with them associated problems, disputes and tensions' and that Liverpool 'has for many years fulfilled her [*sic*] reputation as a tough, violent city, to the present day' (ibid.: 4–5). In his report Oxford (ibid.: 54–6) defended the 'frequent use' of stop-and-search powers as 'an essential operational requirement' to stem the rising tide of local violent crime variously referred to throughout the report. Constructing this negative stereotype of sections of the Liverpool population, with its undertones of genetic and cultural pathology, denied the legacy of casual labour, high rates of unemployment and a police force that was out of control as well as the previously unacknowledged 'uniquely horrific' racism pervading every aspect of the city's life (Gifford *et al.* 1989: 82). The Gifford Inquiry reported that the geographical demarcation of Liverpool's black population was particularly 'staggering'. Formal and informal racism were combined with the established form of aggressive and hostile policing which further reinforced the exclusion of the black population: 'Even in the city centre, only a mile away from Liverpool 8, the absence of black people is strikingly noticeable to the visitor from any city with a substantial black population ... Black people are not even doing the low-level jobs like sweeping the streets' (ibid.: 71).

During the 1980s the struggle for the control of the streets in Liverpool became subject to a series of debates that scrutinised the police role. In the mid-1980s, a local report recommended a variety of measures for police adoption to reduce further damage to police/public relations that included overhauling relations between police and other public agencies; disbanding the operational support units; paying closer attention to community needs; improving relations with young people, blacks and women; and a general move to improving conduct in public order situations (Kinsey 1985). These recommendations were made in the light of other findings suggesting Merseyside has one of the highest rates of victimisation, a high fear of crime and one of the least satisfactory rates of public co-operation with the police (ibid.). In the decade after 1974 recorded crime increased by 60%, compounded by a fall in detection rates which were down 23% between 1983 and 1985. The use of stop-and-search powers was seen to be particularly ineffective in and around Liverpool with only 4% resulting in arrest with a resultant increase in resentment towards the police (ibid.: 52). Within this context of rising crime, falling detection rates and disaffection felt by significant sections of the local population a wider mistrust developed between police on the one hand and council officers and local media on the other.

These developments took place within the continuing economic and political difficulties faced by the city – not least in terms of its reputation and image as a strike-ridden, bankrupt and derelict area. As the *Daily Mirror* reported in 1982: 'They should build a fence around [Liverpool] and charge admission. For sadly it has become a "show-case" for everything that has gone wrong in Britain's major cities' (cited in Lane 1987: 12). During the 1980s the peculiarities of the local economy set in motion a cycle of decline which was manifested in the rise in vacant land and buildings, population loss (from 750,000 in 1961 to 490,000 in 1985), decreasing personal income and spending, local authority revenue loss, declining taxation, and increases in social security spending to meet the Liverpool unemployment rate of 26.1% compared to the national average of 14% (Parkinson 1985: 14; Liverpool City Council 1987). In this climate of economic instability the service sector dominated Liverpool's economy into the late 1970s and accounted for 70% of all occupations (half these in the public sector with a third of this category employed by the City Council). Within this context Liverpool City Council challenged central government fiscal policy in the 1980s under the banner of defending local jobs and services. Between 1983 and 1987 the City Council was dominated by the Militant Tendency, which had gradually gained control of the local Labour Party through the 1970s. Their strategy was one of confrontation with central government through threatening to bankrupt the city if extra public funding was not forthcoming. During this period the council funded – from central grants and foreign bank loans – a 'constrained' Urban Regeneration Strategy that focused on its working-class heartland and paid little attention to the retail and tourist potential of the city centre. This created a marked gulf between the city's political and business elites (Parkinson 1990: 250–1). By 1987, the 47 Militant Labour councillors had been pushed from office and were replaced by a more moderate Labour group who sought to reverse the climate of hostility towards the private sector that had meant local 'regeneration' lagged behind national trends in developing the increasingly fashionable public and private partnerships.

Against the backdrop of structural decline, local and national commentators continued to reinforce commonsensical understandings of Liverpool's demise as a city without order and embroiled with violence, self-pity, militancy and communal self-destruction (Scraton *et al.* 1995: 270). Such negative images became a major obstacle for regenerative partnerships working towards promoting the city as a business and tourist destination (Madsen 1992). Three particularly outstanding events, and the consequent media reporting of them, helped reinforce the image of a city beyond control. The 1985 Heysel Stadium Disaster resulting in the death of 39 Juventus football fans and the 1989 Hillsborough Disaster resulting in the death of 96 Liverpool fans marked a watershed in the representation of Liverpool people as 'riotous', 'violent' and beyond redemption (Scraton *et al.* 1995: 226–92). After the events at Heysel Liverpool was held up by those on the political right as the model of an ill-disciplined society as Richard West argued in *The Spectator*:

> The collapse of teaching and discipline in our schools ... is nowhere more evident than in Liverpool ... [where] a whole generation of pampered, undisciplined children has grown up with the habit of petulance, envy, greed and wanton cruelty – as seen last week on the television screens of the world (cited in Edgar 1985: 26).

The third event – the abduction of two-year-old James Bulger from a local shopping precinct and his subsequent murder by two 10-year-olds – became the pinnacle of the extensive media campaign that focused on Liverpool as the centre of Britain's perceived moral and social decline. The interweaving of the city's 'unique' problems was encapsulated in headlines such as 'Heysel, Hillsborough and now this ...' (*The Guardian* 20 February 1993).[6] During 1996, a spate of drug-related shootings in the city led to national headlines reporting the 'mean streets of Liverpool' encapsulated in *The Independent*'s (23 August 1996) 'Greetings from Gun City, UK'. Again, the article linked a number of themes in reinforcing the special 'nature' of the problems in the city that are depicted as representative of urban disorder generally:

> It seems to be Liverpool's destiny always to be setting new benchmarks for urban barbarity. The city that brought you the Toxteth riots, Heysel, the murder of James Bulger and, last spring, the rape of a five year old girl by a 14 year old boy, has in the past year staked a plausible claim to being the gun capital of the country (ibid.).

Such representations have weaved a maze of 'problems' at all levels of Liverpool life that are perceived as uniquely 'self-inflicted' by the people and place. The construction of the city as a 'problem place' aided its positioning as an icon for national de-civilisation. One article, as part of a supplement on Liverpool, summarised the problems facing investment managers in the city during the 1990s:

> Merseyside has long suffered from an image problem, much of it self-inflicted from events in the past: the Toxteth riots of 1981; the vicious political infighting between left-wing groups which all but wrecked the Labour party in the 1980s; the Militant Tendency's orchestrated confrontations with the second Thatcher government; the Liverpool city council workers strike of 1991; crime, gang warfare; and the apparent inability of a divided community to help itself (*The Financial Times* 3 April 1997).

The impact of such high-profile constructions upon strategies of local economic recovery became increasingly apparent in the 1990s. The label of 'problem city' became a problem in itself for city managers, marketing strategists and policing agencies concerned with restructuring the city's political economy under the auspices of urban regeneration. The perceptions of the locally powerful, working to re-order a strategy of rule in the city, are elaborated in Chapters 6 and 7. However, the next section introduces and outlines the contours of contemporary policing and social control in Liverpool city centre that were developed during 1990s.

Recivilising the streets (again): social control from the 1990s

> Liverpool city centre has a lot going for it ... There is a natural partnership of interests between the public sector, like Liverpool City Council, Merseyside Police and Merseytravel, and the private sector. Neither can succeed without the other ... over the next year exiting new developments will come on stream. *Alongside these we must see 'zero tolerance' within the city centre of anything but the highest standards. Promoting and planning special events and attractions is important. So too is the more mundane responsibility of keeping streets clean, policing unauthorised collectors and street sellers* (*Liverpool Echo* 14 October 1997: Editorial, 'working together', emphasis added).

Throughout the 1990s and today a new vernacular permeates the channels of local rule, propelling a debate about 'partnership' – what it could mean and why it is a necessary form of rule for the city. The next chapter deals fully with these developments in contemporary partnership rule in Liverpool. Underpinning the partnership process, a vernacular of renaissance is helping to galvanise locally powerful networks in setting a trajectory – or a 'collective will' – regarding the objects of local partnership power. Within these debates the 'look' and 'purpose' of the city streets have remained central and, arguably, have intensified their significance within the organs of rule. Debates and experiments in local order maintenance take shape in a changing city that is now going through a process of what could be termed 'Disneyisation' (Bryman 2002). As a corollary of entrepreneurialism discussed in the previous chapter, Disneyisation refers to a number of inter-related developments in advanced capitalist cities, and includes the theming of cities, the differentiation of consumption, merchandising or branding of urban spaces and an investment in emotional labour to 'talk up' places. As processes that underpin urban entrepreneurialism, these developments forge a 'politics of image' that is fermenting within locally powerful networks in a way that reworks the rationale for urban order and control. The new politics of image is providing the police, as the established symbols of authority, with a renewed language of legitimacy as well as providing a rationale for the development of new agents and technologies of control, such as street CCTV.

In Liverpool camera networks are developing alongside other policing initiatives that are being positioned under a broad rationale of *urban renaissance*. This rationale is activating a complex nexus of social regulation related to 'aggressive place marketing strategies' that implicate a commitment to 'civilise cities' (Ward 2003: 117). In the middle of the 1990s the surveillance network developed when Merseyside Police and other partners launched a series of initiatives under the umbrella of Citysafe, which brought together a number of agencies including Merseyside Police, the City Council, Merseytravel and Liverpool Chamber of Commerce. Launched in 1997, the initiative anticipated the Crime and Disorder Act in 1998 and instigated a series of policing initiatives aimed to 'improve quality of life' within Liverpool (Liverpool City Council 10 February 1999: press release). In order to tackle crime and disorder in Liverpool, partnerships were established, under the Crime and Disorder Act, between police and other agencies to implement 'neighbourhood policing, which can encourage ownership, reduce the fear of crime and bring new investment to the city' (Merseyside Police 2 February 1999: press release). In drawing up its

Crime and Disorder Strategy for Liverpool, Citysafe produced an audit purporting to show an increase in disorder-related calls to the police, from 51,390 in 1995 to 57,844 in 1997 (Citysafe 1998: 2). The release of these figures forms the basis for understanding developments in policing the city centre during the 1990s and today. The focus on street disorder coincides with the re-politicisation of street aesthetics in the city of renaissance.

Concerns expressed for street order in Liverpool city centre have to be placed alongside a number of region-wide initiatives that have included local police resourcing projects and wider partnership schemes that emerged in the 1990s. During this time, Merseyside Police began seconding senior police officers to engage in local partnerships including the Safer Merseyside Partnership and the Urban Regeneration section in the Government Office for Merseyside. Merseyside Safer Cities (with an annual budget of £100,000) and the Safer Merseyside Partnership have worked at responsibilising and encouraging co-operation between public and private agencies by targeting resources for crime prevention towards vulnerable individuals and communities. The latter partnership brought together Merseyside Police Authority, Merseyside Police, Merseyside District Council and a range of voluntary and statutory agencies to secure £10 million between 1994 and 1997 through local fund raising and successful bids from the Single Regeneration Budget. During the 1990s, Merseyside Police engaged in a number of fund raising exercises that included encouraging local businesses to contribute to the under-funded Crimestoppers phone line and to take up seats on the Crimestoppers board (*Liverpool Echo* 28 January 1997: 'Call for crime line funding').

In 1997 Merseyside Police embarked on more fund raising and unveiled a 'pioneering cash for constables scheme' for patrols to be made available to specific institutions and residential areas that would be prepared to pay for the service.[7] In 1998 a 'unique' trust fund to raise £1 million was established by the Chief Constable and the High Sheriff of Merseyside[8] to 'enable businesses to make a contribution to community safety and crime prevention' (*Liverpool Echo* 25 February 1998: 'Crimebusters to trust in cash aid'). Such developments have to be seen in the light of dwindling local police resources compounded by a 1997 public perception survey undertaken by the police that purported to show the majority of those surveyed thought that Merseyside as a whole was 'unsafe', a significant proportion only felt safe at home, 72% wanted to see more officers on the beat and that the numbers of those dissatisfied with their dealings with the police had risen on 1995 figures (*Liverpool Echo*, 7 March 1997: 'People feel safe at home'). Furthermore, the cost per head of policing on Merseyside was the second highest in the country, at £152 per person. In addition, throughout the 1990s, the council tax police precept for Merseyside remained at over £29 million. In terms of the levy imposed on residents, these policing costs were the fifth highest in the country (Charted Institute of Public Finance and Accountancy 1999). Merseyside Police continue to maintain high operating costs in public order policing, incorporating a number of high-profile policing strategies.

These costs are met by consistent annual rises in local council tax precepts for Merseyside Police. In 1999, there was one officer for every 331 people living on Merseyside. This compared with a national average of 427. Merseyside has, with the exception of the Metropolitan force, remained, by this indicator, the most heavily policed area in England and Wales since its inception. Since the 1970s, Merseyside has had the highest number of police per head of population outside London. In 1997/8 the force cost the public £158 per person, 38% higher than the average cost per person for all forces in England and Wales. Between 1996 and 1999, Council Tax contributions for the police rose by 34% (Coleman et al. 2002). Furthermore, the council now funds 12 extra police officers to patrol the city centre at a cost of £350,000 'with officers' time being rented for shifts during the most disorderly parts of the day and evening' (the Guardian 6 October 2000). According to a Liverpool City Council Executive Member for Community Safety: 'These 12 police officers, along with a radical CCTV system ... will make the city safer for our citizens, visitors and for business. That will help Liverpool's continuing regeneration' (Liverpool City Council 2001: 26).

The 'funding crisis' of Merseyside Police is undercut by police and media representations of pockets of lawlessness in and around the city, which have led to a number of initiatives aimed at street cleansing. Local police investment in hand-held video cameras to film 'overtly in areas identified ... where there is a problem with youths misbehaving' is based on the principle 'that there is a wealth of evidence to show that filming people has a strong deterrent effect' (Merseyside Police Inspector cited in Liverpool Echo 10 April 1996: 'Police video to target youths'). Under 'Operation Tranquility' committed to 'keeping unruly youngsters off the streets' the police targeted and filmed youthful disturbances associated with under-age alcohol consumption and showed the film to parents (Liverpool Echo 17 October 1997: 'Caught on camera'). In the spirit of partnership the police work closely with Merseytravel to improve safety on public transport through schemes such as 'Travelsafe' and more proactive initiatives like 'Operation Forensic Cult'.[9] The kinds of policing initiatives discussed here were fuelled in 1999 by the launch in the city centre of the 'Citysafe War on Crime'. As well as unveiling a number of signs publicising the presence of CCTV, the launch set out an agenda to tackle 'yobbish behaviour'[10] in the city centre which included truancy, street muggings, drunkenness and vandalism (*Liverpool Echo* 10 May 1999: 'Citysafe war on street crime').

As part of a £315,000 government and European-funded scheme, the City Council and the police launched Liverpool's 'biggest crackdown on school truants' that involved a massive advertising campaign aimed at young people and their parents. As part of the crackdown, the police role was to 'round up pupils in the city centre and major shopping areas' (*Liverpool Echo* 19 April 1998). By autumn 2003, 132 round-ups had resulted in 671 stops of children in Liverpool whose parents face an immediate £50 fine if their children are stopped more than once (*Liverpool Echo* 4 May 2004: 'City in bid for truancy fines'). Since 1998 the police helicopter plays its part in looking 'for pockets of school crime' in order to monitor 'school vandals' and 'teenage thugs' (*Liverpool Echo* 27 July 1998: 'School prefect'). These 'experiments' in the policing of youth have culminated in the recruitment of a 'Yob Tsar' who works with police, landlords and community groups to 'speed up' the process of bringing anti-social youths to justice (*Liverpool Echo* 13 April 2004: 'Hunt for city yob catcher'). The management of troublesome behaviour in city space is formalised under the Anti-Social Behaviour Act 2003 that enables community safety officers to work with police in issuing tickets and fines to control graffiti, fly posting, truanting and begging. Moreover, the Act has been taken up in Liverpool to enforce a number of 'no-go zones for yobs' where 'police can banish youths congregating' in particular areas (*Liverpool Echo* 2 April 2004: 'No-go zones for yobs').

These developments are supported by the police crime reduction campaign 'be-street-safe'. The campaign has all the hallmarks of a corporate public relations strategy and is carefully aimed at building collective solidarity around 'tactics to identify, confront and arrest offenders' (www.bestreetsafe.co.uk.). Photographs and descriptions of 10 of 'Merseyside's Most Wanted' (mostly unconvicted) appear on the campaign website.

The campaign draws attention to the dangers of street robbery and street violence and issues the usual diet of crime prevention advice: to avoid high-risk areas, not to wear expensive jewellery prominently and so on. It also seeks to responsibilise potential victims into action:

Know your rights: You may use as much force as you need to stop yourself or somebody else being attacked, or to detain the offender, but you must not use more force than you need. You must use

anything or anyone to help you however you must not carry a knife
or anything else you intend to use as a weapon (ibid.).

This tone of cautious intervention is carefully repeated: 'don't fight back
unless you are certain that you can overpower the offender without
injuring yourself', while warning that prospective 'have-a-go heroes'
should 'avoid getting so drunk that it adversely affects your decision
making reactions' (ibid.). Using public focus groups to test out publicity
ideas and high-profile advertising campaigns, be-street-safe is aimed
explicitly at 'education of the public' and 'improving public reassurance'
using its corporate brand name to promote high-visibility patrols in
fluorescent jackets supported by dogs and officers on mounted horse-
back (ibid.). It is also the vehicle for the launch of new high-visibility
(fluorescent yellow) mobile patrol CCTV vehicles that can record footage
on location as and when required. This strategy has two clear aims: to
build a consensus around the ever-expanding deployment of coercive
and invasive technology in order to mitigate a supposed growing threat
to law and order; and to use the rhetoric of self-responsibilisation to push
forward this consensus.

The intensification of street surveillance and monitoring has,
predictably, targeted the homeless. In August 1995 the local press
inaugurated what is now a well established war against homeless people
in the city with its 'City plans to clampdown on beggars' headline. The
clampdown, in bringing together police and council, is set to, as one
councillor put it, 'improve the city's image'. The City Centre Commander comments, 'we would be happy to work with the city council to
get rid of them' (*Liverpool Echo* 11 September 1995: 'City plans to
clampdown on beggars'). The control practices to spring from this are
explored fully in Chapter 7.

The idea and practice of regeneration have not been lost on
legitimatising the intensification in militarised policing. From the mid-
1990s, Merseyside Police have invested millions in proactive policing
that included a £1.5 million surveillance helicopter, £600,000 spent on
bullet-proof vests for 2,500 officers and the piloting of CS gas (*Liverpool
Echo* 16 January 1996: 'Vested interest'). From 1996 Merseyside Police,
under the flag of 'Operation Goldwing', deployed 11 armed response
vehicles and 72 trained marksmen carrying semi-automatic weapons
supported by riot vans from the Operation Support Division containing
snatch squads and teams of special dog patrols. Such visible and
paramilitary policing tactics caused tensions between the police and
other partnership players (these tensions will be discussed in Chapter 8).

This show of force, focused on the city centre, was justified through local newspaper headlines such as: 'Crackdown on armed raiders' (*Liverpool Echo* 31 January 1996), in combating 'Gun law on the streets' (*Liverpool Echo* 17 April 1996), as a response to a 'Christmas bombs offensive' by Irish Republican groups (*Liverpool Echo* 4 December 1996), and as part of a general 'safety' initiative:

> This is not in response to any specific threat … This is all part of our policy of a safer Merseyside. Crime has the potential to increase over the Christmas period but we want people to feel safe to come and shop and socialise in Liverpool city centre (Assistant Chief Constable cited in *Liverpool Echo* 4 December 1996: 'Christmas bombs offensive').

In 1997, in Birkenhead, half a mile from the city centre, the police regularly deployed 100 officers on the streets in an £800,000 'Townsafe' initiative to target 'anti-social behaviour' that included rowdiness, truancy, prostitution, shoplifting and drug selling. The 'experiment' in zero tolerance-style policing was 'set against a back drop of massive investment in the town. But the regeneration was – and is – threatened by the perception of rising crime. So we had to confront this' (Superintendent, Merseyside Police cited in *Liverpool Echo* 11 March 1998: 'The force is with you').

The visibility of hard-line policing has its detractors within the locally powerful organs of rule and certain methods of policing were subject to attack against the backdrop of prevailing definitions and meanings attributed to the city's 'regeneration'. These tensions within the local state are discussed in the second part of Chapter 7. The initiatives described here bare witness to continuities in targeting the control process within what may be termed a renewed re-civilisation of the streets – albeit a civilising process associated with a reconfigured political landscape of entrepreneurial urbanism discussed in the previous chapter. In Liverpool such initiatives are underpinned by a move towards zero tolerance policing strategies in and around the city centre, representing an 'all out war on street crime', the establishment of which was financed by £30 million from the Home Office Crime Hotspot fund (*Liverpool Echo* 13 November 1998: 'All out war on street crimes'). Zero tolerance on the streets of the city is further fuelled by a liaison scheme initiated in 1998 between senior Merseyside Police, council officials and the New York Police Department. The liaison gives these developments a trans-local character in terms of lessons to be learnt from

New York-style 'quality of life' policing. As one senior police officer in Liverpool sums it up, the initiative with New York is important because 'from Liverpool's point of view we need to keep crime low to encourage tourists to keep on coming' (*Liverpool Echo* 15 August 2000: 'Big ideas from the Big Apple').

Conclusion

This chapter has charted how the struggle for street order and control over 'unruly' groups in Liverpool city centre is a feature of the city's historical, political, economic and social development. Discourses of censure constructed by fractions of the locally powerful continue to play a role in the political management of the city. As the next chapter will show, the contemporary regeneration effort has intensified a focus on the streets of the city and conflated aesthetic considerations with issues of social regulation and control. One of the key promises made for the 'renaissance' of the city is precisely an idealisation of the 'orderly street'. Powerful constructions of 'regeneration' and 'renaissance' are themselves cited as justifications for particular social control practices that delineate the desired urban aesthetic.

To reiterate: the rationalisation for street order in Liverpool during the 1990s has been informed by discourses of regeneration and urban revitalisation couched in neoliberal ideology. This ideology, and its role in shaping Liverpool's urban fabric, is discussed in the next chapter. The so-called Disneyisation of the city is forging a process that contrives city centre spaces in such a way as makes them relatively predictable, and hence subject to control. It is the new primary definers of the urban form who are the undertakers of this task in constructing 'a new urban frontier' (Smith 1996). The vernacular, which constructs the streets of the city, ushers in fresh justifications for new technologies of control as well as reinvigorates the necessity for an eclectic exercise in 'street cleansing'. In attempting to forge an image of a 'crisis-free' civic realm, the contemporary vernacular of entrepreneurial urbanism is reorientating concerns of 'safety', 'crime' and 'disorder' in the city centre and tying them into more all-encompassing notions of 'quality of life' and 'regeneration'. These discourses emerge directly out of the strategic thinking of the city centre partnerships as the rationale and site of contemporary state management. It is to the role and perceptions of the new primary definers that the book now turns.

Notes

1 The political hegemony of the city was thus assured through the dominance of the Tory Party that was able to gain substantial working-class support by playing the Protestant card and appealing to the small numbers of skilled working men (Waller 1981: 18).

2 The drive against drink and prostitution in 1876 resulted in rises in arrests for all crime to 27,529 (20,551 for drunkenness alone), of which 12,156 were women (Waller 1981: 24, 109). Over 5,000 drunks who were convicted were aged between 12 and 21. Stealing, violence, riots and drunkenness were often depicted within police, media and reforming circles as peculiarly Irish crimes (ibid.: 25). This led a prominent local reformer to observe that 'this human despot of vice and poverty is hereditary' and that assisted emigration should be encouraged forthwith (Samuel Smith cited in ibid. 1981: 24).

3 However, the social control of the streets did have a significant impact on levels of incarceration in the city. By the end of the nineteenth century, the prisons in Liverpool held one-ninth of the total prison population of England, 1 in 7 of all those sentenced aged between 16 and 29, 1 in 3 of all reformatory inmates and just under 1 in 3 of all reconvicted ex-reformatory inmates (Waller 1981: 170).

4 Some years later the police in Liverpool acknowledged that the camera experiment resulted in no arrests though 'the effect was preventative but largely psychological and therefore the camera had to be moved around' (Home Office report 1969, cited in Williams 2002: 3).

5 The disturbances in Liverpool drew witness to the spectacle of the Liberal leader of the City Council unsuccessfully petitioning the Home Secretary, William Whitelaw, to send troops to defend the city centre. During these events, 59 CS gas projectiles were fired by police to disperse crowds – its first use against British civilians outside Northern Ireland. Officers believed that the city centre was about to be taken over by rioters. Four people were seriously injured after inhaling gas along with one disabled man who was killed, with others injured as the police drove Land Rovers on to pavements and into the crowds (Kettle and Hodges 1983: 173).

6 This kind of reporting helped establish a negative national and international reputation for the city, which allowed the German Chancellor Helmut Kohl to comment that the unification of East and West Germany was 'like inheriting twelve Liverpools' (cited in Scraton et al. 1995: 226).

7 A local chief inspector justified the proposal in that it would be preferable 'to have trained and accountable police officers patrolling the streets than private security officers' (Liverpool Echo 15 October 1997: 'Rent-a-cop').

8 Since late in 1999 the office of High Sheriff has been filled by an ex-vice chancellor from John Moores University where the research for this book was based.

9   The first of these operations involved a month-long 'purge' involving police carrying out 911 station checks and 2,322 spot checks on buses resulting in 29 arrests for criminal damage or possession of drugs, 206 passengers 'thrown off' buses and trains and 1,011 fare increases made after ticket inspections. More operations were planned in conjunction with Merseyside Transport's Rapid Response Unit (*Liverpool Echo* 19 February 1997: 'Vandals are tracked down').

10 Under the Crime and Disorder Act, partnerships in Liverpool have utilised sophisticated geographical information systems (GIS) used to create so-called 'yob maps' that have detailed a 'top 130 yob zones' each with an estimated one youth disorder incident for every 40 people (*Liverpool Echo* 16 March 2001: 'Yobs map targets streets of crime'). See Coleman *et al.* (2002) for a fuller discussion of GIS in Liverpool.

Chapter 6

State, partnership and power: excavating neoliberal rule in the city

We are talking about the drive toward a twenty-four hour city. What we mean by that is that people will come here for perhaps a day's business and then do some shopping and then go for a meal, go to a show, then go onto a night club and then to a hotel to stay overnight. That's what we are after – all of it generating wealth and prosperity in Liverpool and improving the quality of life here for people who live and work here (Superintendent Merseyside Police, Government Office for Merseyside).

Unless we constantly ask 'who builds, develops and governs; and why?', we shall not understand the scope and limits of present institutions and programmes or appreciate why every definition of a social problem or its solution should trigger in our minds the further questions: 'A problem for whom?' 'A solution for whom?' 'Whose city is this?' (Donnison and Soto 1980: 185).

The camera surveillance network in Liverpool is central in the development of a social ordering strategy that emerges out of a locally powerful strategic vernacular that emphasises a spatially coherent, politically viable and image-friendly city centre. This part of the book explores more closely the emergence and impact of neoliberal discourses of urban renaissance that took root from the middle of the 1990s and began to delineate the trajectory of social control and order maintenance in Liverpool city centre. It is the local filtration of neoliberal vernacular and rationalisation for urban rule that this chapter explores in order to illuminate the precise politicisation of the urban form and the shifts in state and city rule identified in Chapters 3 and 4 respectively. In charting the institutional matrix through which the state is in motion in Liverpool, the chapter draws attention to the normative sense of order articulated by the 'new primary definers' as they attempt to imbue this state form with meaning and strategic direction.

What are these wider visions for order and how are they helping to reshape the city centre? In answering this question, it is possible to explore how the move towards a neoliberal cityscape is not without its problems and is part of a hegemonic struggle taking place within the local power bloc. This struggle is not exclusively local and is encouraged by perceptions of what other 'competitor' cities are doing as well as the availability of government and other funds that have, as part of their operating rationale, encouraged the changes to political rule described in this chapter. It is to the 'politics of vision' shaping the city centre – its 'look', idealised uses and ambience – that the chapter draws attention to as a precursor to exploring the street camera network. Indeed, the latter can only be understood as a constituent component of, and indeed an expression of, local social order. Though not necessarily 'successful' in terms of their realisation, the visions for order discussed here represent political strategies that are representative of an attempt by the locally powerful to bring problematic activities and people under surveillance and control.

Studying up the social and political hierarchy

In taking this view, the agents involved in the camera network are understood as engaged in a process of 'interpretive construction' (Lacey 1994: 30) across a range of sites regarding the identification of suspiciousness, wrongdoing and illegality that involves information sharing and the development of tactical intervention. As already indicated, these interpretive decisions can only make sense and, indeed, be operationalised, within the broader social relations of urban rule that are discussed in this chapter. The interpretive basis for 'suspiciousness' therefore is understood as a normative process 'made in the context of underlying features of the social order' which also contain 'locally dominant ideologies' pertaining to the nature of that order (ibid.: 30–1). The preferred meanings of an orderly city centre express desires for the 'rational' and 'proper' governance of the city. The representatives of the neoliberal state not only indicate preferred techniques of control but their responses also denote the persistence and reworking of long-standing moralising discourses of censure aimed at problematic categories. As Chapter 5 shows, the streets of the city centre have historically provided the modus operandi of policing alongside discourses of censure and order. The contemporary attempts, therefore, to promote order in the city demonstrate both continuities and dis-continuities in *who* and *what* is to be targeted and the means by which targeting has taken place.

Entering the world of the locally powerful enables a focus upon the inter-relationships between local state agencies, together with an understanding of the ideological frameworks underpinning the notion of urban 'regeneration'. 'Partnership' continues to provide the rhetorical framework within which the locally powerful co-ordinate interagency relations and establish a rationale for their rule. More critically, formal and informal normative orders constructed in the neoliberal state ensemble guide trajectories of 'partnership' and 'regeneration' and permeate these categories with meaning and a measure of coherence. These normative discourses play a role in the construction of social order and – through their careful construction – endeavour to 'command the support of a critical mass of citizens or officials who see the relevant norms as expressing quasi-moral judgements' (ibid.: 31). What follows is an exploration of the interests and cultural sensibilities of locally powerful actors in order to reveal the dynamics of ideological unity and fracture across the neoliberal state form. In this sense, the surveillance system can be understood as part of the wider social processes that govern the city centre. The chapter deals first with the development and relations between the formal and informal partnerships in the city centre. The focus here will be on how local ruling interests are reorientating themselves (institutionally and ideologically) in relation to each other, and in doing so constructing and fostering circuits of power in the trajectory of city centre regeneration. Following this the chapter explores the process of 'spatialisation' (Ryan 1994: 40), how partnership power is spatialised, and, in so being, aids and reinforces the city-building process.

Orchestrating partnership

> It is a common recognition that we have got to get a grip of the situation and do something about it. We can't all sit around saying 'it's not my problem, I'll look after my little bit' (Chairman, Merseyside Development Corporation).

Neoliberal statecraft brings forth issues and problems around the development of city-building partnerships that, in Liverpool, hinge on issues of negotiating a strategy and constructing a vision for regeneration in the city centre. This section examines the notion of partnership in Liverpool and what this means in terms of tackling differences in local institutional political outlooks. The notion of 'orchestrating' partnership points to the processual nature of state building as a strategically selective endeavour that seeks to establish 'feasible', 'credible' and authoritative channels in the task of city centre regeneration. The social and political processes involved in the propagation of partnerships in Liverpool city centre take place in formal and informal settings. The establishment and strategic direction of partnerships in Liverpool are structured through avenues of central government funding, local funding initiatives, the outcomes of conferences on the future of the city, as well as local interagency connections formed via more established avenues. With the ending of City Challenge and the Development Corporation programmes in the middle of the 1990s, more localised solutions to the problem of city management and strategic growth were found. On the formal level, Liverpool Vision (formally Liverpool City Centre Partnership – LCCP) and the Government Office for Merseyside (GOM) (whose work has moved under the ambit of the Regional Development Agency) are central to the development of initiatives aimed at promoting coherence in regeneration generally. The variety of initiatives, funding regimes and partnerships underpinning Liverpool's regeneration necessitated the formation of the Government Office for Merseyside. The office was established to 'provide a single point of contact' for partnerships and to 'promote a coherent approach' to competitiveness, quality of life and regeneration (Government Office for Merseyside 1995: *A Brief Guide*). More established bodies like the Stores' Committee and Merseyside Police have regular senior-level contact through the Officer Partnership Group (established through the Government Office) which is responsible for finding out what bodies exist in the city centre and co-ordinating their efforts towards the marketing and promotion of a secure and orderly city centre. The group's main partners in the city centre are: Merseyside Police, Liverpool Chamber of Commerce, Liverpool City Centre Partnership, the Stores' Committee, Mersey Partnership and Liverpool City Council. The group aims to co-ordinate the partners and identify problems for action within the regeneration agenda.

It is the Government Office and development agencies that make decisions on funding local projects based upon criteria laid down at both central and European government level. Another important point of contact is Liverpool Vision. This body marshals public and private funding for city centre projects. As the chapter makes clear these developments in neoliberal statecraft did not easily come together in an unproblematic manner. Those involved in these processes often articulate historically formed and negative perceptions of relations between agencies that include perceived threats to institutional authority and patterns of leadership. In other words, problems are thrown up in this process concerning who should run the city.

'Policing' and partnership

A big factor with the cops now is their willingness to talk. It isn't generally known that they are now talking to people like us [Government Office] at a strategic level because they do influence the process of regeneration. If something is going to adversely impact on the image of Liverpool then we need to know, as do the city fathers (Home Office adviser, GOM).

This section examines how particular institutional hurdles are overcome within the process of establishing a partnership between agencies that had previously regarded each other with a measure of institutional closure, even mistrust. These hurdles are managed through normative ideals and the creation of visionary discourses to do with 'renaissance' and the promise from this of benefits accruing from resource allocation. The processes involved in the instigation of partnerships bring to the surface problems in the negotiation of roles and responsibilities between various agencies that at the same time involve the attempt to reconcile competing interests and perspectives. Partners, therefore, engage in constructing a form of official discourse through which a rationale and legitimacy of rule can be forged along with the construction of the objects of partnership power. At this stage, it is important to point out that these discourses of partnership 'are not neutral' in the sense 'that they construct problems, solutions and actions in particular ways that are congruent with existing relations of power, domination and distribution of resources' (Atkinson 1999: 70). Thus in Liverpool city centre a great deal of ideological work is undertaken by the new primary definers in building coalitions of interest in the name of the wider interest of what is deemed strategically necessary for the 'city as a whole'. The building of 'workable' partnerships in Liverpool needs to be co-ordinated and 'policed'. Underlying the vernacular of 'common goals' and 'getting a grip' are changes in the balance of power underpinning the strategic alliances that make up the political decision-making process.[1] The

Government Office has provided the nodal point in the process of creating a perception, if not an actuality, of stability among the key players in the regeneration process:

> If the police are not talking to the city council and the council are not working with the private sector then we lack credibility in the eyes of everyone else. Regeneration has given this city the impetus to move forward, leave the past behind and challenge some pretty outmoded ways of thinking (Home Office adviser, GOM).

Writers have noted the labour and effort that need to be carried out to 'make partnerships work' with regard to finding common ground and agreed goals (Crawford 1997). The negotiation of trust and management of conflict between partners in Liverpool are manifest within the discourse of 'regeneration' as signified through the network of interests most centrally involved in the city's renaissance. The struggle to make partnerships coherent and workable is routinely fought out at the highest strategic level in the attempt to reconcile organisational differences and establish common goals:

> Although partnership may be a fairly hackneyed expression, one thing that is coming out of it is a tremendous learning curve as far as partnerships are concerned. There are still people in many organisations who think that partnership means having your name on a list somewhere and saying 'that's a good idea, we support you'. It's not. It's actually about committing resources to the common goal of the partnership – to the agenda. Problems happen where the goals of the partnership are in tension with the objectives of your organisation. But it's about commitment; it is about honouring promises and delivering what you agreed to deliver. It is also about negotiating sensible terms of reference when you get involved in a partnership. But this is a growth area with much work to be done (Home Office adviser, GOM).

The establishment of terms of reference, common goals and a sense of unity is most actively fought out and negotiated at the local level. 'Responding to the need of the partnership' (Chairman, Stores' Committee) involves processes that both realign and reinforce existing local networks of power as they impinge directly on the meaning of 'place' and space in the city centre. However, through the discourse of partnership, the ascendancy of the city as a marketable place in tune with modern consumer patterns and investment trends is not a phenomenon orchestrated by the locally powerful alone, but is worked out in conjunction with centrally administered rules and procedures (see Department of Environment, Transport and the Regions 2000).

As Chapter 4 made clear, the shift to the so-called 'entrepreneurial city' is encouraged through the formation of public and private partnerships and competitive, centrally co-ordinated bidding regimes. Moreover, the very vagueness with which central government continues to define 'partnerships' (Atkinson 1999) is sidelining issues to do with broadening democratic local decision-making and allowing more established actors to set agendas. It is these agendas that form the basis of feedback chains between local and central decision-making agencies. It is the government offices that act as a means of communication between local and central governmental actors. One interviewee describes the process of partnership in Liverpool city centre as:

> a method for delivering on a local basis. But the policies, the significant policies, are still set nationally by central government but it's left to local government and other organisations ... to actually deliver things on the ground and to feed back to the central policy making machinery about what works, what doesn't and why (Chairman, Merseyside Development Corporation).

As a forerunner to practising and initiating regeneration projects, local state managers organise conferences in an attempt to stabilise and promote effectivity in the working relations between key players.[2] It is perceived that only with a measure of stability and coherence among the key players could regeneration take place. Outside perceptions of local political infighting and instability 'do not bode well for building and sustaining the investment machinery Liverpool has in place' (ibid.). The process of developing new ways of thinking across various agencies is forged through appeals to both particular agencies and the benefits that would be gained in partnership as well as appeals to the 'city interest' as a whole. This is exemplified by the position of Merseyside Police who are reorientating themselves in relation to other local agencies at a strategic level through the secondment of senior personnel to the Government Office. Alongside this, other initiatives are in place that position the police in closer working proximity to other city centre regeneration agencies on both formal and informal levels. First, Merseyside Police in the form of the Area Commander for the city centre sits on the monthly meetings of the Stores' Committee to keep senior store representatives up to date on policing in the city and to listen to the concerns of retailers regarding issues around crime and disorder. Secondly, crime prevention officers and undercover police attend a subsidiary of the Stores' Committee – Crime Alert. These closer working relations at an operational level between police and business have come about through pressure from local businesses for the police to take their concerns more seriously around crime and disorder in the city centre and a police recognition of the benefits of being involved in the move to partnership:[3]

> In the past the perception from the business side was 'what the hell has this got to do with you' [the police]? Now there is the sudden realisation that the police do have a real role to play. They can be instrumental in initiating the regeneration process and in maintaining it by policing effectively and by consent (Superintendent, Merseyside Police, GOM).

'Policing effectively and by consent' can be a source of tension between key players regarding what this means in terms of 'effective regeneration', and will be discussed in the next chapter. In Liverpool the police and businesses have close working relations under the auspices of regeneration that requires the passing of expert information deemed necessary for 'successful renaissance'. Here the police role takes on a 'knowledge-risk-security' perspective in providing expertise to other governmental agencies concerned with wider aspects of 'social development' (Ericson 1994: 168):

> I think the cops have become more receptive to the sharing aspect that they were not renowned for before. Since around the time of the Morgan Report in 1991 the perception among police officers was that it was probably within their interests to acknowledge that crime prevention can't just be left to the cops and by implication opinions spread wider and people wanted to know more. People are much more informed now than they were and the police are a lot more open about the recording of the reality. They recognise that perceptions of safety and un-safety [sic] are factors in the regeneration process (Superintendent, Merseyside Police, GOM).

In this sense the police are able to 'provide local intelligence and information crucial to the planning stage on all manner of funded projects' (city centre crime prevention officer, Merseyside Police). In Liverpool, the notion of the police as information brokers extends to meetings of the Confederation of Trade and British Industry (CBI) in the city. It is in this forum that the Assistant Chief Constable addresses investors and potential investors on the merits of setting up commercial ventures in the city:

> Our Assistant Chief Constable now carries a stronger message to business. It is now a case of saying 'look – the CBI needs to know that things in Liverpool are not as bad as they are perceived to be. You need to take this message to your organisations and not miss out on this window of opportunity under Objective One simply because you think Liverpool is not a safe place (Superintendent, Merseyside Police, GOM).

Having the police involved at a strategic level in the regeneration process materialised as an outcome of pressure from local businesses and developers. From their perspective, the police are able to furrow a new language of regeneration that denotes what they do. In this way partnership with the police attempts to redress the fallout between the police and the local council after the street disturbances of 1981 and the local Militant politics of the 1980s:

> In the Liverpool of the 1980s we had the problem of council officers criticising the police and the police refusing to talk to the council. What seems to have happened during the 1990s is that businesses and developers have gained a greater say. They've been able to bridge the impasse and point out the futility of wrangling when we should all be working for the renaissance in the city (Marketing Director, Mersey Partnership).

Persuading the police of the benefits of being at the centre of the regeneration process has a two-fold appeal. Firstly, it appeals to the local political position of the police regarding strengthening their involvement in local political decision-making. Secondly, and related to the above, the police's ideological hegemony on issues of local crime and disorder is also strengthened. In this sense the discourse of regeneration provides the cement with which to reconfigure locally powerful agencies and smooth over old enmities:

> The fact that we have senior police officers on board – most crucially in the Government Office – shows Merseyside Police as willing to take a gamble. But the way we sold it to them, and I have been at it for years, is by saying you really ought to be involved in the policy process because there will be policy dividends for you down the track. I mean if we are successful in delivering Objective

One and the Single Regeneration Budget and attracting business and people there are operational implications for the police service. As they are involved in the planning stage they will have the edge over other organisations that are not (Home Office adviser, GOM).

'Having the edge over other organisations' means the police being involved in the bid-approval process through the Government Office and regional development agencies. The work of such bodies concerns itself with the construction and propagation of a consensus among locally powerful and 'responsible' agencies regarding the 'good governance' and strategic rule of a particular locality. For the police as well as other institutions this means experimenting with new cross-agency roles and, at the highest level, engaging the police in constructing discourses and implementing management procedures around local social development strategies:

> The police organisation wants to be involved in the regeneration process as partners and we want to see the place as a vibrant region, which is attractive to inward investors and supports a high quality of life for citizens and visitors. Having a police officer in here has been able to make a change in the bid approval process and helps deliver policy objectives around quality of life and freedom from crime. It is actually a good thing for the police as an organisation as well as a good thing for the people of Merseyside. It's an example of good practice (Superintendent, Merseyside Police, GOM).

Development and business managers are enthusiastic about senior police involvement in the regeneration process in that it helps smooth the process and enhance its credibility in the eyes of potential investors:

> To be effective, urban profiling has to have all the key players involved and at the highest levels and we are way ahead of other areas on this. It is not every investor that wants a low down on crime, but a major investor who does, wants to see the sheriff not the deputy. So yes, it's very good, very good that they [the police] are part of the whole partnership thing – *they listen to us and they actually understand that their role is now part of the investment machinery.* The Chief Constable has actually been to business receptions with me and explained the picture – they have got totally into that (Chairman, Merseyside Development Corporation, emphasis in original).

Within this process, police symbolic power is a central component in a wider corporate strategy to lever investment and sustain local economic growth. The cementing of local power relations through the discourse of regeneration opens up a space for the police in Merseyside to take forward their own agenda around the issue of police funding. In this sense police involvement in the process bolsters their position in terms of their 'symbolic authority' to make 'legitimate pronouncements' on crime and disorder (Loader 1997: 2). Indeed such authority manifests itself in, and is processed through, the authoritative coalitions that are emerging around regeneration. Crime and disorder are articulated in terms of a wider notion of 'social development' and the 'quality of life we are trying to promote in this city' (Superintendent, Merseyside Police, GOM):

> It seems to me an anathema that in a region in England and Wales that qualifies for Objective One status and where we are trying to do the socio-economic regeneration work with the police on board and through secondment, that the funding for the police is being cut – particularly when crime and safety are the big issues blocking inward investment. It is absolutely crackers and we will be saying so to the Chief Inspector of Constabulary (ibid.).

Responsible partners and the responsibilisation process

David Garland's (1996) notion of a 'responsibilisation strategy' highlights a series of political processes in which state agencies were divesting responsibility for crime control to other public and private agencies at a time when problems of management overload and legitimisation were particularly acute. Indeed, as Garland argues, the responsibilisation strategy takes place across a range of social policy fields in an attempt to redraw and reconstitute the management of diverse social problems. In the context of regeneration in Liverpool and the reordering of local power relations, the notion of 'responsibility' takes on a political and ideological significance. The meanings attributed to 'responsible partner' and the empowerment of such a partner – through funding and political recognition – point to broader processes concerned with the co-ordination of the local state ensemble in a manner that seeks to expand its scope for action and influence. Police expertise is central in these definitional processes and provides leadership in this area. Having the police involved in the bid-approval process, with the information and intelligence they can bring, is articulated as a means to enhance the credibility of local partnerships with respect to those who manage urban funding regimes, such as the Single Regeneration Budget:

> All partnerships like to have the police involved – it lends legitimacy to what they do. There is an issue of trust here about who is actually going to be the banker, handle the money and, you know, is it going to get ripped off? This has happened in Liverpool in the past. Some of the government-funded organisations, for example, involved in the regeneration of Toxteth have ripped the government off and there have been a number of fraud investigations. So having the police involved is a step towards making that harder and making partnerships do the right thing rather than what suits their own agenda (Superintendent, Merseyside Police, GOM).

The co-ordination of partnerships involves 'policing' the discursive contours as to the meaning of 'reliable' and 'credible' partners. More particularly, this involves the attempt to shape definitions of 'responsibility' and 'responsible partners' in the regeneration process. Thus partnerships in Liverpool city centre are engaged in a process of determining the ideological parameters of partnership power in terms of *who* is authorised to speak, on *which* issues and at *which* time. This process can be seen as an attempt to define a localised 'collective will' and to promote strategies judged to serve it. In this sense, 'partnership' in Liverpool involves processes towards 'the focusing of minds and the negotiation of sensible terms of reference' along with the 'commitment of resources to agreed packages' (Home Office adviser, GOM) that, at the same time, redraws notions of the public and private interest. The responsibilisation of agents and agencies takes place on a selective institutional and ideological terrain underpinned by the notion of 'empowerment'. Key players focus on who is 'empowered' to speak for particular collective interests and, therefore, able to assume a measure of 'responsibility' to receive funding:

> We need to check with potential partners whether they are empowered to speak for a community. It operates like a checklist: Accountability – to whom? Responsibility – how much of it do you have? Information – how much information is available you and how much do you have to pass to other players? (city centre crime prevention officer, Merseyside Police).

Accountability, responsibility and information set the discursive and institutional parameters for the process of partnership building and access to centres of power and decision-making. 'Useful' information, in particular, was defined within the context of regeneration and, as indicated earlier, definitions of what were in the interests of 'the city as a whole'. Importantly, the building of partnership and, therefore, the state ensemble itself, does not represent an open free for all that eschews contemporary and more traditional networks of ideological and institutional power. As one interviewee candidly stated:

> One of the biggest problems has been around consultation in Liverpool and the transparency of the process itself. The temptation is when you are setting something up you go and talk to somebody *who will respond to your need.* You take the easy way round (Home Office adviser, GOM, emphasis added).

As elsewhere, partnership in Liverpool operates through a series of constraints to do with the identification and targeting of key players deemed appropriate and necessary for 'successful' regeneration, tempered by definitions of who is responsible and who is not. In this sense, new and old sets of power relations are reinforced through the building of alliances that at the same time reconfigure the contours of locally powerful networks of rule.

Getting the message across: re-imaging and the local press

The notions of the 'entrepreneurial city' or the city as 'growth machine' each highlighted the development of locally powerful coalitions whose concern to 'talk up' a sense of place and instil a growth mentality has led to alliances with local press agencies. The local press 'can play an invaluable role in coordinating strategy and selling growth to the public' (Logan and Molotch 1987: 72). The strategic importance of such agencies in regeneration projects is grounded in the dissemination of information and images that potentially construct a sense of place favourable to potential investors and are geared towards cultivating 'local pride' among the local population. The construction of an urban aesthetic through local press organs is an important component in regeneration for businesses, local developers and police. In Liverpool, the local press[4] (consisting of the *Liverpool Echo* and *Daily Post*) are pressed by city centre partners to attune their role and become agents of regeneration. The position of the local press in representing 'quality of life' issues is deemed to have a major impact on smoothing the wheels of the investment machinery. This is born from recognition that the local press can produce negative and positive images of the region and of particular institutions within it – images that will have a direct bearing upon regeneration. Those involved in city centre partnerships are particularly resolute about the impact of 'negative' reporting around both the City Council and Merseyside Police:

> We are not trying to have a go at investigative journalism but the presentation of a story does not have to be couched in negativity. Potential investors will want a flavour, a snap shot of things in the city and they will want to see the local press. Sometimes I cringe at some of the stories in there, which only reinforce images we need to overturn – 'Liverpool is politically unstable, the City Council is crap, that Liverpool people are bolshie and thieving'. Some sections of the press have done nothing for this city and Council Officers have a bad taste in their mouths from the past, they're terrified they might get a bad press and so won't talk (Marketing Director, Mersey Partnership).

This situation has in the past led local partners to form alliances with sympathetic national newspapers in order to promote the city through, for example, national conferences such as 'Merseyside: the future', sponsored by *The Guardian* in 1997. In other areas, agreements with the local press are inaugurated in order to bridge perceived mistrust. This is exemplified by the negotiation of press–police relations regarding the reporting of policing and levels of crime in the city. One interviewee described these negotiations as 'about building trust with the media' after a series of 'damaging articles for Liverpool'. These articles

> were basically along the lines of 'crime is out of hand and the police are unable to cope with it'. At the end of the day it is as much in the interest of the *Echo*'s Editor as it is in the interest of Merseyside Police that we repopulate, have prosperity and vibrancy. I mean he'll sell more newspapers if there are more people living here, working and with money to spend (Superintendent, Merseyside Police, GOM).

The production of news around issues of local crime and disorder is being reshaped, in this instance by the building of a collective will around regeneration that helps cement relations between key players within which issues of policing assumed paramount importance. Again this involves negotiation and co-operation between locally powerful players at a corporate level:

> Now I would like to think we have got our act together here. If something is going to happen that we [the police] know about we brief the media first. If things happen that we don't know about and the media get a story we have negotiated protocols with them so that we can actually say when a story is published it must portray things fairly. We can actually go as far as to contact editors directly via the Chief Constable. 'This is the Chief Constable of Merseyside on the telephone – if you do not publish a retraction of what you have just said we will issue writs today.' We have done that and they have backed off (ibid.).

Alongside these coercive tactics there have been moves to strengthen a political image-building process to help shape and reinforce particular definitions of the 'public interest'. This kind of coalition building, involving the local press, increasingly endeavours to link the notions of 'good business practice' with the proactive management of images of crime and its incidence. In a contrived statement the editor of the region's biggest-selling newspaper recently commented:

> Merseyside is no worse than other cities – in fact our crime trends are probably better than most. But we seem stuck with an undeserved reputation as a hotbed of criminal activity … To say Merseyside is a safe place to do business requires a sense of proportion. Perhaps nowhere is truly safe in the sense of being completely crime free, but Merseyside is certainly a sensible place to do business … and I am delighted to have the chance to put the record straight (editor of the *Liverpool Echo* cited in Merseyside Police Community Strategy Department 1998: 4).

The aim here is not to contest the accuracy of such statements but to note the closer alignment of the local press to the regeneration process that is also in evidence through headlines to do with 'talking up' Liverpool and the new entrepreneurial spirit that partnerships wanted to represent. The attempt to normalise the service-based economy, as discussed below, continues to be hailed as a success for Liverpool and its people. The local press do play a role in getting a positive message about regeneration to the wider public: 'Partners doing the business' (*Liverpool Echo* 20 May 1998); 'Mersey fortunes in hands of experts' (*Liverpool Echo* 12 September 1996); 'Progress – here and now' (*Liverpool Echo*

11 September 1995); '21st century city' (*Liverpool Echo* 17 September 1997); and 'Mersey is leading the way!' (*Liverpool Echo* 1 November 1996) are earlier examples of positive local coverage.

The next section deals with partnership and the issue of leadership. Locally powerful agents identify leadership as an important issue – and this is central to the process of state transformation.

Leadership: who runs the city?

> The trick is; this is never going to be a properly democratic process. We use democratically elected representatives where appropriate and where possible, but there has to be a point where you say, 'we've done as much as we can' (Marketing Director, Mersey Partnership).

The shift to a more business like approach to urban rule and the establishment and inter-linkage of bodies such as the Government Office, Liverpool Vision and Mersey Partnership generated initial mistrust between these 'catalysts for change' (The City Centre Manager) and other local actors, particularly the City Council and Merseyside Police. Initially the latter agencies viewed the former as political outsiders – 'parachutists' or 'prefects' (Home Office Adviser, GOM) – who were appropriating and reordering, both discursively and materially, the mechanisms and rationality for urban rule from outside older, established local political frameworks. Mistrust was tempered by the feeling that power was sliding away to other bodies, a perception recognised by the Government Office:

> The government view of regeneration and the Government Office's view is that it is about arresting the demographic slide, improving infrastructure, improving the quality of life and improving the ability of the local authorities to deliver their services more effectively. The subtext ... is about politics and the view rightly or wrongly that central government have an almost pathological dislike of local government – that it wasn't going anywhere. The Government Office is about striking a balance between local and central. We are here to make the process of change easier (ibid.).

For the Government Office and Liverpool Vision things became easier with changes to Liverpool's ruling Labour group in the run-up to and after the 1997 General Election and the Liberal takeover of the council in

1998. Under a co-operative approach the 'spirit of regeneration' became more tangible. The processes of bringing agencies into the 'spirit' of the regeneration agenda are at the same time attempting to facilitate trust between agencies. The perceived failure of past forms of urban management under the auspices of an urban welfare strategy was sharpened for new governmental actors in Liverpool by the spectre of 'hard left' council politics in the shape of Militant in the 1980s:

> Something that we are working for and is coming over the horizon is trust, which is growing between organisations like the City Council and the police. You must realise that in Liverpool it was not that long ago since the Fraud Squad were arresting the Deputy Leader, Derek Hatton. Time is a great healer but you need more than time. It's about building bridges at the highest level in both organisations where you can have a strategic impact in trusting each other with knowledge about each other's organisations and priorities (Superintendent, Merseyside Police, GOM).

The prospect of gaining funds through competitive bidding and the arrival of Objective One funding 'has provided the glue where we have had to sit round the table and thrash out strategies – but it has not in itself solved the leadership issue' (Chairman, Stores Committee). Leadership issues go hand in hand with trust and raise questions for urban managers about who is 'capable', 'responsible' and 'charismatic' to fill the role:

> One of the themes that came through is that leadership is required and leadership is something that has been lacking. This lacking is not a reflection of the individuals involved but it points to the problem of council officers having to serve the needs of politicians and the politicians in Liverpool, dare I say, are of a widely varied calibre. Some of the more charismatic, who possess qualities of leadership, have actually shot Liverpool in the foot with the rise of Militant and so on. As I've indicated this is one of the things in the minds of potential investors (private developer 1, affiliated to Liverpool Vision).

The perception was that 'old ways' of governing were at odds with what is deemed necessary for effective regeneration:

> Party politics whether left or right is a Stalinist type of approach and can get in the way of real politics. The only thing that gets in the

way in Liverpool as in other cities is party politics – that is, who has the right to decide. Until a system is in place that people see as being the right system, not all the people but the few that count, you are always going to have that party politics (Marketing Director, Mersey Partnership).

'Educating' elected local representatives to new learning curves regarding the nature of local economic and social development involves moving beyond what is characterised as 'political infighting' or 'turf politics'. In establishing an authoritative context within which partnership for regeneration can operate, a carrot and stick approach has been favoured as a means to bring agencies into line. Merseyside Police and the Government Office play a key role here:

Building trust is very, very important. It's about having the police actually saying to Liverpool City Council here is access to our information, our database that you can use for deciding what you need to do to engineer out crime when rebuilding parts of the city. It's about focusing minds and getting local politicians to think across the city and not just their own wards and that they might get some of the cake next time (Superintendent, Merseyside Police, GOM).

Thus building strategic ways of thinking in the governance of the city goes hand in hand with the allocation of resources through Objective One and the Single Regeneration Budget:

What is bringing people together is the prospect of having some money to spend on what they want to see done. Realistically that is quite fair and legitimate because if you live in a crappy environment you want to do something about it. If something like the Single Regeneration Budget or Objective One is in operation you are told that if you want to spend X million pounds on something, you get yourselves into a partnership, show us that you mean it and have some strategic thought behind it (Home Office adviser, GOM).

Within the processes of defining and refining 'strategic thought' there is a related process to do with getting agencies to think within an ideological framework that prioritises what is in the interests of 'the city as a whole'. This incorporates the idea of 'sustainable projects':

Partnerships will get the money and continue to get it providing they deliver what they said they would deliver. But all of these projects have to identify succession strategies – what are they going to do when the money runs out? Have they thought about budgeting in the future? (ibid.).

In establishing a framework of governance that moved beyond 'parochialism' (ibid.), a series of regeneration strategies were initiated to re-orientate the meaning of urban renewal in terms of *who* would be responsibilised, *what* kinds of projects took precedence and *where*, in geographical terms, funded projects would occur:

People are beginning to get a much better idea about seeing how things can work in strategic blocks. So rather than saying 'I want this in my area', they can actually see that there are over-spill benefits from one area to another. In Merseyside there has always been those who get and those who don't and there is a perception among residents that the city centre and south Liverpool are getting all the money and the north of the city is not (Chairman, Merseyside Development Corporation).

It is the city centre that provides the hub of regeneration. The assumption is that what is good for the region of Merseyside would be provided for in promoting the city centre, re-scaling it and re-ordering it within a framework of 'sensible governance'.

The emphasis, therefore, on partnership between public and private sectors and the shift away from traditional postwar models of urban government throws into sharp focus the issue of leadership. This issue percolated through the local press, which provides a forum for local elites to air their views on the subject. For example, in an article entitled 'Who runs the city centre?' (*Liverpool Echo* 15 August 1997) a series of 'key players' expressed the need for leadership that encompassed a range of related issues – including external image, city marketing and street cleanliness. 'Our city's heart: clean sweep for the streets of shame' was the title for another article which identified a 'new confidence' expressed by city managers in tackling anti-social activities in the city centre including litter, graffiti and fly-posting. In the article the City Centre Manager expressed the new confidence thus:

if we want to attract the big players to the city then we have to clean up the environment … I think pride in the city is what we need to have, unless we instil that pride, unless people take ownership of their own city, we are not going to make much of an impact (*Liverpool Echo* 9 October 1998: 'Our city's heart: clean sweep for the streets of shame').

The article trumpets the collaborative efforts towards 'street cleansing' between the City Council, City Centre Manager and the Stores' Committee and mirrors other well received collaborations in the press that sought to manage order in the city centre. Indeed, it is within this context of reordering, re-imaging and establishing responsibility and leadership in the city centre that Liverpool's camera surveillance system emerges. The system continues to be positioned as a flagship development in the regeneration process and is born of out of the coalitions of interest discussed here. Before discussing this in the next chapter, the following section explores the emergence and consolidation of the neoliberal state form and the city centre regenerative visions that are emerging within it as expressed by interviewees. It is to these 'new primary definers' that the chapter will now turn.

The politics of attraction

'The Perception of Merseyside and the Client Problem' – a local survey that shows an all too familiar problem. Those surveyed listed crime, poor industrial relations and political unrest as the key major factors in decisions to invest. This is the client pool of our potential inward investment. Those are the perceptions of outside of what's inside (Marketing Director, Mersey Partnership).

Liverpool and Merseyside are unlikely to succeed if the city centre fails (Liverpool City Council 1997a: 11).

As examined in Chapter 5, the political, ideological and economic climate of Liverpool in the 1980s meant that the city's regeneration lagged behind developments that were underway in other cities throughout the UK. However, the trajectory of the regeneration strategy followed the substantive contours concerning the shifts in urban governance identified in Chapter 4. This section discusses the key agencies underpinning Liverpool's regeneration as a means of introducing and contextualising the emergent strategies for order in the city that have witnessed shifts in the institutional configuration and responsibility for enacting social control. The creation of an urban aesthetic landscape encompasses the growth of a local politics of attraction that has both an ideological and material dimension. Underpinned by orderly visions for the city centre, the politics of attraction cultivates a sense of place and, running alongside, perceptions of threats to the aesthetic order. In sharp contrast to the 1980s, and moving more in line with national trends, the contemporary restructuring of Liverpool focuses on the city centre and designated key spaces for renaissance that include retailing and consumption, commerce, leisure and tourism, culture and the arts.

As in other cities, the renaissance of Liverpool is permeated by a more business-like approach to urban management that has incorporated now outmoded bodies such as City Challenge and the Merseyside Development Corporation. The latter body, established in Liverpool since 1981, was responsible for a series of initiatives (costing £400 million up to 1997) to regenerate the city's docklands. Stressing a more business-like approach to urban governance involves the setting up of 'visionary' institutions to market localities and construct a 'distinctive' city image to lure inward investment. The Mersey Partnership brings together over 300 local partners to invest millions in marketing campaigns through a proliferation of brochures, seminars and conferences and a series of targeted initiatives aimed at national and international media and at potential investors. The work here hinges around promotional strategies that construct a local 'quality of life' and publicise information on business services, local infrastructure, labour costs – sold as 'lower than the national average for virtually all grades' (Mersey Partnership 1997) – culture, arts, education, housing, and architecture and scenery. In a climate of global competition, local marketing strategies are attempting to promote a distinctive city image: 'Liverpool – A Maritime City', 'A Pool of Talent' and 'Local and Proud' are examples. Today, a marketing campaign to reverse the negative undertones associated with the regional name 'Merseyside', and to change it to 'Liverpool Bay', is being put together with the support of local business with an aim of selling the region to the USA, Canada and Japan where 'Liverpool' is thought to be a 'recognised brand name' (*Liverpool Echo* 2 July 1998: 'New name plan for Merseyside'). In addition, tourism forms a major plank of the local economy and it is estimated that it will be worth £1 billion a year (*Daily Post* 12 November 2003: 'Where will all the tourists go?'). The Merseyside Development Corporation's crowning glory, the Albert Dock shopping, arts and museum complex, receives 5 million visitors a year and houses Liverpool's bid at 'cultural differentiation' in the form of the Tate Gallery. In attracting capital and investors local partnerships have been planning and funding improved telecommunications, infrastructural support, tourist attractions and leisure services (notably around the Beatles mythology reported to be worth £50 million in spending alone), café-bar culture and sport. One of Europe's biggest city centre developments at the Bluecoat Triangle exemplifies future visions for the city in incorporating an international shopping complex costing over £750 million and largely funded by one of the world's richest men in the Duke of Westminster. The mushrooming of private developments in the city is underpinned by Merseyside's Objective One funding status whereby £630 million has already been claimed from the European Union to encourage private investments in technology, exports, marketing and small business (*The Times* 5 March 1995: 'Merseyside to benefit from European fund'). Objective One funding is granted to Europe's poorest regions – those whose per capita gross domestic product is less than 75% of the European Union average – and has been instrumental in encouraging partnerships as a prerequisite for funding. The city is currently 33rd out of 80 European cities in terms of wealth creation. In terms of gross domestic product per head (an index of real wages), the city lies 72nd (*Daily Post* 11 May 2002: 'City shops ban Big Issue sales').

More recently the European Capital of Culture crown bestowed upon Liverpool for 2008 is used to trumpet further successes with an 'over-estimate' that 14,000 jobs will be created and £571 million of revenue generated for the local economy (*The Guardian* 4 June 2003: 'Benefits of Liverpool's culture crown "over-estimated" '). Crucially this latest renaissance signifier is reinforcing the trends discussed in this chapter: that is the *re-imaging* and *re-branding* of the city centre around a commercial project of spatial reclamation. As part of a recent intensification towards a decline in so-called 'unmarketed space' (Klein 2000: 59) in advanced capitalist cities, the Chief Executive of the City Council in Liverpool is keen to target the likes of McDonald's, Coca-Cola and Microsoft as city sponsors to provide revenue for activities under the Capital of Culture banner (*Daily Post* 30 October 2003: 'A brand new day for city as search begins for sponsors').

These ways of orchestrating a sense of public space and its 'regeneration' are impacting upon the city centre in particular as 'the driving engine for the whole region' (City Centre Manager cited in *Liverpool Echo* 20 May 1998: 'Partners doing the business'). Drawn up in 1997, the *Ambitions for the City Centre* document involved public and private agencies that included the City Council, the police, the Development Corporation and the Tourism Bureau. The document took a 'hard headed' view of the city's potential in utilising Objective One funds to become a world-class player in insurance, tourism and media, arts and culture (Liverpool City Council 1997a: 9). The creation of a 'safe and secure' 24-hour, 'European city' is a central theme in the document. Furthermore, the council 'cannot and should not itself lead in all courses of action' (ibid.: 3). The 'success' of the strategy was to be 'measured by indicators such as the level of private sector investment, improvements in the appearance of the city centre ... *but most importantly by the city centre's image and level of confidence in its future*' (ibid.: 7, emphasis added). Thus the strategic revitalisation of the city centre is, following this document, prioritised as the drive to regenerate economically, socially and culturally the region as a whole.[5]

These shifts to public–private partnerships, image dressing and responsibilisation have slowly evolved in Liverpool and point to the way advanced capitalist cities have attempted to redefine the role of particular cites in the face of shifts in the global marketplace, accompanied by inter-city competition. As early as 1987 the reformed Labour majority on the City Council published a major *Economic Review* that highlighted 'the need for a strategy' regarding the city centre that would promote its centrality as the hub for regional regeneration. The review flagged up a number of 'only too well publicised problems' that included the environment, security and pedestrianisation that would need to be tackled if the city centre was to stave off competition and build a 'total package' that accommodated shoppers' preferences for 'an overall leisure experience – the day out in Liverpool' (Liverpool City Council 1987: 4). The Liverpool City Centre Plan (1993) extended these observations and noted that 'competition is intense' and that public and private sectors must work to a common purpose in establishing the 'strategies, policies and proposals needed to help create Liverpool as an international city'. The instigation of 'proper management' through harnessing public and private interests became the prescribed role of the Liverpool City Centre Partnership (Liverpool Vision), established in 1992 (ibid.: 30). As part of a patchwork of local bodies this agency is loosely connected to elected local government and concerned with the promotion and regeneration of Liverpool city centre. The agency operates to help implement various schemes 'working towards maximizing the city centre's potential as a regional centre, and enhancing its attractiveness to all those who use it' (Liverpool City Centre Partnership 1995: 1). This body acts as a catalyst for public and private partnerships both to fund, and become responsible players in, city centre projects that include transport facilities, area ownership schemes, redevelopment projects, anti-litter campaigns and, as a central focus, street security. From this platform, local and outside interests are targeted for potential investment in local projects that include the provision of security initiatives such as CCTV, which is discussed fully in the next chapter. The growth of such city centre management agencies extends the neoliberal drive of the 1980s that implies lasting economic, social and environmental regeneration can be best secured through giving a key role to the private sector and in making urban places more attractive to business. Hence Liverpool Vision is established as a local initiative with an administrative team and the un-elected office of City Centre Manager, which to date has been filled by seconded, private sector businessmen. This 'flexible' and more 'efficient' approach to urban management is described in the following terms: 'The City Centre Partnership exists at the behest of the City Council but it is not another layer of bureaucracy. It is an open channel of communication, a catalyst and a means of getting things done that need to be done' (The City Centre Manager). The impetus behind the City Centre Manager idea originated from the Stores' Committee in Liverpool who, as an affiliate of the Chamber of Commerce, see the position as an opportunity to voice business interests in managing the city centre.[6] The Area Commander from Merseyside Police attends committee meetings to listen to requests for police action on behalf of the stores and to brief store managers on relevant aspects of policing and criminal activity. Its members account for over 80% of city centre turnover and its aims are 'to assist in provision of a clean, safe city centre environment', and 'to further the interests of all its members who trade in Liverpool city centre' (Liverpool Stores' Committee 1992: 1).

The committee has a subgroup, 'Crime Alert', that has developed since the early 1980s into a sophisticated information and surveillance forum for store detectives, private security and police. Indicative of building partnerships towards regeneration, the Stores' Committee is now an active player in the city centre:

> The committee was originally formed to look after the interests of retailers, but more recently it has become a body concerned with general issues in the city centre. We see ourselves, because of our voluntary status, as facilitators and a body tuning in to the groups of people who run the city and lobbying them, cajoling them and advising them on what direction the city should take. We now have a strong power base, in that we represent a large number of staff and a large turnover and large purpose for visiting the city centre – but we feel frustrated because the city does not share our vision (Chairman, Stores' Committee).

With these concerns in mind, the Stores' Committee actively pushed for the establishment of a Liverpool Vision-type organisation as a more 'representative' body of city centre interests that would be able to draw upon the expertise and knowledge of the private sector:

Yes ... we were the founding members ... because our frustration had always been that we have this untapped resource of ideas. We were working on shop floors ... we know what is going on in the city and we know what the demands of the public are as well. We continue to have strong feelings on issues in the city such as street cleansing, security, street trading through to the management of the city centre. There was no representative body to channel this through; it was just a slanging match between the city council and the stores on a regular basis (ibid.).

In general terms, these shifts in the rule of the city centre have established new networks and alliances within which the objects of that rule are defined. As part of these developments in the realignment of governance in the city centre, more sophisticated forms of social control have evolved through the establishment of partnerships and strategic alliances that precipitated a greater role for the above agencies in the task of securing order in the city through camera surveillance. The next section will consider, in broad terms, the visions for the city as the new primary definers express them.

Spatialisation, city visions and street reclamation

Toxteth is not Liverpool; it is not the city centre just like Brixton is not London. The urban problems of the twenty first century are going to the suburban areas. They are moving to the outer city and this brings us back to the necessity of success for the renaissance of the city centre (Chairman, Merseyside Development Corporation).

David Harvey's notion of 'attracting capital and people of the right sort' (1990: 295) has been particularly apposite in Liverpool's regeneration strategy. This part of the chapter contextualises the politics of attraction in Liverpool and the general meanings attributed to regeneration in terms of a 'city centre ambience' that key partnership players seek to promote. The impact of business and development agencies in the local decision-making process opens up forms of dialogue around the nature of order in the city centre, and reconfigures locally powerful agencies in realising that order within the public realm.[7] The regeneration process sets in train a series of initiatives in the form of annual conferences which bring together elected representatives, developers, local businesses, churches, educational establishments and police. The purpose of such conferences is to create a sense of coherence to the work of the various partnerships across the city and to produce progress reports for developers, investors, businesses, elected representatives and 'other agencies and groups who contribute to the future of the city centre' (Liverpool City Council 1997a: 4). Two of the most high-profile conferences – 'Ambitions for the city centre' and 'Merseyside: the future' – set themselves the task of identifying a number of themes 'as a means of guiding and focusing action' (ibid.). These themes are laid down in the City Centre Strategy and include building upon retailing, cultural design and media industries; enabling private sector development by improving transport links and providing new buildings, repair and refurbishment; creating a quality environment by improving maintenance and design and security; developing as a leading cultural and tourist centre with an emphasis on business, tourist and short-stay products; communicating a positive image to build the confidence of operators, investors, developers and visitors; and, lastly, linking opportunity with need by giving the most needy better access to employment (ibid.).

As part of these strategies for regenerating the city centre, a new ideological terrain is being constructed that emphasises a re-imaging and marketisation of the urban landscape. Agencies charged with this function can be understood as belonging to what Thrift (2000: 252–3) terms the 'capitalist circuit of cultural capital', the use of which is central to the dissemination of knowledge used in the construction of place identity. The form of discourse invoked in this task plays a role in cultivating belief among the locally powerful regarding the reshaping of place identity. In some respects 'it is *belief itself*, rather than what is believed, that counts as important' (ibid.: 254, emphasis in original), but it is belief in a shared past and shared future that is being cultivated here. References made by urban managers in 'talking up' Liverpool, 'making the place look better' along with the construction of 'spectacular' urban landscapes through design, play an important legitimating role in 'lubricating the transition ... to urban entrepreneurialism' (Hubbard 1996: 1442). This is done, for example, through attempting to foster 'civic pride' that appeal to both local audiences and external investors. Belief in the regeneration programme for Liverpool is orchestrated through a commercial vernacular that attempts to promote 'confidence in the city' while, at the same time, trumpeting a form of locally powerful self-promotion. General references to the urban landscape with an emphasis on existing and new architecture, as well as the 'look of the place', form an important starting point for understanding the articulation of social order within the city centre. As the literature produced by regeneration agencies themselves indicates, there is an increasing emphasis upon the catch-all category of 'quality of life', within which a number of interlinked programmes for action are spotlighted for urban managers. Some cities, however, find it more difficult than others to market 'successfully' a sense of 'place'. In Liverpool, this has a particular resonance in terms of redressing negative perceptions of 'place':

> In Liverpool you have got the problem of perception and the actuality – there is a big gap here. If somebody is looking for a place to set up business, which will mean employing people and paying taxes, they will look at it objectively and subjectively. Objectively – and we are doing very well on this – they ask 'where will we be in commercial terms if we move here'? Subjectively they ask, 'do I really want to be in *this place*'? Here we are losing at the moment. It is part of the image problem of the city (Superintendent, Merseyside Police, GOM, emphasis in original).

The problem of image sets in train a series of objects for action that include perceptions of political instability; poor labour relations; inadequate leisure, cultural facilities and consumption facilities; a problem of street trading; land litter; and crime and disorder. Each issue was seen to contribute to negative perceptions of place. Although these issues were qualitatively quite distinct, they all fell under the remit of the Mersey Partnership as issues to be marketed.

The partnership evolved from the late 1980s through the efforts of Liverpool Chamber of Commerce and the Stores' Committee who felt frustrated at the City Council in its refusal to give voice to, or work with, the private sector:

> The history of the Mersey Partnership starts at the back end of the 1980s. There was a lot of disquiet amongst local companies around the question of who speaks up for Merseyside. Some worthwhile work was being done but not in a co-ordinated manner. It started with the problem of perceptions, out of which stems the problem of inward investment. All city regions in the UK have had to develop new mechanisms, new vehicles to promote and attract investment for all sorts of reasons. More importantly, it is a realisation that this is not just a public sector job, the private sector can probably do it better and can actually physically create and fund an organisation and, critically, use their network to actually make things happen. I think there is always going to be a role for the City Centre Partnership and the Mersey Partnership. They can do publicly

what businesses have always done privately – and give people a kick up the backside. So there is always going to be a role for that kind of lobby and if we are going to be an efficient smooth running machine as a region, the key elements, including the City Council will have to be able to run at whatever speed the market wants it to run at (Marketing Director, Mersey Partnership).

The Mersey Partnership orientates its campaigns both at intra-region and inter-region levels and defines 'hard' and 'soft' marketing issues. The 'hard' issues include strikes, productivity and political stability, and campaigns that aim to redress 'misconceptions that this is not a sensible place to do business' (ibid.). 'Soft' issues:

> are beginning to become more important as regeneration takes hold. Softer issues include crime – that's the top issue – crime and its perception. Second is the issue of 'am I going to live here'? That's the social stuff around education, housing and leisure. These soft issues are about quality of life, which in turn are about security. Security runs like a vein through both hard and soft issues. For our potential inward investors security has political and social dimensions – a secure environment means looking at the political regime, the culture of the workforce and then it runs through into issues of social security and personal safety. We try and deal with all of these things, though different clientele seek information on different aspects of the equation. What we are marketing here, across the board, is stability (ibid.).

Addressing the problem of image provides a focal point for partners in initiating and channelling the regeneration process in the city centre that focuses upon a generalised 'look' and 'feel' of the urban fabric:

> The regeneration is wonderful because the place was looking very sad and sorry for itself and it has a reputation it doesn't deserve. We need the place to look significantly better and the city has a lot to offer – there are some beautiful buildings here, the museums and theatres. We need to get people to realise that this is a beautiful city (Superintendent, Merseyside Police, GOM).

The focus on the condition of the urban fabric pulls together themes around 'pride of place' and the potential for economic development within a recognition of competition between cities at the national level. The Officer Partnership Group provides a forum where issues under this general theme can be aired. The articulation of 'place attractiveness' allows the new primary definers to impact upon the processes of rule in the city:

> One mechanism that is most likely to achieve success is the Officer Partnership Group. These officials provide an important guide to policy. But the group has gained a very powerful argument to take to the politicians whom it has been left to grasp the nettle (Chairman, Stores' Committee).

The hegemony of image and attractiveness provides a means for focusing minds across partnerships and plays a cementing role in directing urban governance. As one interviewee stated:

> Indeed, if they [local politicians] fail to grasp these arguments and begin to think holistically they may well lose their seats because our consultation process has been very wide indeed. For example, the Stores' Committee, Marks and Spencer, the Chamber of Commerce, the Mersey Partnership and the Community Safety Officer in the council itself, have contributed to the agenda. The council are beginning to recognise that, on a par with unemployment and education, perceptions of un-safety [sic] are important (ibid.).

In its *Action Plan,* the Officer Partnership Group related image to 'the development of a safer city' and partners were encouraged proactively to market Liverpool in a positive light:

> The strategic importance of the image of Liverpool cannot be over-emphasised. The whole regeneration opportunity and process could be thwarted if people from within and outside Merseyside do not perceive Liverpool as a safe place and market its many qualities actively (Liverpool City Council 1997b: 6).

This marketing goes hand in hand with situational measures placed in the urban fabric such as the 'disguise and screening of derelict sites' and 'improving the appearance of the gateways to Liverpool'. These measures were important 'to improving the image of Liverpool, not just in terms of safety, but to stimulate wider regeneration in the city', as 'first impressions are very important' (ibid.: 3).

Just as the main routes into the city are receiving makeovers to disguise the poor estates that lie either side from visitors (mass tree planting on artificial hills and renaming, such as from Street to

Boulevard) – so forms of social control such as CCTV can be understood as an attempt to disguise-through-exclusion the flip-side of neoliberal city building. Crucially, the enforcement of a new-fangled social hygiene and the class-based cues and norms that underlie it is not neutral. For the locally powerful, the focus on the urban fabric occupies an initial stage on a continuum that seeks to re-image and re-order the city centre under a ubiquitous discourse of 'safety' within which CCTV plays a central role.

In broad terms, those at the centre of regeneration in the city centre express their enthusiasm for 'talking up' Liverpool in terms of its architectural and cultural heritage and as a 'European city':

> I recently hosted a visit from the Chief Executive of Paramount Parks in the USA. They run theme parks, well controlled and organised, sanitised Disney-like spaces, which are state of the art in terms of security and hospitality. They are a top ten world company and I showed them the Pier Head and walked them through the Albert Dock. They thought it was awesome as it is older than anything they have. They thought it was a fix, you know – like Disneyland done for real. What struck me is that they thought we had it made and that we do not realise what we have got here. Put simply, our job of reclaiming the city centre as an economically viable place will be a lot easier than the American approach, which starts from scratch (Chairman, Merseyside Development Corporation).

The notion of 'reclaiming' the city centre as a viable commercial entity is expressed through a variety of strategies aimed at tourists, shoppers and investors. The vernacular of 'reclamation' targets specific audiences and attempts to revert negative images of the past that play upon and rework 'older' discourses of class. This process contrives to appeal to a 'new' constituency in Liverpool: an upwardly mobile, prosperous and entre-preneurial citizenry. Reworking images of Liverpool from a 'working-class city' into a representative 'European city' focuses not only on how city streets 'look' but also *what activities take place in them*. For example, the drive to instigate a café society in the city centre takes place alongside campaigns that seek to cultivate a café culture clientele:

> Our image campaigns are aimed at addressing local audiences as much as outsiders. The self-perception of Liverpudlians is negative even when they are being funny. The best burglar jokes are about Liverpudlians, but Liverpudlians tell them best! So that is why

there are Mersey Partnership campaigns aimed inwardly to address Liverpool people and their relationship to the city. We are saying to Merseysiders – 'you are not just poor or self-pitying'. We have to get across that Liverpool people are not all scallies [i.e. 'reprobates'], they have flash and well dressed young people who drink cappuccinos (ibid.).

In this sense, the local population as a whole are a category to be 'educated' in line with 'quality of life' and 'lifestyle' issues, defined within regeneration vernacular. These themes run coterminously with a desire to evoke a notion of self-governing subjects, choosing autonomously, aspects of 'lifestyle' and culture offered by the regenerated city. Furthermore, and in contrast to these new urban desires, other aspects of city centre business which attracted a rather different citizenry within the network of market stalls, street traders and the 'bargain-basement sector', are deemed out of step with the new urban façade and indicate a perception of a 'downgraded economy' (Marketing Director, Mersey Partnership), thereby attracting people of the 'wrong sort'. These new ways of representing the city marginalise other discourses and experiences of city life that score low on marketing indices. The need of local people for lower-end priced products and so-called 'bargain shopping' is borne out by the fact that Liverpool was ranked the poorest area in the UK in terms of average incomes with a high proportion of families surviving on around £8,000 a year (*Liverpool Echo* 25 October 1999: 'We're still the poor relations'). For local marketers, this reality of the working-class city presents difficulties to the re-imaging process.

As part of this process of rearticulating the urban order, a range of issues are targeted as suitable objects of a strategy of responsibilised self-governance. These strategies aim to instigate a zero tolerance culture of civility. Intolerance of litter, vandalism and damage to the physical environment, along with 'courteous, knowledgeable advice to customers and visitors', are the desirable qualities of 'a town-watch culture where people advocate their own responsibility' (Chairman, Merseyside Development Corporation). North American theme parks and European cities such as Amsterdam are held as exemplars in this respect:

North American hospitality industries have developed a whole level of management expertise and training – a philosophy of customer relations, which is still to reach our service industries. I mean they are selling a themed product – it's not just about what is

sold but how it is sold. But it does not stop there. If you go to the
Magic Kingdom in Orlando you cannot put a fag end out on the
ground – a park employee would have picked it up in ten seconds
and binned it. It is that kind of quick response we are working
towards here. So people won't stub out a fag or drop a crisp packet
because they are totally intimidated by doing it. I ran a similar
scheme in London Docklands – if something happens you hit it
instantly. I would like to think we did it here as well (ibid.).

Initiatives such as Town Watch underpin the material drive towards a
service-based economy and are taking place alongside a recognition
among locally powerful partners of the particular need to train the local
service-based workforce in 'customer care':

We want to make people feel inclusive when they come to
Liverpool. So what we are doing is about creating jobs within the
services but also it's about creating a town centre culture of
responsibility on behalf of those who work here, day to day. It is a
way of getting everyone who is working in shops, cafés and bars to
know what they are part of – that they get the bigger picture and
appreciate what is going on around them (Chairman, Stores'
Committee).

Liverpool Vision is at the forefront of campaigns to establish an Academy
(dubbed the 'charm school') to educate service staff in the treatment of
customers and visitors to the city (*Liverpool Echo* 25 April 2000: 'City must
turn on the charm'). Instilling a culture of civility among front-line
business personnel is seen as a necessary step in the move to a service
economy and as a response to competition from other cities. For
example, a more business-like approach in managing the city centre has
allowed the Government Office and the Stores' Committee to challenge
the City Council to take a more proactive stance over its workforce
regarding street sweeping. The perception of an 'unclean' urban fabric
for these new urban managers is critical to the process of attracting
investment, and used as a means to bargain with council officials and
change council employment practices that were often described in
Liverpool as based on a 'jobs for the boys' agenda:

If we want people to come and shop, go for a meal and to a show,
we don't want them to have McDonald's wrappers blowing round
their ankles at 7.00 pm in the evening – but that's what happens. At
a much more cynical level if the City Council adopts and signs up to

the regeneration agenda it will give them the leverage they need to challenge some of the inertia and worst customer practice in the council workforce. This is the case with the street sweepers, who finish at 2.00 pm. They should be working shifts. If we are to get a 24-hour city they are going to have to re-negotiate a deal with sweepers so they are cleaning up 24 hours a day (Superintendent, Merseyside Police, GOM).

The process of regeneration opens up spaces of manoeuvrability for key players in order to articulate interests, roles and responsibilities both within and between agencies. The cultivation of a 'growth mentality' has at its kernel a drive towards civic pride coupled with educative discourses directed at particular agencies and segments of the population. This educational aspect of neoliberal rule, along with marketing campaigns, forms the basis of a responsibilisation strategy that is legitimated through an official discourse aimed at both constructing and addressing 'self-governing subjects'. A campaign such as 'Your City, Your Choice' is directed at both businesses and individual citizens, as responsible categories, to be made aware of the benefits of a clean city centre environment and the impact this is presumed to have on tourism and investment (*Liverpool Echo* 9 October 1998: 'Our city's heart'). These discourses of empowerment are central to strategies of city centre rule and represent techniques that seek the promotion of neoliberal state architects and the social reproduction of their power to rule. The above discussion illuminates how the discourses of responsibilisation are not neutral or divorced from particular visions of space. Instead, they prioritise a commercialisation of city centre space and the promotion of certain activities within it. In their promotion of a political strategy for the city the agents and agencies of neoliberal rule evoke a set of spatialised discourses within which is found a moral, as well as technical, utopia of the ideal city. Out of these wider visions emerge the conditions for a series of debates calling for a more exacting social control of city centre streets.

Conclusion

The issues raised in this chapter reinforce a body of work discussed in Chapter 4 in examining the ways that neoliberal landscapes are ideologically constituted and, in addition, are capable of organising space and mobilising its meaning so as to give it a veneer of democratic legitimacy. The governmental logic that permeates the neoliberal state in Liverpool hinges upon what Zukin (1996a: 45–6) calls 'a collective belief in the growth of the symbolic economy', images from and about which circulate through to the wider public and underpin 'both a landscape of power and a vernacular'. It is Liverpool's European Capital of Culture status for 2008 that crystallises many of these developments and, with an air of cosmopolitanism, within the 'inclusive' slogan, 'The World in One City'. In attempting to get behind such representations this chapter has explored the role and self-interest of the new primary definers who articulate the meaning and the benefit of the city's renaissance and cultural status in a manner couched in terms of the 'city as a whole'.[8] As representatives of a contradictory and discordant particular social bloc, these agents of the rescaled state are engaged in local political struggles to forge a 'hegemonic project' (Jessop 1990: 260) across institutional boundaries that have, as discussed in this and the next chapter, thrown up contradictions and tensions between powerful interests. However, ideas of what are deemed to be in the interests of 'the city as a whole' are married with a particular meaning of 'regeneration' in order to forge a consensus and legitimacy *within* and *for* the mechanisms of state building. The meanings and visions outlined in this chapter are central to a hegemonic project that is constructed 'through particular spacialized discourses and practices' in a series of attempts to resolve '(albeit temporarily and unevenly) the conflicts between particular interests within a particular spatially imagined and demarcated space' (MacLeod and Goodwin 1999b: 720). The development of the street camera network in Liverpool, discussed in the next chapter, can be seen as an attempt to render a visionary and demarcated space, both thinkable and practicable, for the locally powerful.

It is within the 'new' urban spaces explored here that 'the popular press has focused on the economy of play … [while] few writers have examined the security imperative that lurks on the dark side of "culture" based regeneration strategies', or 'policing the theme park city' (Parenti 1999: 95). The 'economy of play' and the politics of city renaissance discussed in this chapter set the context for the forging of normative orders that delineate city centre space. The neoliberal discourses that construct, address and hail the 'active' and 'responsible' subject discussed here are central to understanding the establishment of a landscape of power and its regulation and control. Within the articulations of an orderly urban fabric emerge the objects of power as construed by the locally powerful who, as new primary definers, take on a role best described as 'judges of normality' (Foucault 1977: 304) in relation to delineating desired and proper conduct in city spaces. In this sense a re-moralisation of city spaces permeates the institutions of rule in Liverpool and sets the state in motion through the building of interagency co-operation.

The objects of partnership power discussed here include the development and sponsorship of an effective network of surveillance over the city streets. As the next chapter will show, this development is occurring alongside an institutional expansion in relation to the definition of deviance that concerns not only legal categories, but extra-legal formulations of 'danger' and 'threat' that constitute the intended targets of surveillance. An exploration of these developments will focus upon the politics and materiality of risk within which street camera surveillance occupies a nodal point. In focusing upon those social forces charged with reconstituting city centre spaces, the powerful processes out of which a landscape of risk is being constructed can be illuminated. How a normative sense of city centre space is authorised and how this authorisation reflects the visions of space negotiated between coalitions of the locally powerful can also be opened up for scrutiny. The next chapter examines the development of the camera surveillance network that stems from within the processes discussed here and, as an extension of these processes, marks out the moral geographies upon the landscape in a manner that inscribes the values of the locally powerful upon the materiality of city space.

Notes

1   For some, these processes are characterised as 'decentred' in the sense that locally elected governmental structures are becoming but one of many governmental actors involved in promoting a place-marketing ethos which sits alongside the fragmentation of centrally funded and administered services. Thus funding regimes such as Objective One and the Single Regeneration Budget, which are ostensibly administered outside established city politics, lead to a shift in power to government offices and regional agencies. It is in such bodies that decisions are made about the funding of city centre projects and whether applications for funding cohere with strategic thinking about the regeneration of the 'city as a whole'.

2   In carrying out field research for the book I attended two major local conferences indicative of these attempts to align local key players.

3   Both the Stores' Committee and Crime Alert were central to the establishment of the camera network. These organisations and their relationship to Merseyside Police are discussed in Chapter 7.

4   It was the local press as opposed to other media that interviewees highlighted as a concern in the process of building partnerships. In their study, Logan and Molotch argue that 'because newspaper interests are tied to growth, media executives are sympathetic to business complaints that a particular journalistic investigation or angle may be bad for the local

business climate' (1987: 72). Thus a ready correspondence of interests exists, but has also to be negotiated and forged, between these intuitional domains of local power.

5   Indeed during Liverpool's postwar decline, discussed in the previous chapter, the city centre remained the hub of the area's economic activity. The slow decline of the economic and political power of the merchant class became gradually replaced by the city's retail sector (Midwinter 1971). Out of the 240,000 jobs located in Liverpool in 1981, 101,000 (or 42%) were in the city centre, notably in the commercial, retail and local government service sectors. Despite decline elsewhere in the local economy the city centre during the early 1970s had the highest retail turnover of any shopping centre in England and Wales outside London (Liverpool City Council 1987: 3–6).

6   The Stores' Committee in the city has been in existence since the Second World War and holds monthly meetings for its 40 members who pay an annual subscription of £1,200.

7   This is not to argue that because 'private' interests and fractions of capital are increasingly involved in these processes that a 'new' shift towards privatism is occurring (Johnson 1992; Goss 1996). As Chapter 3 illustrated, the scale of corporate involvement and capacity for influence have fluctuated historically. Thus nostalgia among some critical commentators for a lost, more authentic, 'public' space has forgotten, as Goss argued and the historical material in Chapter 5 highlighted, 'the modern bourgeois revolution and its conception of the public sphere was built on private property and commerce' (1996: 240). The transformation and management of these social relations are inscribed into the neoliberal state that is scaling its interventions and scope for action around the powerful coalitions discussed in this chapter.

8   Within hours of the announcement of the cultural prize property prices rose by as much as 20% in the city centre and the local media heralded the coming of 'Boom Town', with increased tourism, hi-tech investment and property development (*Liverpool Echo* 6 June 2003: 'Boom Town'). Though trumpeted claims by city marketers in Liverpool may be overestimated in terms of the City of Culture and   impact on job creation (see *The Guardian* 4 June 2003: 'Benefits of Liv   culture crown "overestimated"') the Chief Constable made   omise of a 'safe culture', where tourists will be 'delighted wit'   dy way the city centre is policed' (*Merseymart* 19 June 2003: 'S   or culture year'). The circumscription by business led-agenda   ool's 'culture' continues to be attacked in alternative local new   e *TVS Magazine* Spring 2002; *Nerve* Issue 3, 2004).

Chapter 7

Reclaiming the streets: the techniques and norms of contemporary social control

At the high-profile launch of Liverpool's street surveillance system in 1994, David MacLean, the then Home Office Minister for Crime Prevention, invoked the infamous murder in 1993 of local two-year-old James Bulger to illustrate the need for, and advantages of, CCTV, not only in Liverpool but in towns and cities up and down the UK. His justification for cameras was picked up in the national press.[1] National coverage of the launch underpinned assumptions about the preventative capacity of the cameras regarding the safety of women and children in public spaces (LCCP 1994: 1), along with the much-publicised claim that the cameras would reduce crime in Liverpool city centre by 20% (*Daily Post* 5 July 1994: 'You've been framed ...'). The vernacular around CCTV in Liverpool promised a 'more secure environment' and 'particularly in a city like Liverpool where the fear of crime is not borne out by the statistics' (City Centre Manager cited in *Liverpool Echo* 5 July 1994 'Crime busters'). At the launch, the Home Office Minister praised the 'excellent common sense' of the people of Liverpool in responding positively to the system, adding that formal regulation of CCTV is unnecessary:

> The controls [sic] are that if people are behaving themselves, not committing crime on the streets, then nothing actually happens. It is rather fanciful to suggest that we need special controls just because we are using the latest high technology which actually stops crime ... and that's what the public want (*Liverpool Echo* 5 July 1994: 'Crime-busters').

So began the cultivation of a 'common sense' around contemporary street surveillance in the UK that has continued to reflect and cultivate a popular anxiety around particular forms of street crime and victimisation. The construction of 'risk' for women and children in the public realm justifies massive expenditure on street camera networks and yet this same construction denies the *reality* of victimisation for these groups.[2]

As this chapter will reveal, the official rhetoric around CCTV distorts more than illuminates our understanding of the development of street cameras. As a techno-fix for an array of urban problems camera networks have been able to assume the mantle of 'city saviour'. This chapter explores the deeper political changes behind the establishment of the camera network in Liverpool while, at the same time, bringing into view the trajectory of those shifts in political management that crystallise the desire to reconstruct the city's image, bolster consumer and business confidence, and censure certain forms of criminal and non-criminal activity. In seeking to construct a new 'collective will' for the running of the city, key players in the neoliberal state have mobilised locally powerful support for a comprehensive surveillance system. As one urban manager puts it: 'The Bulger case served to focus attention but it was not the prime cause in establishing CCTV. It's a much longer-term thing than that' (City Centre Manager). In marshalling support for a street surveillance system, the social forces that espouse a neoliberal urbanism rework and reinforce a power to punish in the city. The self-styled role of the new primary definers finds expression in the development and targeting of the camera network. Their political and ideological position in the institutions of neoliberal rule provides a powerful position for the articulation of 'crime', 'deviance' and 'social order', and a focal point for the instigation of social control practices. Within the context of definitional struggles over the meaning of 'partnership' and 'regeneration', the 'proper objects of power' – to borrow Fiske's (1993: 235) phrase – emerge as salient components in a strategy for sociospatial order that endorses the visionary landscape of power discussed in the previous chapter.

In contrast to many of the previous studies (highlighted in the second part of Chapter 3), this chapter examines more closely the ideological underpinnings of the techniques of social control in Liverpool city centre. In particular, the focus is on the role of street cameras in the promotion of a social ordering strategy that is filtered and organised through a project of urban renaissance. Taking this track illuminates the cross-agency alliances involved in the definition, management and targeting of 'risk' that underpin the CCTV network. It also provides an indication of how that targeting is refined through its coupling with a morality of power. The range of problems identified by and within the vernacular of the powerful – for example, 'the homeless' and 'street traders' – are real problems that, as we shall see, are 'understood' as well as *transformed* into subjects requiring action through the pathologising language within which they are conceived by the locally powerful.

The role of the street camera network in Liverpool is pivotal in that it is identified as a flagship development in the promotion and maintenance of an orderly city. The first part of the chapter overviews the establishment of this flagship network, its broad rationale and targeting. As Chapter 3 argued, bringing the state back into an analysis of social control does not mean resurrecting a view of state institutions as monolithic, reductionist and overdetermined, but does mean viewing the state as a contested, often contradictory, terrain of power that responsibilises some actors and activities and censures others. Thus the second part of the chapter explores the tensions and contradictions within the neoliberal state around the social ordering strategy and the conflicts that arise around the means and ends of such a strategy.

Street camera surveillance and renaissance in Liverpool

During the 1990s, what was conspicuous about public and private policing initiatives in the city centre was the development of an underlying rationalisation for such initiatives that was mobilised around the notions of 'regeneration', 'renaissance' and 'quality of life'. As discussed in Chapter 5, public order policing in and around the city centre was, throughout the 1990s, increasingly articulated through a discourse of urban 'renewal' and 'regeneration'. These discursive themes play a significant role for the agents in the neoliberal state in rationalising the social control initiatives and primary definition of problems discussed in this chapter. The discourse of city renaissance provides a platform for the locally powerful to promote their visions for the city out of which a variety of strategies for rule in the city centre are articulated. For example, the establishment of CCTV in the city symbolises a new-found confidence for the new urban managers who are central to the regeneration process, and consolidates their belief in the process. As one manager states:

> CCTV is a fantastic thing. Liverpool was one of the first major cities to establish a comprehensive surveillance system and it has helped produce dividends across the board. We had been arguing for it for

years, and finally we pulled it off. It is marketed here so people know it is there. We had one of the biggest launches in the UK and as the Home Office minister said at the time people have nothing to fear from this technology and it will prove a tremendous asset to the city of Liverpool. Why? Because it can help induce confidence; a confidence in this city for all manner of people. And confidence in this city is something that has been lacking (Chairman, Stores' Committee).

The expression of 'confidence' through CCTV points particularly to the increased power and influence of the private sector in local decision-making and the process of urban management generally. It is the new primary definers who, as will become clear, provide a central ideological and material base for the introduction of CCTV in the city. The development of CCTV in the city centre takes place within a wider set of debates concerning the city's renaissance and future prosperity and therefore is situated materially within the network of alliances and strategies of rule that shape the meaning and direction of regeneration. The surveillance system is developed and managed in order to appeal to a range of audiences – namely, consumers, local businesses and potential investors. In this sense, CCTV provides a focal point for agents of 'vision' and 'change' whose modus operandi crystallises under the attempt to re-image the identity and reputation of the city:

We can reassure already existing businesses, which may have felt isolated – let down even by crime being unchecked in the city centre – that we are keeping an eye on their frontage day and night. We can also reassure the consumer, and tourists, that this is a safe place to enjoy and spend some time. And of course, we can show potential investors into the city that we have our act together with efficient and open partnership forums, which care about business in this city and are prepared to provide the necessary safeguards (City Centre Manager).

It is important, then, initially, to contextualise city centre CCTV as a key policing development implicated *in a series of regeneration strategies on a number of fronts.* Following on from this, the next section examines the establishment of CCTV through the various networks of partners that were introduced in the previous chapter. This illustrates how these partners are able to cultivate a *raison d'être* and management structure for the surveillance network.

Establishing the camera network in Liverpool: roots and consolidation

CCTV is the flagship development in promoting a 'secure' city centre in Liverpool and providing the vehicle for initiating a more extensive form of partnership policing in the city. Tracing the trajectory of Liverpool's CCTV scheme further illuminates shifts in urban rule under a neoliberal mantra together with changes in responsibility for the provision of social control in the city.

In 1989, a report drawn up by the Liverpool City Centre Crime Prevention Panel looked into the feasibility of establishing a CCTV system in the city centre in terms of mobilising cross-agency support and securing funding. The report signalled the start of a responsibilisation strategy concerned with the governance of crime and disorder in the city centre. Early in the report it is stated that:

> It is recognised that the prevention of crime is not just a matter for the police. If we are to succeed we must all accept responsibility. The support and co-operation of all in the community is essential. Local authority departments, business and commercial interests and the individual citizen all have a part to play. It is equally recognised that solutions to crime need to be based on sound knowledge of local problems and needs. To this end the Crime Prevention Panel is a non-political organisation representing the public (Crime Concern 1989: 2).

In supposedly representing 'all sectors of the city community' the panel consisted of the City Council, Crime Concern, Merseyside Tourism Board, the Stores' Committee and Merseyside Police. In a move that promised a 'safer city for all', the report contextualised the need for CCTV within:

> The changing face of the city centre [which] has received wide media coverage following press releases from the Leader of the City Council. Private sector investment in the city has also gathered momentum through the development of new shopping precincts and large-scale refurbishment. Installing CCTV as an initiative for crime prevention will register support for all. It will prevent and reduce crime and disorder. It will reduce the 'fear of crime', restore confidence and encourage greater city centre use. It will be helpful to business in that they would not have to present a siege image (ibid.: 9).

Initially, the report proposed an initial six-camera network to be located in the main retail area and hoped that funding would be shared across a range of agencies, notably central government, the City Council, Merseyside Development Corporation, the police and large corporate bodies. It was proposed that the system would be maintained by yearly subscriptions from commercial and business enterprises and that it would act 'as an additional aid to the police':

> At the end of the day it was concluded that to obtain the most effective and beneficial use of the system, the only body capable of monitoring is the police. The value to be gained, it was felt, would be derived from the speed of communication with, and operational response from, police officers on the ground. The police have the training, skill and experience unique in this field and the statutory power to take the necessary action. We are cognisant to the fact that we would be adding to the burden already carried by the police, but feel that the benefit to be derived would outweigh the costs and resource implications (ibid.: 7).

As noted above, the original intention was to seek funding from the City Council, Merseyside Police, central government and large corporate bodies. In effect no money was forthcoming from the council (whose budget deficit was the largest in the country throughout the 1990s), nor Merseyside Police. Insurmountable problems around funding and responsibility for the system meant that CCTV in the city as envisaged by the Liverpool City Centre Crime Prevention Panel was abandoned. As one of those involved in the process explained:

> Part of the debate we were having at the time was setting up CCTV which many of the people felt was an essential element in trying to improve the product of Liverpool city centre – primarily as a shopping base but also as a safer place for people to walk around … [and] drawing upon the experience of other cities who have pushed ahead – particularly Newcastle. We put forward this proposal for CCTV through the Urban Crime Fund but we could not sort out the management of it and it was eventually abandoned at that stage. One of the reasons I was unwilling to push forward with it was I and others felt very strongly that Merseyside Police should have accepted long term liabilities for the maintenance and management of the system. Okay, it's an expensive system – high quality fibre optics – but unless someone took ownership of it, whether it be the City Council or Merseyside Police – who did not

have much money, but realistically it was a policing tool (private developer 2, affiliated to Liverpool Vision).

CCTV did not arrive in the city for another five years, with the configuration of relations and responsibilities between key partners considerably changed from the initial plan. The conflict between the partners flagged up difficulties over responsibilities for the funding, monitoring and location of the system. It was not until July 1994 that Liverpool's camera network was established with a total capital funding of £396,000. Central government, through the Urban Programme, subsidised local capital to the tune of £100,000, the European Regional Development Fund contributed £158,000 with the private sector inputting £138,000. Though the system now has over 240 cameras (see Introduction), it initially comprised 20 high-resolution pan, tilt and zoom cameras with full night-time capability that were installed within a two-square mile area, covering the central shopping and office districts. Then, as now, a private security company in a secretly located control room monitors the system. Monitor and audio links are installed in Merseyside Police Headquarters and in the Police Shop on Church Street (the city's central shopping street). The system is part of an extensive surveillance network that links the police, private security and in-house store security via a radio link 'early warning' system that makes possible the monitoring of persons through both open public space and private shop space. The cameras are located on police advice in 'recognised trouble spots and escape routes' (LCCP 1994: 3).

Rationalising CCTV in Liverpool

If Liverpool is to become a hotbed of industrial activity it is essential that we can effectively attract new businesses here. All forms of grant assistance to Merseyside are allowing companies to make considerable improvements to their premises, not only to make them more appealing but much more secure against crime. Most of our major town centres now have comprehensive CCTV systems and many businesses are participating in various schemes that upgrade their security (Community Strategy Department, Merseyside Police 1998: 1).

Official rhetoric may focus on the popular fears around street crime but the deeper motivations for the introduction of surveillance cameras in the public realm can be found in the glossy brochures produced for corporate audiences. The roots of the system are found in the ascendancy of the private sector within the developing neoliberal state form, from where new circuits of power are opened up: 'CCTV did not come about just because retailers were bleating. But it is a fact that they were in the best position to bring all of this about' (Chairman, Stores' Committee). For this manager of the CCTV system, the cameras form part of an attempt to reverse the city's negative image and its perceived impact on city centre business: 'Perception is the biggest single burden Liverpool has got in terms of regeneration. There is a lot of information and disinformation, which can feed back in locally. The core trading area can be seen by some as a dangerous place (City Centre Manager, LCCP).[3] Moreover, the network had

> been evolving for the last 10 years. My experience of towns and cities is that it [CCTV] came out of horrendous store losses ... up to 3% straight loss. We have long been particularly concerned about security with regard to stores *but also external security of the environment in which we operate* (Chairman, Stores' Committee, emphasis added).

As active lobbyists in establishing LCCP, the Stores' Committee articulates a powerful argument regarding the need for a CCTV scheme:

> We were the leading advocates of CCTV. We had been pursuing the issue for 4 or 5 years before the establishment of the LCCP in 1992, but when the Partnership was formed the number one priority of the City Centre Manager was to establish a CCTV system, which he did successfully ... housed in the city centre and run predominantly by the private sector (ibid.).

The major retailers in the city argue that policing and prosecution of offenders in the city centre are ineffective. The main problems they identify are summarised by one interviewee as the 'lack of resources to patrol the streets; the lack of communication on criminal movement from one area to another; and the lack of the courts to give meaningful sentences given to the convicted offender, which can have a knock-on effect on the morale of the police and Crime Alert members' (Stores' Committee August 1997, pers. comm.). At the time, the Stores' Committee were concerned about cut-backs in police foot patrols in the city centre from two sergeants and fifteen officers from the Shop Theft Squad to one sergeant and six officers based at the Police Shop on Church Street. This lengthened the police's backup response time from 90 seconds to 5 minutes. Within the context of dwindling public resources for the police, the pressure on the private sector to carve out a political space to responsibilise themselves in matters of managing local crime became acute: 'My biggest concern for the police is that their power base has been undermined, their authority undermined, the conviction rate has fallen. The simple fact is that the criminal seems to be winning the war' (Chairman, Stores' Committee). Within this context a 'siege mentality' (ibid.) emerged within the Stores' Committee who felt, at best, let down by public authorities in the city:

> Our organisation has security bills of £270,000. That suddenly becomes an acceptable cost and do I feel comfortable with that? Well I can control it and become master of my own territory instead of relying on a public service body. This came about because of a deterioration in the quality of the police force – under-resourcing and motivational problems. We decided to take control of our own situation and because our insurance companies demand it – you don't get cover unless security is sorted out (ibid.).

Funding the CCTV network

The central government handouts for, and the grant-aided subsidisation of, public–private CCTV networks is often unremarked upon, but has fostered a flagging surveillance industry in a post cold war world and aided the ascendancy of the new primary definers into the processes of local statecraft.

In Liverpool, funds to establish and extend the CCTV network come from central government and European sources and make available funds on the proviso that private sector funding and input are available also. Thus the role of the Liverpool Vision from 1992 was to lobby various businesses in the city to generate capital funding. This was done without any long-term planning regarding the maintenance of the system: 'At the beginning the primary goal was to get the system up and running while the capital funds were available through European and government money, with no plan for operating costs. The initial funding was capital not revenue' (City Centre Manager, LCCP). Lack of planning regarding future funding towards maintenance costs contributed to tensions within the security network; these are discussed in the final section of this chapter. For one CCTV manager, the rise of CCTV in Liverpool was a process of 'metamorphosis' and the raising of private capital involved targeting the larger traders in the city: 'All the people that were approached were pretty sold on the idea. I'm not saying they parted with cash easily but the issues were well known. They all had the same problems as previously outlined and there was a general move towards this' (ibid.).[4]

The ongoing maintenance costs of the system were secured through lobbying activities directed by the City Centre Manager and aimed at local businesses. As pointed out earlier, the surveillance system in Liverpool links the control room with private security via a radio link, which is monitored by police along with camera pictures. The combat radios – of which there are nearly 100 on the network – cost £350 each and are funded through the Urban Crime Fund. It is the Stores' Committee who issue them to members on payment of an annual subscription.

The management, control and public credibility of CCTV

Chains of command and lines of accountability are often obscured in the management of CCTV schemes (NACRO 2002). In Liverpool, management of the system involves the City Centre Manager and Merseyside Police. The police control access to taped information for reviewing, evidential and publicity purposes as laid down in the local codes of practice (Liverpool City Council 1994). The handbook states that the police may request cameras to be directed to specific locations and that such requests must be complied with unless the operator deems otherwise, in which case the police must be given an explanation (ibid.: para. 6.9).[5] The objectives of the system include: deterring crime; enhancing detection; reducing the fear of crime; making the city centre more attractive to business, shoppers and tourists; improving communication and response times of police patrols; and creating a safer city for all (ibid.: para. 1.3). The codes of practice state that private operators of the system must discharge their duties in line with the key objective so as 'to keep wrong-doers off the streets' (ibid.: para. 1.5). The local controls surrounding the system cohere around an informal triangle or chain involving the City Centre Manager, the security management team involved in Crime Alert and the City Centre Commander for Merseyside Police:

> Although everything we do has to be closely worked out with the police – they don't control it, only over evidence. This is all part of maintaining the system's integrity and confidence with the public. So there is not a lot of need for detailed control ... I'm not saying it's not there because there is a management chain (Chairman, Stores' Committee).

The day-to-day operation of the system is directed through Crime Alert, the subgroup of the Liverpool Stores' Committee. This group performs functions in the front line of targeting surveillance in the city centre and is discussed in more detail below.

Official guidelines state that the 'effectiveness' of CCTV as a finely targeted mechanism of public surveillance needs to be communicated to the wider public. Home Office guidelines urge scheme managers 'to get the local press on your side from the start' and 'ensure they realise what your objectives are' in focusing 'them on the safer shopping/ walking element' (Home Office 1994: 32). From the outset, a key component in the management of CCTV is its reception in the local media and therefore its credibility and legitimacy among the wider populace. As one CCTV manager stresses, 'there is no need for detailed controls; as long as we've got Mr and Mrs Bloggs on board – great' (City Centre Manager). Another interviewee stressed the need to 'constantly sell the benefits of CCTV; though this must be done carefully' (private developer 1, affiliated to LCCP). 'Keeping Mr and Mrs Bloggs on board' (i.e. the public at large) is achieved with the minimum of organisation and expense. At the launch of the scheme a three-question survey was used to show over 90% public support for the system. Six years later a very similar survey using a regularly consulted 'Citizens Panel' numbering 2,000 reported that 85% responded positively when asked 'would you feel safer with CCTV?' Only 6% thought it might constitute 'an invasion of privacy' (City Safe 2000). Neither the constitution of the panel nor how its members were selected are known. The phrasing of just three questions on the subject is problematic and reflects the methodological flaws indicative of surveys around camera networks (see Short 1998).

The location of the cameras in Liverpool is decided on the basis of 'police crime patterns and knowledge of incidents' along with the 'hands-on experience' of store security so that 'escape routes and access points' would be covered (City Centre Manager). Crime Alert, along with the City Centre Manager, defines the role and use of CCTV in the city: 'That is what is most effective about CCTV ... It is effective when you know *who* you are looking for' (Chairman, Stores' Committee, emphasis in original). Furthermore: 'You need somebody to monitor the system, somebody available to react and to be seen to react – then it has got credibility' (ibid.). This involves triggering an 'appropriate police response' using picture relays and the two-way radio. This acts as an 'early warning deterrence':

> The criminal element is not stupid. They have a pretty good idea about what's covered, where and how ... and they can tell that by testing it ... but once they've been picked up on the radio and then on camera – it cramps their style – there is virtually no escape (ibid.).

Importantly, a message 'must go out' to those targeted by the system so that 'known shoplifters and people who are banned cannot walk around the city centre with impunity' (ibid.). This message is relayed replete with video stills through local and national media to promote claims of the system's 'success' in deterring and apprehending potential and actual offenders.[6] The Area Commander, in a much-publicised comment, maintains that 'The system is like having 20 more officers on duty 24 hours a day who make a note of everything, never take a holiday and are very rarely off sick' (*The Times*, 6 July 1994: 'Security cameras zoom in on crime'). The police position on CCTV in Liverpool is returned to below, as it took a more ambiguous line than such official pronouncements suggest. In summary, and as the City Centre Manager articulates, CCTV provides a broader vehicle for social ordering in the city centre: 'Hopefully the cameras will deter criminals. But we also hope the cameras will reassure potential investors' (*Liverpool Echo* 13 June 1996: 'Spy at night').

As outlined in the Introduction this street surveillance system is significantly extended and enhanced. Today the system is promoted as one of the most advanced in the world and is firmly integrated with two other initiatives in the city centre with a security function. Firstly, Crime Alert takes a key role in targeting the system. Secondly, the Town Watch initiative became operational and is envisaged as a visible street-level accompaniment to the effectiveness of street camera surveillance. It is to a consideration of the development and role of these organisations that the chapter now turns.

Working the cameras: Crime Alert

The work of Crime Alert has been briefly alluded to above in this chapter. What follows is an exploration of the work of the organisation, its rationale and position within the overall camera network. This section utilises field notes and interview material accrued from the group. The group initially used to consist of store detectives only, but with the proliferation of in-house security guards, security managers and in-store CCTV the meetings of the group became operationalised on a monthly basis with 30–40 attendees. These meetings provide a central focus for local businesses, police and private security in defining risks and gaps in the network as well as prioritising policing objectives for the city centre. In bringing together private and public interests this closed forum constitutes a network whose authority stems from the Stores' Committee and its larger offshoot, the Liverpool City Centre Partnership. Out of these bodies developed the city centre CCTV system, Crime Alert and Town Watch who, collectively, form the pillars of the network. The work of Crime Alert is described as 'letting the criminal element know that we know they are there … it is about making it harder for them'. This body acts as a catalyst for store security and attempts to 'get people into the spirit' (Chairman, Crime Alert). The chair of Crime Alert reports back to the Stores' Committee, which the Area Commander from Merseyside Police attends. Crime Alert exists as part of the Stores' Committee and is one of several inter-related subgroups with responsibility for promoting retail interests and working with interested parties in the city centre:

> The Stores' Committee is like a brotherhood organisation and from that we have set up Crime Alert. There are groups responsible for tourism, street lighting and street cleansing. But we all work as a team and each cultivate working relations with the likes of the City Council and Merseyside Police (ibid.).

Within Crime Alert, Merseyside Police crime prevention officers and operational support, private security and store security meet to discuss intelligence and the targeting of activities in the city centre.

To be a member of the group the annual fee of £1,200 is paid to the Stores' Committee whereby access to the radio link and monthly meetings is granted:

> Crime Alert, in conjunction with the Liverpool Stores' Committee, has an aim to make Liverpool a safe and clean city for visitors and shoppers alike and to this end works closely with many organisations, including the City Council, Liverpool City Centre Partnership and the Chamber of Commerce (Private Communication from the Stores' Committee 11 August 1996, pers. comm.).

Crime Alert identifies problems in the city centre, but these problems are subsumed under a key concern with that which was detrimental to trade. The main problems are defined in the following manner:

> We have problems with terrorist threats – the Animal Liberation people for example. Of course we have shoplifting, damage to

property day and night. From a personal point of view and from the Stores' Committee point of view we also believe the street traders do not enhance the city centre. They force people in certain directions so you have not got any freedom to move through Church Street at will. Street beggars, street musicians and collectors give the same problems. We seem to have people collecting for all sorts all the time. We don't believe there should be so many and that licensing should be tightened up and inspected (Chairman, Stores' Committee).

Initially the group was organised through the larger stores 'to get information passed amongst retailers of who was operating in the city centre to the detriment of trade and with a view to working with police to curtail the problem' (Chairman, Crime Alert). From this fairly ad hoc and informal communication channel 'the idea progressed to an organised monthly meeting with a full sixty radio communication system connected to the city camera room and "Cop Shop" along with meetings with the Police Intelligence Unit, Crime Prevention, Shop Lifting Squad with regular attendance of the Crime Prosecution Service' (ibid.). The larger numbers of attendees at Crime Alert are private security. Most of the security staff are hired on an individual basis by particular stores, while others belong to national security firms con-tracted to particular retailers (ibid.).

The aim of working more closely with the police is a concern of the larger retailers who advocate such a move on a national scale. In this sense, the cultivation of both formal and informal national feedback chains helps to plan and initiate action at the local level. For example, in Liverpool, Marks & Spencer, who spearheaded the move to install a City Centre Manager and who take a leading role in the Stores' Committee, developed senior and board-level links with Home Office ministers concerned with crime prevention. In this context, meetings occurred around issues to do with the role of retailers in 'contributing to the local environment in which we operate' (represenative of Stores' Committee). The aim of such contacts is to encourage and galvanise local co-operation between business, local government and police on matters of crime prevention and to 'improve the environmental quality of life within which business operatives work' (ibid.). In forging these links, Marks & Spencer are central in that they had been able to utilise their national security provision that consists of six divisional security co-ordinators and extensive databases of known and potential shoplifters including a regularly updated and distributed 'national top ten'. The utilisation of this provision to aid local policing is encouraged by the Home Office and supported by major retailers themselves who, in Liverpool, want to see more done in terms of policing crime as perceived from the retail perspective:

> Other stores are very interested in what we are doing because we tend to be the high street leaders in these things – probably because of the size of our operation and the high levels of loss we incur, we have invested a lot in security. So we tend to know if and when there is something going down somewhere. So if we have got a pattern of something happening we can get the regional crime squads involved (ibid.).

From the perspective of Merseyside Police the pressure to become involved with local retailers took place in a context of criticism from the latter over the perceived decline in police presence in the city centre and lack of understanding regarding retail issues. For the police, the more effective targeting of their resources provided a rationale for the existence of Crime Alert and their working with them. However, crime prevention officers initially expressed their concern about engaging with such bodies in that 'normal' policing issues, resources and time may be diluted in having to engage with the business community. One crime prevention officer states:

> Some years ago when the police were invited to attend local traders' meetings I would sit for hours listening to people talk about the state of the pound and what a Labour government would or would not do for the local economy. This can't be justified – it is a waste of police time and so, yes, we encourage subgroups that focus on the issues the police can be useful in. These partnerships with local traders come out of the fact that the police cannot do it on their own. So we, and others had to get on board with this. Crime Alert is a classic example of how we cannot police the city centre as we once did – because of resource issues and the like. So we rely on those others to be our eyes and ears and bring things to our attention, so if we do have an incident we can allocate resources accordingly (city centre crime prevention officer, Merseyside Police).

As the previous chapter highlighted, the police role in the city centre changed from a situation of relative isolation from other agencies to one of closer co-operation and liaison. In this context, information becomes a prime commodity and negotiating tool in inter-partner relations:

Fifteen or twenty years ago we would not have even entertained the idea of engaging with the likes of the Stores' Committee. I mean, two separate organisations, right? The level of information exchange and formalised meetings that we have today was unimaginable then. For example, as a crime prevention officer I would have to seek higher approval for releasing crime figures and even if they were released there was the worry of how they would be used – how would they reflect on the police? With the arrangements we have now this is not necessary and we can be a bit more honest. We have nothing to hide and if people say those figures are terrible, we say yes they are, and that is why we are doing this and that to rectify the situation. The more information we release the more we can explain ourselves and influence people (ibid.).

Information gathering and sharing are also a key function of Crime Alert. The information it gathers through CCTV footage and intelligence from the radio link is channelled through the chair of Crime Alert to be used in helping to guide police action. This information channelling through the private sector is necessary in order to get the police to act – 'they'll only proceed if there's intelligence, not because we want them to' (Chairman, Crime Alert). From the police point of view, this is crucial for them to get involved in criminal or potentially criminal activities and to target resources accordingly. For Crime Alert, a process of learning to gather information and collate it in accordance with police criteria of 'usefulness' is set in motion:

We have day-to-day contact and monitoring procedures aimed at street beggars, Big Issue vendors, acts of criminal damage, fly posting – anything of that nature. We know when it has become a problem. The more information they [the police] get, the more that is fed to them, the more they can decide upon what resources they need to put in. If we can get our act together information wise, they are quite willing to receive the information, estimate it and act upon it (ibid.).

Within Crime Alert all security managers are regularly encouraged to write to the Area Commander within Merseyside Police informing him of all incidents in order to 'keep piling on the pressure for increased police manpower in the city centre' (field notes). Again, lower-level crime prevention officers were initially reluctant to become involved with Crime Alert in that a sense of an 'independent' policing rationale for particular policing operations was being taken away:

As the business partners became more organised through things like Crime Alert and CCTV they were obviously able to command a certain amount of information about crime in the city – *at least crime in the way they see it*. These associations tend to evolve with a crime component in their day-to-day activities and there are always victims amongst them and so we get dragged in. Dragged sounds terrible, but you know we tend to get pulled in their direction (city centre crime prevention officer, Merseyside Police, emphasis in original).

The police response at a more senior level was to establish specialist units to work more closely with local businesses in the city centre. Thus the Police Intelligence Unit, a crime prevention officer for the city centre and the Shop Lifting Squad regularly attend Crime Alert and supply information and operational support when appropriate.

Although tensions arise on technical matters between police and private security, members of Crime Alert have an organisational bonding through the cultivation of a normative sense of purpose that engenders loyalty and cohesion around the aims of the group. This normative underpinning aids the various agents within Crime Alert to define their work as well as cement relations between agency representatives. These normative processes are manifest in the discursive exchanges between group members and represent an integral part of the front line social ordering activities the group were engaged in. Such exchanges construct and demarcate the users of city centre space between the 'respectable' and 'non-respectable'. Members of Crime Alert characterised the objects of their power as 'dross', 'scallies', 'knobs', 'hawkers', 'urchins' and 'fake homeless' (field notes). These constructions complement and reinforce, albeit in less sophisticated tones, the broader visions for order in the city centre discussed at length in the last chapter and underpin a spatialisation strategy aimed at street reclamation.

In the process of constructing the proper of objects of power, the members of Crime Alert collectively compound a process of negation and othering directed at known and potential shoplifters, street traders, homeless people and young people who are regularly the subject of ridicule, contempt and objects of fascination and frustration.[7] These aspects of Crime Alert are discussed more fully below.

Working the cameras: Town Watch

Alongside the city centre camera network and Crime Alert, another inter-related scheme plays a key role. Town Watch (also known as the City Representatives) stemmed from discussions between the Government Office and the Stores' Committee and was described as 'a reassuring, visible presence that is uniformed but recognisable ... to stand in public places with no special powers' (Home Office Adviser, GOM). Town Watch became operational in January 1998 and recruited 20 persons from the long-term unemployed. The problems in establishing Town Watch were considerable and involved negotiating relations with the police and city centre funding regimes. The issues with the police were down to operational matters:

> The possibility was they [the City Reps] would be perceived by the regular police as the thin end of the wedge to a two tier police service ... They [the police] told us what they would not be prepared to tolerate that and we had to construct a path through it. So we had to avoid things like using the word 'security' and the word 'control'. You have to avoid words like 'residential areas' (ibid.).

The Government Office took on the role of selling the idea to the Association of Chief Police Officers through Merseyside's Chief Constable. For the police, the idea became realistic when it became clear that Town Watch personnel would not be a policing substitute. Furthermore, from the police point of view, Town Watch would be an independent policing aid, with specified links with the policing apparatus and untainted by links with the private security industry:

> They would have to be employed through or by the local authority and would have a communication network that was independent of the police. We [the police] might help in their training and so on. The deal is that they [Town Watch] will have service level agreements with a broad spectrum of agencies. So for example, if they found uneven paving stones and asked the Highways Department to come and sort them, they would sort them in an agreed number of days. If they find crime, vandalism or anti-social behaviour and they report them to the police, the police will respond within agreed time periods. The key thing is they would have no special powers. They would not be expected to use their civil powers of arrest unless it was in circumstances were they would do it anyway as citizens. On that basis we are happy to go with it because it is very much not for profit like the private security industry and will employ people responsibly (city centre crime prevention officer, Merseyside Police).

The role of Town Watch emanates from concerns within the Stores' Committee regarding the declining police presence in the city centre, alongside the separate issue of the competition wrought by the rise of 'out-of-town shopping' areas. Out-of-town shopping complexes, are seen to be one step ahead of the city centre regarding street security, cleanliness and order. Town Watch is envisaged as a response to these issues as well as a facilitator to the tourist industry:

> Town Watch is a group of people from the long term unemployed who are trained in knowledge of the city. They have maps and car park information. They are also trained in non-aggressive communication skills with the general public. The training is extensive in making sure Town Watch is non-confrontational. They can move on street traders unlawfully trading and move on beggars. They can check the validity of Big Issue sellers and they can even challenge people who drop litter on the streets. They are radio linked to the CCTV control room so that if they see something untoward they would be able to call the police very quickly. They are literally a presence; they are not another police force. They are not vigilantes (representative of Stores' Committee).

Town Watch emerged from negotiations between key players at local and national level and fitted in with the regeneration strategy, giving the personnel of the watch a broad remit. As well as 'protecting the City Council's assets and the streets' (ibid.), Town Watch must give visitors 'a sense that they feel comfortable and not fearful from crime' (ibid.). The managers of Town Watch are concerned to counter negative perceptions of the group as 'yet another layer of surveillance and policing in the city centre' (Home Office Adviser, GOM). Town Watch represents one component in the network of order maintenance in the city centre. As one interviewee expresses it:

> What you have to realise is it [Town Watch] is only part of the solution. Town Watch feeds in with an agreed strategy between city centre occupiers; it involves linking in with CCTV; it involves linking in with the police. It also involves a significant publicity campaign so people know why they are there. It's got to be marketed right (ibid.).

Thus far the chapter has discussed the inter-relationship between CCTV, Crime Alert and Town Watch, and the problems identified by urban managers pertaining to the dynamics of this inter-relationship and the promotion or marketing of these aspects of social control. The next section of the chapter outlines the role of the security network as a vehicle understood not just in terms of the *techniques* implicated in contemporary control processes but understood also for the *moral* and *normative* dynamics that underpin these techniques of control. Moreover, the position of CCTV, Crime Alert and Town Watch within these processes is tactically important in that these techniques of order form the basis for future ordering strategies:

> The long-term vision for a structure that would include CCTV and Town Watch is having a system that is in a position to make qualitative interventions, positive interventions in the cyclical process of offending. It is actually resourcing that system and then *getting the players in that system to recognise problems and then intervene* (Chairman, Stores' Committee, emphasis added).

Targeting the cameras: the proper objects of power

The CCTV surveillance system developed within, and out of, a wider set of debates taking place that concerned the trajectory and management of the regeneration process. The purposes of CCTV in the city centre, and thus how it is used and targeted, are articulated within the formal and informal networks of the neoliberal state. The locally powerful, and those who administer the camera network on a daily basis, understand the problems before them in the context of city renaissance. 'Risky' places, 'risky' people and 'risky' activities are identified in this context. Those engaged in this process also transform these risks into distinct subjects requiring particular forms of action.

As noted in the previous chapter, the Stores' Committee, Liverpool City Centre Partnership, the Office of Partnership Group and Merseyside Police played a key role in this process. These same partners play a determining role in establishing the bodies and mechanisms that are charged with consolidating and extending camera networks and, from their point of view, rendering the network effective. Thus the responsibility and management of CCTV and its attendant organs lie within the network of these partners. It was the Stores' Committee and the City Centre Manager who initially pushed and developed all the links in the network and gained a greater hands-on control and responsibility for the targeting of the network. The issue of leadership and responsibility regarding the CCTV network is not a clear-cut one and exists as a source of tension for the partners themselves. However, understanding the objects of city centre surveillance requires both a recognition of the trajectory of neoliberal urban management and the social relations out of which this trajectory was born and, indeed, constructed. In other words understanding the day-to-day operation of the surveillance system is achieved by placing that system within the underlying features of the emerging social order. The taken-for-granted assumptions of those operating the CCTV network pertain to what constitutes 'suspicious' and 'incongruous' activity and are reliant on, and take their cues from, the broader ideologies that construct a sense of place.

In constructing the objects of their power the agencies involved in the network are engaged in a process of defining categories of 'responsibility' and 'appropriateness' that delineate who can use the city centre – what practices and behaviours are permissible against the backdrop of urban renaissance. The historical material in Chapter 5 highlights the concerns of Liverpool's governing classes as they were directed at particular groups and activities in the city centre. Defined as disorderly, these activities were thought to undermine the city's sense of civic propriety. The governing classes were not only involved in defining disorder but also took a role in shaping the police response to it (Brogden 1982). The following discussion draws attention to historical continuity regarding these processes, focusing on the targeting of problematic activities in the city centre by the city's governing fractions. A historical narrative of the practice of social control questions and challenges just exactly what is 'new' about a supposed 'new penology'.

In 1997, a move to bring coherence to the process of securing the streets of Liverpool developed through the Officer Partnership Group. Here a strategy document was drawn up which derived from meetings between the key players and circulated to them. This document, introduced in the previous chapter, was entitled *Action Plan – Regeneration Agenda for Liverpool: To Develop a Safer City.* The document placed 'safety' as central to the regeneration process:

> Experience and perceptions of safety in Liverpool fundamentally affect quality of life across the whole of Merseyside and impact on inward investment and wider economic regeneration of the city. Developing a Safer City is an essential element of the holistic approach to promoting Liverpool as a safe, vibrant, regenerating city, which is attractive to inward investors and supports a high quality of life for residents and visitors (Liverpool City Council 1997b: 1).

The document identifies 'key elements' defined as 'situational measures' to 'make Liverpool city centre more attractive for work, commerce, leisure, shopping and tourism' (ibid.: 6). The document consolidates the role of the partners discussed so far in this chapter in placing CCTV in a pivotal position regarding street management. The key elements it notes for development are the 'raising [of] a visible, uniformed presence in the city centre; improving litter and graffiti removal services; encouraging leisure and healthy life style opportunities; a focused media campaign; controlling street traders'; the catch-all category of 'street management and cleanliness'; and 'extending closed circuit television' (ibid.). Against this backdrop the chapter turns to the themes and issues that the objects of partnership power identify and of how the targeting of the camera network takes place.

Purification of the streets

> The pavements here are a disgrace. They do not encourage investment (field notes: senior business executive addressing local conference, 'Merseyside: the future' 4 July 1997).

The streets of the city centre form a focus for the attention of the locally powerful in general and the security network in particular. The concern with 'the look of the streets' and the 'ambience of city centre life' was central to the architects of regeneration discussed in the previous chapter. The focus on the streets as an object of power is conflating a range of problems subsumed under an 'orderly regeneration'. Threats to the local urban aesthetic are identified as the problem of litter; individual and travelling groups of shoplifters; the prevalence of litter and graffiti; sellers of the homeless magazine (*Big Issue*); young people; licensed and unlicensed street trading; and busking. As problems hindering the process of regeneration, these categories are positioned in opposition to a more orderly vision of street life that is prioritising particular culturally defined notions of 'carnival' and 'fun'. These are highly circumscribed notions of culture. The streets are a locus for the new primary definers to instil 'spontaneity' and 'playfulness' as well as to advertise, through the use of banners on special posts, officially sanctioned cultural and other events in the city centre. Alongside the CCTV system, LCCP promotes various campaigns to promote a city of civic propriety:

> It all stems from our 'Local and Proud' initiative, which sparked off a number of other projects. The city centre was obviously in a bad state, a free for all, if you like; buskers, fly posting, litter and all

manner of collectors – none of it controlled and some of it down right offensive to visitors, tourists and shoppers. It gave the impression of wider dereliction and impoverishment. We needed to counter these kinds of things and salvage the architectural and cultural heritage of this city; if you like – marketing the city's heritage splendours, and building a more family friendly environment. We're giving the city centre back to the people (Chairman, Stores' Committee).

Reclaiming the city centre as a managed and controlled environment forms a key renaissance platform from which to lever inward investment. 'Street cleanliness' is the directive phrase through which a series of initiatives concerned with street order is enacted:

I am not spouting a prejudice here but as any one who cares about the future of this city will tell you the people of this city are so untidy. The streets are always filthy and that just gives us a bad name. Just how many more letters to the [*Liverpool*] *Echo* do we have to read slagging us off for the state of our streets? It's a big put off for shoppers and tourists (Economic Development Officer, Liverpool City Council).

Street cleansing took root in an initiative entitled 'Gold Zone', launched in 1998. The initiative relies chiefly on private sector backing and has the support of key players that include the Stores' Committee and Mersey Partnership.[8] In attempting to make businesses and citizens responsible for their own environment, Gold Zone extends the notion of Town Watch and takes a step in the direction of responsibilised self-governance and underpins the shift to re-order the city centre as a Business Improvement District (BID). An important component in the armoury of these neoliberal strategies is the creation of BIDs, much in evidence in the USA and now on the agenda in the UK. In return for paying annual subscriptions, commercial property owners are able to fund a private body charged with managing city centres. Within BID partnerships 'street cleanliness' becomes the catch-all category under which problems of marketing, environmental improvements and 'street safety' become conflated. BIDs are publicly unaccountable bodies set up to police and monitor the 'debris' of neoliberal urban visions – litter, graffiti, the homeless and prohibited street trading. Alongside these developments, Merseyside Police and the City Council now enforce a by-law to extend 'alcohol-free zones' in the city centre. This 'important weapon in the war against street crime' applies to the drinking of alcohol on all main streets.

Street signs are erected warning people that drinking in the streets will entail the risk of being fined up to £500 and the possibility of police arrest. The exceptions to the by-law were the new designated pavement cafés (*Daily Post* 24 March 2000: 'Street ban on drinkers') much in evidence in renaissance cities. The by-law is suspended during officially sponsored festivals and events, such as the annual Matthew Street Beatles Festival. The instigation of a café bar culture brings with it contradictions for urban managers. With the proliferation of bars, the fear of a city centre blighted by drunken disorder is seen as a threat to the desired urban ambience and must, therefore, be countered with street controls. In this sense a careful management of street order is enacted in an effort not to offset the trajectory of urban growth but to reorder the nature, timing and location of activities in the streets.

The mushrooming of street management schemes is tied to discourses of image and safety and the logic of investment, whether through tourism, shopping or attracting new businesses. Within this, the role of CCTV is to oversee a ubiquitous construction of 'street cleanliness'. This role is articulated in a manner that refers to and evokes a notion of 'the people'. As one CCTV manager puts it: 'The city centre is a people's place first and foremost and CCTV is a people's system. It's got to be otherwise it could not be successful in terms of what we are trying to do' (City Centre Manager, LCCP). For this interviewee, CCTV was described as one of 'the vehicles' through which the new primary definers operate. CCTV is important in the process of 'sustaining the pedestrian flow of traffic' (ibid.). In sustaining this flow, a number of obstacles to street order are identified by those who manage the camera network. These obstacles are discussed below.

Homelessness

The reality of homelessness is an important factor for those partnerships concerned with image management and the creation of favourable business climates. In September 1995, Liverpool City Council's Social Services Committee considered a motion in the name of a Conservative councillor. The motion read as follows: 'That the City Council, in conjunction with Merseyside Police, initiate a programme to remove from the streets of Liverpool all professional beggars in order to prevent residents of the city and visitors being harassed and accosted' (Liverpool City Council 1996: 2).[9] The subcommittee approved the motion.[10] The motion formalised random police 'checks', using the Operational Support Division, on those found begging and selling the *Big Issue* magazine in the city centre. The problem of homelessness in Liverpool is now firmly articulated as one of rooting out and ridding the city of 'aggressive beggars' as distinguished from the 'genuinely homeless'. One councillor fuelled the 'debate' in saying that 'some of these people are earning up to £500 a week. It doesn't improve the city's image' (*Liverpool Echo* 11 September 1995: 'City plans to clamp down on beggars').

In joining the Office of Partnership Group, the Stores' Committee is able to articulate the problem of the homeless in Liverpool that dovetails with its, and others', concerns about street cleanliness and the quality of the environment. Hostility towards the homeless is not uncommon and underpins a hostility towards the presence of this group for seemingly contradicting the re-imaging of the city centre:

> Oh yes, there is a 'big issue' [laughter]. When people come out of Lime Street Station to do some shopping they've already passed seven or eight *Big Issue* sellers and it really pisses them off. People then think this city is seedy and full of beggars and homeless people; *like something you stand on* (Superintendent, Merseyside Police, GOM, emphasis added).

The problem of homeless persons in the city centre is articulated most forcibly through the Stores' Committee, the City Centre Manager, and Crime Alert:

> Well you see we have this problem with *Big Issue* vendors. They stand right outside the more popular stores in a manner intrusive to those entering and leaving. Some of them even go into a store causing mayhem. Some of them we've banned because it has been in our customers' interests (Chairman, Crime Alert).

Initiatives from the partners aimed at the problem of the homeless vary from covert surveillance to 'educational' approaches that brought together police and Stores' representatives to meet with the *Big Issue* vendors in order to discuss 'sensible selling strategies' (Home Office adviser, GOM):

> It is not politically acceptable to say to the *Big Issue* sellers 'get lost'. All we can do is negotiate with them and say 'do you realise the impact this is having on people?' I know some of them have taken this on board and try to sell their paper in a manner that is non-threatening or overtly intrusive. *But some of them just look wrong.* They do not look like someone who has fallen on hard times and are

trying to do something for themselves but [look] like they are getting money for the next fix. Perhaps the *Big Issue* should consider who they accept as a vendor and where they are placed (Superintendent, Merseyside Police, GOM, emphasis in original).

These educative strategies include discussions among key players as to the possibility of responsibilising *Big Issue* vendors with tasks deemed more appropriate and attuned with neoliberal sensibilities. These tasks include recruiting and training the vendors as tourist guides alongside Town Watch (*Liverpool Echo* 8 January 1997: 'Big Issue on city agenda'). At the same time, other initiatives include the undercover surveillance of the homeless in the city centre undertaken by Merseyside Police. Crime Alert provides the forum for the conduct of such operations that involve police officers posing as homeless people in order to ascertain intelligence on their movements, involvement in criminal activity and whether or not they were 'genuinely homeless' (Chairman, Crime Alert). Intelligence is then passed around private security staff regarding the identification of 'problem' homeless persons, which is then used for targeting them in the city centre. As indicated earlier in the chapter, Crime Alert provides a forum within which a normative bonding is nourished between private security and police personnel. This bonding underpins an open hostility towards identified groups, and this is particularly visible regarding the homeless. For example, during one Crime Alert meeting, two police officers engaged in undercover operations led a debate about the homeless problem in Liverpool:

Chair: It is just annoying when you read in the *Sun* about the *Big Issue* vendor who moans if he makes £800 a week.
Police officer 1: Yeh, but as we know 99.9% of them are known criminals.
Police officer 2: Only 1 in 50 that we spoke to are actually homeless.
Police officer 1: We've nailed the original aggressive beggar now. He can't come into the city because we know him. He can't move outside his front door!
Chair: The problem is there are just too many of them. They are always aggressive, threatening and selling at our doors ... shop-lifters, drunks, dirty sods, wandering in and out of stores.
Private security guard 1: They shouldn't be allowed in stores. We should always check their identification.
Private security guard 2: She's awful (pointing to photo). You can smell her before she comes round the corner (field notes, Crime Alert).

Crime Alert focuses its own surveillance measures using the radio link and CCTV to monitor the movement of *Big Issue* vendors around the city centre. This is felt necessary, as vendors in particular are, it is thought, trying to avoid surveillance and becoming known to security staff. This concern is placed alongside the futility of the 'educative' measures mentioned above:

> We had meetings between the Stores' Committee and the *Big Issue* office, where they put their side of the story and we put ours. But the situation gets no better; they just seem to be an uncontrollable group. They swap and change their identity badges amongst themselves and change pitches – it can be difficult to keep tabs on them. They probably have a good knowledge of security in the city centre but we are on to them (ibid.).

The positioning of *Big Issue* vendors outside store entrances is also deemed problematic in that they could overhear information passed over the radio link: 'It has been known for them [the homeless] to pass on this information and even tip off shoplifters, some of who have managed to get away' (security manager 1, Crime Alert). The monitoring is felt necessary as 'they are a potentially criminal group – we have examples of them stealing and dealing in drugs – and they intimidate the public in entering our stores' (ibid.).

It is the targeting of beggars who mingle with the crowds around the bars and major shopping malls that presents the biggest challenge. 'Operation Change' launched in Liverpool in 2003 aimed to reduce 'anti-social behaviour' among beggars and, in the words of a Chamber of Commerce spokesperson, target 'people who allegedly can't speak English, using their children to ask for money' (*Daily Post* 13 March 2003: 'Crackdown on street beggars'). Publicity posters (titled 'Fact: Nobody needs to beg for a bed') have a picture of a fake model homeless person, crouched on a city street, whose face is covered by a cardboard sign that reads 'Help them make the change, keep your change'. This process of silencing the experiences of homeless people is reflected in the poster campaigns, which discourage local people from talking to and handing over loose change to street people. In Liverpool, this has been coupled with undercover policing and targeted surveillance resulting in the arrest, caution or charging of over 800 people in 2002 in relation to begging offences. Nationally, begging is now a recordable offence in recognition that 'the public do not want to see beggars on our street [*sic*]'. In moving begging into the realms of 'anti-social behaviour' those arrested are routinely finger-printed and placed on the Police National Computer (Home Office 2003).

The problem of homelessness as it is conveyed here conflates the problems of orchestrating a desirable image with the perception of drug use, drug selling and shoplifting. As elsewhere in cities of the UK, *Big Issue* vendors have now to stand within a stencilled selling pitch painted on the ground measuring about two foot square. In Liverpool, sellers of the *Big Issue* magazine are banned from the main indoor shopping mall and the stores of the larger retailers, and are subject to a 'curfew' on sales after 8 pm (*Daily Post* 11 May 2002: 'City shops ban Big Issue sales'). As part of a larger campaign against the homeless, this embargo denies freedom of movement around the city and denies basic access to food, drink, shelter and facilities for cleanliness that others who work and visit the city take for granted. Homeless people are the subject of intense surveillance underpinned by hostility towards this group for its perceived attitude in either attempting to avoid surveillance or in merely 'looking wrong'. In an unprecedented move in October 2003 all 130 *Big Issue* vendors were banned from selling in downtown Liverpool after 200 police swamped the city centre and arrested 57 people on suspicion of drug offences, 30 of whom were sellers of the homeless magazine and only 12 were actually charged. The City Centre Manager heralded the move as a 'major step forward in creating a cleaner, safer and more attractive environment' (*The Guardian* 18 October 2003: 'Big Issue sellers held in drugs crackdown'). After threats of legal action by the homeless magazine 'the ban' was lifted after one week but had served its purpose in sending out a message of censure towards homeless people that consolidates the developments outlined in this section. This fits with a wider assault on the homeless as oppressive monitoring on a national scale is leading to outright social removal as court injunctions are set to lead the way to a national ban on begging (*The Independent* 22 August 2003: 'Court ruling may lead to national ban on beggars'). In the neoliberal cities of the USA and UK the normative demarcation of space robustly targets the homeless who have been successfully defined (along with other poor people) as just 'so many "broken windows" ', the idea being 'not to repair them but to remove them altogether' (Mitchell 2001: 83).

Street trading

As Chapter 5 highlighted, Liverpool city centre has a long tradition of independent street trading which dates back to the early nineteenth century and has been the subject of concern and regulation by the locally powerful and the police.[11] Licensing, along with the requirement of traders to pay for the square footage of their pitch and parking and refuse fees, had the impact of cutting the number of traders as well as forcing others unwilling or unable to pay the licence fee off the streets and into local pubs to sell. During the 1990s, a number of issues emerged that underpinned a reinvigorated and concerted effort by city centre partners to remove the street traders from the main city centre consumption zone of Church Street. Based as they are on the door-step of the big city centre retailers, the Stores' Committee along with the Government Office and the City Centre Manager vocalise a number of concerns that provide a focal point on which partners have agreed to as the 'unsightliness' of the traders, the rubbish they leave behind, the minimal licence and pitch fees compared to the business rates of mainstream retailers and the insinuations that traders are involved in criminal activity. As one senior security manager puts it: 'They are taking trade away from respectable retailers and we also feel that it is having an effect on people feeling safe within the city centre. Why be crowded out by people like that?' (Chairman, Crime Alert). The problem of street trading is expressed in terms of the negative image for the city centre and can be compared directly to the favourable response afforded to the European Market occasionally set up in the city centre as part of the Liverpool's image-conscious claim to be a leading European city. Powerful censures aimed at local traders whose livelihoods depend on street stalls reveal a disdain for any image that conjures up an 'older' and therefore less relevant Liverpool. The problem of street traders condenses around the issue of licensing and violations of pitch size allowable under the licence. For those involved in the security network the battery of powers available to regulate traders is felt to be inept at addressing the problem:

> The regulation of pitch sizes needs to be enforced, as does the vetting of traders by the police. No trader should be allowed to operate with a criminal record. Enforcement orders against these people should be used without fear of a backlash. This laxity has led to our belief that there is a mafia out there (representative of LCCP).

This 'mafia' seems particularly well organised, with one local Labour councillor among the 51 licensed traders. The traders fought and won a High Court battle against having them removed from the city centre, despite much pressure from the Stores' Committee and the Government Office. The victory of the traders is seen as 'creating a crisis of confidence in the way our city is run' (*Liverpool Echo* 24 May 2000: 'What a way to run a city'). The issue of street trading is prominent in local press articles and is a central feature in debates around the 'proper' governance of the city and what counts as the 'public interest'. In defiance of those seeking to create a new urban aesthetic, the traders articulate a sense of tradition clearly at odds with the position of the new primary definers:

> What people should realise is that the traders survive because people shop at our stalls. People want the barrow boys and flower sellers to stay. We are part of the furniture in the city. Not every one in the city can afford to shop at Marks and Spencer (street trader cited in *Liverpool Echo* 20 July 1999: 'Not everyone can afford to shop at Marks').

In challenging the power of the new urban aesthetic, the traders argue that 'if traders were removed [from the city centre] ... it would become a soulless and sterile place much like high streets in other cities, but Liverpool, the "pool of life", is no other city and we do not wish it to be' (leaflet, *Street Trading: The Facts*, distributed on the streets of Liverpool May–August 1998). The local press, however, is a key vehicle for orchestrating a campaign against street trading. In one particular editorial, street traders in the city centre are derided as nineteenth century throwbacks belonging to a 'monstrous era'. Street traders are characterised as a 'species' and a 'pox on our city' who, because they represent 'a curse' on the city, should be located 'somewhere more appropriate ... like the [River] Mersey, perhaps' (*Daily Post* 19 May 1998: 'Our view'). In the local press traders are, at best, described as an 'eyesore' and at worst as 'swagmen'.[12] For the traders a process of criminalisation is underway as a perquisite to their removal: 'We would suggest that words used to describe us would normally be reserved for Nazis, rapists and child molesters and not people who after all, are only trying to earn a living' (Leaflet: *Street Trading: The Facts*).

From the point of view of the Stores' Committee and the other key players, the longevity of street trading in Liverpool has been tempered by successive City Council administrations granting trading licences:

> These issues go back to when Adam was a lad. Rightly or wrongly the licensing has given the traders certain rights, which has bounced back on us. I know as a city we have had to set up this situation properly and responsibly but the other side of it is that a lot of them have not paid any rent for some time. There are not many people in this city getting anything for nothing. These guys are out there giving us straight competition and paying nothing (representative 2, Stores' Committee).

Other partners outside retailing express similar sentiments and spoke of being 'educated' about the issue by other partners. The move at bringing partners together allows the Stores' Committee to place street trading higher on the agenda of city centre regeneration at Government Office level. As one urban manager in the Government Office put it:

> What they [Stores' Committee] were doing and saying about street cleanliness was relevant and that's how they got involved. They were able to tell us about some of their problems like the number of street traders outside their doors. I personally find it difficult picking my way around them but I hadn't thought about how they were taking trade away from stores. Also a lot of stuff that gets nicked from the stores is sold out there as well, which is really galling (Home Office adviser, GOM).

The problematisation of street trading plays a central discursive role in linking issues around 'quality of environment', street cleanliness and the ambience of the city centre in the eyes of potential inward investors:

> We bring businesses to look around Liverpool and it's worrying you know – by the time we get to the core trading area we are faced with the chaos of the traders. Shabby stalls, cheap merchandise and litter that says Liverpool is a low-grade economy (Regeneration Co-ordinator, Liverpool City Council).

As well as the hindrance to investment, the problem of street trading (as intimated above) is also expressed in terms of criminality:

> The stalls are a menace, take up space and undermine the business of established retail. They generate litter and provide an op-portunity for the disposal of stolen goods and the practice of benefit fraud, that kind of thing. There is very little to say that's positive about them; they are in the wrong place (security manager 1, Crime Alert).

Furthermore: 'This problem has been with us a long time and maybe now we are going to sort it. It's common knowledge that merchandise moves from high street chains to the stalls and into the pubs ... but the police, well they don't want to know' (Chairman, Crime Alert). Other partners highlight what they think is the 'real crime' in the policing of the city centre that raises issues of what should be policed at any particular time:

The police will harass someone selling the *Big Issue* who is not doing much harm really other than making £20 a day more than he should. Yet, every one of those street traders is on invalidity or unemployment benefit. Now who is the thief there? (security manager, non-member of Crime Alert).

The use of Liverpool's CCTV system to monitor street trading is undertaken at the request of some of the major retailers, as one security manager sympathetic to the traders stated:

I know people out there who work hard for a living and I also know that some of the stores, including this one, have wanted more to be done about the traders. But yes, we can, and do, use the CCTV system to see what's happening. One store was convinced a particular line of shirts that they sold was lifted and being sold back outside for half the price! So the system can be used to monitor deliveries to traders to see what they're selling (security manager 3, Crime Alert).

The monitoring and recording of violations of pitch space are also undertaken and passed on to licence enforcers at the City Council. The role of Crime Alert in this respect is to scrutinise minutely the activities of traders in order to cajole relevant authorities to take action against them:

We do believe that the stuff that is stolen from the shops ends up on the stalls. All the information we get is passed on to the Police Intelligence Unit. The proof is that street stalls have been raided and closed down for handling stolen goods. We also get members of the public complaining about them. They aren't controlled in any way. The way they take the mickey by infringing their pitch allocation is just a laugh. We record any extensions – how they extend their pitch, by the use of bars and verandas and boxes jutting out over the ground (Chairman, Crime Alert).

Surveillance is also directed at unlicensed sellers who kept mobile around the city centre, selling out of suitcases and backpacks. This group is believed to consist of about 30 'known traders' and posed a particularly difficult problem in that 'they don't just work the streets but inside pubs and clubs' (ibid.).

Merseyside Police supported the City Council and the passing of a by-law to curtail a range of grassroots and spontaneous street protests. The by-law states that 'no person shall in any street or public place, for the purpose of the selling or advertising any article, or obtaining custom tout or importune, to the annoyance or obstruction of passengers'. The broadness of the by-law means it can also be used to attack a range of perceived 'nuisances' that are tied to the secondary economy in the city and that, for the new primary definers, give the city the image of a bargain-basement economy. It is an offence for people to sell or tout for business in the streets or other public places, including flower sellers selling their goods in restaurants and bars. The new law also bans individuals asking for money to mind cars and prevents charities stopping people in the street. This is particularly interesting as Liverpool is one of the poorest areas in the European Union and has had a visible and sizeable part of its population engaged in the secondary economy in the city for over two centuries (Brogden 1982). The by-law also prohibits flyers being given out; people selling draw tickets in the street; student 'rag-mag' sellers; and leaflets being put under the windscreens of parked cars. Liverpool City Council's licensing committee approved a team of 14 Gold Zone wardens to enforce the by-law across the city. Linked by radio to the camera system, these wardens cost £700,000 annually and are utilised widely in tackling 'anti-social behaviour' that has been broadened to include checking the movement and identity of homeless people and those who sell the *Big Issue*.

The use of the camera network to monitor street traders is justified neither in a deterrent nor preventative capacity. Hostility to street trading is intense, and the solution to the 'problem' is, in the final analysis, seen as political. As long as the traders are present the camera network should perform a disciplinary function regardless of whether strictly criminal suspicion is present, and, in that sense, the camera network contributes to the wider political pressure brought to bear on traders, adding to the message that their presence is unwelcome. Street trading, like homelessness, though not illegal activities, are nevertheless coterminous with categories of suspicion defined by normative conceptions of place and associated categories of 'appropriateness' and 'responsibility'. The camera network is mobilised in a disciplinary sense so as to communicate and aid 'the rules of the game' in the regenerating city centre under prevailing definitions of responsibility. Moral objection towards these groups cuts across the institutions for regeneration and underpins the use and targeting of CCTV. The message CCTV communicates is summed up thus: 'they know we are watching'[13] (City Centre Manager).

Youth

> Any child or group of children without a parent with them is bound to arouse suspicion. Just think of the Bulger case. In a sense the kids are the easiest to dissuade. They know they are being watched and it seems like a game to them but once they know we aren't playing they get bored and go elsewhere (Security Manager, Mersey Travel Rapid Response Unit).

Researchers highlight the contemporary targeting of young people by policing agencies in urban centres, albeit with particular reference to targeting black youth (Norris and Armstrong 1998b). This takes place within the process of interpretive construction that highlights constructions as to the proper and legitimate use of time and space. The visibility of youth in public urban spaces is linked to perceptions of disorder among other groups in the population, particularly in the context of urban revitalisation and the creation of safe shopping zones (Beck and Willis 1995; Oc and Tiesdell 1997). Young people of school age constitute a particular concern for security managers in Liverpool, who perceive their presence in the city centre as incongruous with the 'family friendly' environment they espouse:

> There's a tradition in Liverpool of kids bunking school. They roam in and around the city centre on buses and hang out. The city centre has an appeal to the kids; they treat it as a playground but it isn't. They harass shoppers and staff alike. The fact that they aren't doing anything intimidates people and, it seems almost pointless to ask where are their parents in all of this? But there is a time and a place for children to be in the city centre (Chairman, Stores' Committee).

In dealing with these kinds of problems, a number of initiatives focusing on the city centre are up and running. In attracting custom from outside the city centre, public transport, and its image, is deemed a key attribute in regeneration. Mersey Travel and Merseyside Police, with support from the Stores' Committee, are cleaning up the image of public transport in Liverpool. In particular, the aim is 'to rid the system of ticket touts'. This group consists largely of children of school age who 'use the Away Day ticket scheme to move aimlessly around the city, leaving litter and graffiti and intimidating drivers and customers' (Security Manager,

Mersey Travel Rapid Response Unit). Mersey Travel have their own Rapid Response Unit (RRU), a 20-strong security unit who were trained to work with the police:

> One of the reasons the RRU was set up was to deal with kids who actually are becoming more violent. This tends to be a daytime problem; bored kids using the buses as a play ground. But since the 24-hour city initiative our buses have taken on more passengers in and out of the city of a weekend. Rowdiness, drunkenness, physical damage and even urination on the buses have all increased (ibid.).

For Mersey Travel, a senior player in the regeneration process, the problem of youth leads them to argue for linking up the city centre surveillance system with their own camera network covering bus stations and some buses.[14] Within Crime Alert, a special Juvenile Group is in operation to deal with young people to initiate Truancy Watch. This scheme is aimed to 'deal with the scallies'. The CCTV system became a key tool to help police 'round up pupils in the city centre' who presented 'a nuisance to people going about their daily business'[15] (city centre crime prevention officer, Merseyside Police).

As a key tool in the politics of vision, cameras in the cities of the UK are helping to put into effect what can and cannot be seen on the streets. As cameras aid the strategic balance between aesthetics and function, any notion of the city as a space of cultural expression for younger people continues to be highly circumscribed. In Liverpool, skateboarders can be fined from £250 to £1,000 if they break a by-law banning skating passed by city councillors in July 2002. Liverpool council claimed that skateboarding should be an offence as it is giving the city a bad image in terms of scaring off tourists and shoppers, as well as damaging statues and memorials (*Liverpool Echo* 24 July 2002: 'Skateboard ban in city'). In another development, in cities in the counties of Essex, Hampshire, Cornwall and Devon, police and private security enforce a policy that has banned the wearing of hooded tops, baseball caps and hats of various descriptions. For all the techno-hype, cameras cannot identify people accurately if they are wearing headgear. This measure is clearly targeted at young people who are stopped and told to remove headgear if they want to remain in the city centre. As one businesswoman stated: 'it's a brilliant idea [but] some kids get stroppy when we ask them to remove their hoods. As long as it helps in the fight against crime it isn't discriminating against young people' (*The Independent* 23 May 2003: 'Police ban hooded tops from high street'). As well as infringing upon the cultural expression of the young, such measures will further criminalise a generation and reinforce stereotypical discourses around 'dangerous youth' in the public mind.[16]

Race

In his report, Lord Gifford notes the 'strikingly noticeable' (Gifford 1989: 70) lack of black faces as either workers or visitors in the centre of Liverpool. Both local policing and public and private sector employment practices are held responsible for this visible social demarcation in the city. Interestingly the issue of race rarely came up during the course of this research. However, when race is articulated it points to continuity with the observations above and social processes in the city over the last century, in that: 'A colleague of mine works in Bristol [where] they have problems with young black kids. We don't have as many "darkies" as other towns and cities. They're just not here. They stick with their own kind, don't they?' (security manager 2, Crime Alert). This manager, when asked what groups particularly caught his attention, stated simply 'blacks stick out'. When asked what he meant by this, he stated, 'if troublesome black kids are in town they don't stand a chance – we know about it' (ibid.). Notwithstanding these comments, the relative silence on race can be attributed to the findings of local reports that question Liverpool's cosmopolitan image, the role of public agencies and historical patterns of local racial violence that have promoted 'a devastating lack of mobility' for Liverpool's black population and 'confined' them to their places of residence outside the city centre (Gifford 1989: 83). Race, as a relative non-issue for security managers, is understood against the peculiar and historically formed politics of exclusion that has operated in Liverpool. Today, little has changed. Liverpool 8 Law Centre describes the city centre as a 'no-go area' for black people in terms of work and leisure. Only 2% of city jobs were being filled by black people, which amounted to a 1% improvement since the Gifford Inquiry of 1988 (*Liverpool Echo* 3 July 2001: 'Is Liverpool a racist city?').[17]

Nothing to hide, nothing to fear

What can be gauged from the discussion thus far is that the uses and impact of CCTV cannot be understood in terms of the technology alone. The targeting of the camera network raises issues that challenge the commonsense assumption that those who have nothing to hide have nothing to fear from CCTV. The routine targeting of the network, and the discretion within that targeting, is informed by local ideologies of place and social order that display a particular historical trajectory that is rearticulated and reasserted within the contours of contemporary neoliberal rule. As a key aspect of contemporary social control, camera surveillance contributes to a strategy of sociospatial transformation that is fostering the cultivation of urban subjectivities around particular groups and individuals that raises questions over their right to the city.

In Liverpool, wider contemporary discourses pertaining to the legitimate uses of the revitalised city centre are reinforcing some older historical sentiments and normative judgements around what constitutes an 'orderly' city. The proper objects of power are identified not in any straightforward sense of crimes committed, or on the basis of identifying known offenders but, also, through the operation of a set of normative judgements within which legal suspicion may only play a small, if any, part. The ideology of regeneration and neoliberal responsibilisation sets the context for groups and categories to be defined *out* of city centre renaissance: as a threat and visual anomaly to a visionary landscape. For example, surveillance of street traders is deemed legitimate in this context. Indeed, the surveillance of those groups and individuals described above is based on an implicit message to those targeted by the system, which is one of 'they will know we are watching'. The message itself reinforces wider discourses constructed around these 'unwelcome' groups and activities and construes them in entirely negative terms – even pathological – and as a hindrance to the construction of a positive image for the city centre. In this sense, the CCTV network forms a key role in a neoliberal state strategy geared towards the surveillance over, and collation of information about, a given territory. In the attempt, materially, to forge a vision of order in a given territory, the camera network runs conterminous to the ideological power to define and shape that territory.

In a physical sense, street cameras gaze downwards and in doing so symbolise the power of scrutiny and its source within the networks of economic and political authority. The relationship of street cameras to the power of scrutiny and what can and cannot be subject to inspection in Liverpool and other urban centres is often overlooked. Images produced by street cameras reinforce a power of inspection by ensuring the social reproduction of 'the criminal' and a 'criminal class' not only for those behind the cameras but in the public consciousness more generally. In focusing on the politics of surveillance, the domain of the powerful becomes an object of inquiry in order to ascertain prevailing, often taken for granted, discourses that shape a vision for social order and, in doing so, define problems and hindrances for that order. What the discussion indicates is how the proliferation of street cameras is bound up with shifts in the governance of public space and how that space is idealised within powerful discourses promoting preferred and sanctioned uses of space. In problematising the role of CCTV and asking how those agents and agencies that promote the surveillance network come to define the objects of their power, a wider issue relating to 'the right to the city' (Mitchell 2003) comes into view. Closer critical scrutiny of those behind the cameras and city rule more generally reveals that the kinds of surveillance networks being developed in the UK promote a particular and tendentious vision for social order that does little to promote equality of access to city space and in fact does much to reinforce social divisions.

A seamless web of control? Tensions within the neoliberal state

Homogenised views of state institutions and practices have been rightly criticised for their functionalism, rigidity and lack of attention to process (Jessop 1990). The locally powerful are not some monolithic union but a set of class-relevant fractions whose 'unity' depends on struggles and processes found in the political arena. Similarly, overgeneralised views of social control and homogeneity of outcomes do little to advance understanding in the area (McMahon 1990), and certainly this book seeks to avoid promoting a view of social control as a smooth running and seamless expansion of surveillance over public space. What follows therefore is an exploration of how the practices of social ordering in Liverpool city centre are subject to tension and contradiction between key players. Tensions between agencies engaged in social ordering in the city centre are identifiable at two main levels: firstly, at the highest strategic level within the renaissance process, and secondly, among agencies working on the ground in and around Crime Alert. It is to a consideration of these tensions that the discussion now turns.

Locally powerful tensions

There is total agreement among players about the problems that need to be addressed but there are significant differences of priority – about actually doing things to address the problems and what those things should be. The city's renaissance is a very delicate thing and has to be carefully managed. Each player needs to think carefully about what they are doing and why (representative 2, Stores' Committee).

The practice of 'making partnerships work' is not without problems. Bringing together different agencies with different organisational aims, philosophies and working practices may compound tensions between partners around interagency perceptions, designated roles and issues in leadership (Crawford 1997; Loveday 1999). Regarding these issues, Crawford (1997: 133) points to what he calls the 'creative management of conflict' between multi-agency actors which often takes place 'behind the scenes' in informal settings: 'The creativity of practice, more often than not, takes a pragmatic and managerial form. It tends to be about "getting through the day's business" and meeting managerial objectives, *rather than pursuing any moral or political mission'* (ibid.: 135, emphasis added). Contrary to Crawford's argument, the drive to establish effective strategies and structures of city centre rule do not lead to a strict separation between managerial and moral discourses and practices. The public and private interests engaged in the regeneration process forge a strategy of rule that couples a hard-headed pragmatism alongside deeper moralising visions that underpin a set of social ordering practices. This is not to suggest that tensions do not arise among strategists in the regeneration process. In broad terms tensions between the new primary definers arise not in the meanings attributed to 'regeneration' and 'order' but through the strategic actions pursued to achieve these ends. What was deemed as 'good' and 'bad' for the city's image represent benchmark questions that guide senior managerial approaches and their ideological positioning to order maintenance practices. Other tensions arise not out of opposition to particular crime prevention practices but in their management and funding. In short, the problems for order *are not deemed problematic, but the means to achieving order are.*

Tensions between the goals of partnership decision-making processes and sections of the public have been evident (Audit Commission 1999) along with the importance of 'appeals to community' in crime prevention strategies (Crawford 1997). Appeals to 'community' in the city centre are highly circumscribed. The idea of 'community' in the city centre is constructed assertively rather than demonstrably. If 'community' is invoked at all it is as an after-thought: 'People have nothing to fear from CCTV', 'it's a people's system'. These assertions are made without any detailed assessment of which 'people' are being referred to, or what 'the people' think of practices such as CCTV. Marketing and carefully constructed image campaigns are prioritised as part of these processes that underpin *a politics of persuasion* rather than by any open channels of debate. Within the locally powerful discourses explored in the previous chapter, 'the public' are selectively characterised and addressed in a particular fashion – as themselves entrepreneurial in spirit and in tune with the 'playfulness' of the new urban order. This fits with the construction of the city centre as a commercial entity where the 'people' (or public) are regarded as an important potential client base (i.e. a commercial category), but are also absent ('outsiders' to regeneration machinations) – a transitory category to be kept at a distance from the processes of city centre rule. Indeed, forms of partnership rule in the urban centre 'do not need to exert total power *over* the city's population to act effectively (i.e., whether through the ballot box or other means), but rather they merely need the power to act' (Hall and Hubbard 1996: 156, emphasis in original). As discussed in the previous chapter, the ideological basis and scope for this power to act inoculate the workings of local power from outside scrutiny by substituting 'older' democratic frameworks with a form of 'consultocracy' (Fairclough 2000). In this sense, tensions between components of the security network and 'the public' in the enactment of social ordering in the city are construed as non-issues. Instead, however, tensions arise in the networks of rule themselves, in particular, between and within different class fractions within the networks and the structures of political power. It is in this arena that the 'public interest' itself is constructed and made meaningful in relation to the processes of urban renaissance and social ordering.

Militarisation, safe shopping and CCTV

Contemporary writing around social control, has emphasised the management of risk that relies upon actuarial techniques. An implication in that literature has been that these techniques of risk are outmoding 'older' forms of control characterised as state centred, repressive or authoritarian. The characterisation offered by Davis (1990: 223) focuses instead on the range of practices that join up to achieve 'the architectural policing of social boundaries' in a manner that posits a continued inter-relationship between 'old' and 'new' order maintenance strategies.[18] Davis (ibid.) draws attention to important omissions that can be found in urban studies and in criminology regarding the inter-linkage between techniques of policing and control found within urban centres.[19] This is the case with previous studies around camera surveillance. Writings around the impact, effects and uses of CCTV in Britain treat this technology as a discreet entity in policing urban space. In other words, CCTV is not placed alongside other policing and security initiatives deployed in conjunction with camera surveillance systems and it has not been examined how these dialectically inter-relate within a strategy of social ordering.

As discussed in Chapter 5, public order policing in Liverpool has gained a new momentum under the banner of 'Citysafe'. The enactment of zero tolerance measures alongside militarised forms of policing is underpinned by discourses of 'regeneration' that indicate the kinds of authoritarian measures outlined by Davis. In Liverpool, the network of CCTV cameras is reinforced by a heavily militarised police force.[20] However, militarisation is not universally welcomed among all factions of the locally powerful. Coherence and uniformity of purpose regarding policing initiatives in the city should not be taken as given or inevitable. As noted below, the intensification of proactive policing – the use of highly visible and armed police officers on the streets of the city centre – is a source of tension among key players. For the police, however, the issue of armed patrols is represented to other players as 'necessary' to the regeneration process. As one police officer states:

> We had no anticipation [that] the subversive drug trafficking in the seedy side of Liverpool life was going to manifest itself into gunfire on the streets. That was a real kick in the bollocks to Liverpool and the regeneration process. [The shootings] in some respects helped push the issue up the agenda and get something done about it (superintendent, Merseyside Police, GOM).

One local councillor backs putting armed patrols on the streets and calls for the use of the Prevention of Terrorism Act to arrest city gun suspects (*Merseymart* 16 May 1996: 'Terrorism Act call for city'). Armed operations in the city centre were commenced during Christmas in 1996 and received high-profile coverage in the local and national press up to a year after their inception, much to the alarm of the Stores' Committee, the City Centre Manager and Mersey Partnership. The issue highlights differences in institutional logics and power, produces fractures within the channels of communication between key players, and undermines the stability of the unifying potential found within the discourse of regeneration. The role of highly visible and proactive public-order policing is subject to scrutiny among the new primary definers, some of whom feel uncomfortable with certain policing practices against the backdrop of city centre re-imaging. The police are in a situation where they are having to defend certain policing practices to their 'partners'. This problematises the meaning of partnership in the city centre, as one police officer comments:

> There is liaison, yes. At the level of informing them [key players] what we are going to do and why we are going to do it rather how would you feel if we go and do this. There is a statutory obligation on the police to protect life and we couldn't possibly fail to deliver

on that. If somebody was uncomfortable with the sight of a police officer carrying a gun in a public place then they need to see that this is what we have to do operationally. This fact is often much more clear than how we are going to sell that in a positive way (Superintendent, Merseyside Police, GOM).

As identified in the previous chapter, the police's 'willingness to talk' is a factor in building partnerships. This means informing key players of intended police operations because this is recognised as a factor in regeneration and as something that all partners are signed up to. Although other key players welcome the police providing such informal briefings, they also question and express frustration around a sense of exclusivity concerning police operational matters. Alongside this concern is the feeling that this kind of policing is an aspect of order maintenance that, unlike CCTV, is out of formal and informal partnership control. These concerns have developed into a cynicism about police intentions in terms of their commitment to the city's renaissance. As discussed in Chapter 6, police justifications for placing armed patrols on the streets of the city vary. This is not acceptable for other state actors that include local businesses, developers and members of the city council who are working, as they see it, for a more coherent approach across regeneration agencies. As one developer puts it:

> When the police put armed patrols on the city streets it was interesting in that they were saying it was for armed raids and violent crime and this was picked up in the national press. Then after a couple of weeks they said it was because of an IRA threat. *There is a bloody big difference between the two!* I mean having an armed patrol walking down Church Street is bad PR for the city. Okay, they say it is a deterrent but some of us think it is a bit of egoism, bravado by the police to say 'take us seriously'. But in reality, and the way the press used it, it makes Liverpool look like a shooting range (private developer 1, affiliated to LCCP, emphasis in original).

In other words, coherence regarding re-imaging is being undermined. Others express a frustration with the role of the police in the regeneration process in that this role is not only being misplaced but also is contributing to a misunderstanding of the 'fundamentals' of regeneration partnerships. Key players perceive the police as not altogether concerned about the more mundane aspects of policing, as prioritised within a regeneration agenda:

They are [the police] so important to a lot of things that the city needs to happen around enforcement – traffic congestion, illegal parking – as well as aspects of safety, like putting normal bobbies on the street. A problem has been getting them on side and committed; because they will practically say 'we've got more important things to do like chase robbers'. We have to make them understand this is all well and good but we can only do that by working in partnership (representative of Liverpool Vision).

Frustration is evident in that certain aspects of policing – seen as central to successful regeneration – are outside partnership control. The police are widely perceived to be working to their own agenda. As one marketing strategist put it:

I have to talk professionally now in terms of me being an investor walking through the streets. No doubt an investor wants to see the bobby with his sleeves rolled up and talking to the granny on the corner. There is no doubt in my mind that the gangland issue has been exaggerated, fuelled as much by the national as local press. The locals [partnerships] have tried to handle it carefully but the police always need to show they mean business, and are back and in control. So they tend to present things artificially to the media. Like those photographs that they released in 1996 showing the police in flak jackets and carrying submachine guns. As far as the rest of the world was concerned, every policeman in Liverpool was dressed like that. They [the police] did it for very political reasons. They, as always, were saying 'we need more money' but it backfired on the region economically in terms of image (private developer 1, affiliated to LCCP).

The channels of partnership at senior level provide the avenue to pressure the police and debate the merits or otherwise of armed patrols that throw up 'unsavoury' police characterisations of 'rampant' armed criminality:

Senior police contact is, I think, the biggest interrelationship between the investment agencies. So we could say to the Chief Constable that he was going on a bit – with the high profile, gun toting policemen. We said you will kill the industry and that is really awful. He listened to us and put out a reverse script, which said murders are less in his city than elsewhere. I mean we were crying with the amount of adverse publicity the police were putting out to defend their own budget. We know that was what it was all about and there is some sympathy around here on this (Chairman, Merseyside Development Corporation).

As the previous chapter highlights, the police are able to reposition themselves within neoliberal structures of rule through senior secondment to the Government Office. As an example of 'best practice', this provides the means of testing new avenues to argue for increased funding. Within this forum, the issue of armed response is leading to a fine-tuning and a harmonising of relations across partnerships. Here, a partial resolution has been constructed that has established a campaign aimed to counter media stories about Liverpool as a 'gun city' while at the same time recognising that policing operations are left to the police as the statutory authority.

The issue of armed patrols sits alongside concerns regarding public policing in the city centre. The channels of strategic communication in the regeneration of Liverpool aid a process whereby Merseyside Police can be challenged regarding certain practices and operations through the discourse of urban renaissance. A collective will around a 'politics of image' is the key in this kind of criticism, set against the backdrop of a vernacular that constructs a 'family-friendly city' alongside increasing tourism, development activity and investment. The regeneration strategy that CCTV is central in promoting is, it is thought, undermined by other, 'less credible' policing initiatives.[21] As key actors in the regeneration process, Merseyside Police are not immune to these wider state strategies and, as a means of massaging dissent from its partners, now provide 'information' and 'greater openness'.

Politics, funding and CCTV: central–local tensions

As discussed above, the establishment of the camera network in Liverpool was part funded from monies available through the Crime Prevention Agency established under John Major's Conservative administration. Today funding is allocated through New Labour's Crime Reduction Unit. Across the political parties, the process of application for funds both to establish and extend camera networks has set out various criteria for eligibility in the form of CCTV Challenge Competitions. These criteria include the establishment of partnerships, police involvement, parallel private sector funding and the identification of a local crime problem. Despite the discretion allowed under these criteria, limitations and constraints are evident in the establishment of camera networks. These 'real world' constraints are important to recognise for they undermine characterisations of seamless webs of surveillance and a homogeneous view of social control that is evenly dispersing itself into the wider society.

A great deal of local effort in establishing multi-agency links and accruing local knowledge is a prerequisite in the bidding process. Within Liverpool city centre the effort of the partners is strategically directed in line with plans for regeneration. From the perspective of key players at the local level the establishment and continuing extension of CCTV in Liverpool fit in with an agreed agenda for the city's renaissance and underpin both the uses of CCTV and where it is to be located. Those involved in drawing up and submitting applications to central government have expressed frustration at what they perceive as the politicking that governed central policies on crime and law and order. National priorities therefore sometimes appear to conflict with local agendas in terms of support funding for CCTV, and in particular where it could be geographically placed. The 'fickleness' of central government actors has been a target of frustration: 'Around CCTV, as with other central government initiatives, if you have a Minister who is enthusiastic about a particular course of action then that particular course of action will find funding. If a minister says it is a good idea, then it is a good idea' (Home Office adviser, GOM).

It is felt by key players that their local strategies for the uses of CCTV are not always listened to or appreciated within the arena of central government decision-making. It is often perceived that the Home Office and central government generally are subject to ideological constraints and short-term political expediency regarding the allocation of funds for CCTV projects. Frustration expressed by key players in Liverpool has been aimed at the personal complexions of senior ministerial personnel, but these personal idiosyncrasies are placed within a wider context in that 'every government I've seen has beaten the law and order drum and there doesn't seem to be any substantial change in that respect' (ibid.). The changing sentiments underpinning central government law and order policy are seen as obstacles for the 'less ideological' task of establishing CCTV in Liverpool city centre. Tensions have been apparent within the process of submitting funding applications for cameras, as when key players in Liverpool were looking to extend the city centre system in 1997:

The process is, unfortunately, transparently political. Last year in CCTV Challenge we were expecting an indicative allocation in the region of £600,000 to £800,000. We got £34,000 worth of projects funded. I was given the opportunity to comment on the bids before decisions were announced. The only two projects we got funding for, one was in a school, I had commented on as 'not strategically important and should be funded from mainstream education authority funding'. But they [the Home Office] funded it! Like it was a knee jerk reaction – to Dunblane perhaps? These are some of the problems we deal with. Frankly, the bids from Merseyside this year – the temptation has been to throw them in the bin. Why waste time and effort reading them and making recommendations because on previous showings it was working for nothing (superintendent, Merseyside Police, GOM).

The Government Office and the seconded police officer within the office collated and passed comment on bids throughout the Merseyside region, before sending them to the Home Office. The Government Office had a key role in shaping and submitting 'responsible' bids. The office's desire to prioritise bids of 'strategic importance' was, it was felt, compromised by central government tendencies to use grants for CCTV to further their own political advantage.[22]

Earlier in the bidding process it was felt that the office had been impeded by 'beating the law and order drum' at the national level alongside allocating funds to marginal constituencies in electoral terms. Initially, key players felt that competitive bidding for CCTV, although potentially useful particularly in setting up the system in Liverpool, was ideologically driven and could not be relied upon in the long term. Competitive bidding was seen as

> partly public relations and an expensive PR job at that. There have been many millions spent on CCTV through the bid process and this has levered significant sums of money from other sources. So there is an element of added value to it. It is just that the location of some of the funding could be questioned at a later stage (Home Office adviser, GOM).

Local state managers often see themselves as positive instigators of a 'politics of change' at the local level. However, this 'progressive' self-image is cynically contrasted to 'a politics of chance and opportunism' at the national level. However, the 'politics of change' is not always in conflict with 'national opportunism'. The two were married when CCTV was established in Liverpool in 1994, when local and national authorities were able to work together to fund Liverpool's camera network and, as discussed earlier, ideologically represent its 'necessity' and legitimate it with reference to the murder of a local child.

Central government competitive funds for CCTV, when granted, are viewed as a kick start in establishing strategies for local order and encouraging local players to add funds for such purposes. The funding of CCTV in Liverpool city centre and by implication its extension has, therefore, not been without its problems. The levering of local investment to maintain and extend CCTV is the subject of the next part of the chapter.

Funding and levering local revenue

There is a lot of good-will in terms of contributions for the cameras, but this is no way to run a business (City Centre Manager).

The tensions discussed in the previous part of this chapter compound issues of funding, specifically at the local level. As stated earlier in the chapter, the key players in Liverpool had grasped the opportunity of establishing a CCTV system without any long-term funding plan. This has implications for the management and control of the system. The Liverpool City Centre Partnership (LCCP) was charged with the function of generating funds from local interests to secure long-term maintenance costs for CCTV in order to extend further installation. However, dipping into the local capital purse has not been without its problems in terms of funding the camera network. Although widespread ideological support for the camera network continues to exist among local businesses, this is not necessarily extended to financial support. Thus, although 'the Liverpool City Centre Partnership proved that organisations would be prepared to divert funding towards establishing CCTV, it could not easily sustain it' (ibid.). As the City Centre Manager stated, this was a source of frustration between sections of the business community and the LCCP:

Part of the problem of funding for the City Centre Manager is having to go cap in hand and this is not good enough. You know, local businesses who pay rates ask 'why don't local government do it?' I call it the 'they syndrome' – 'they should do, they should do it'. That's not very helpful at all (ibid.).

The battle to maintain local funding is centred on membership of the Stores' Committee. The £12,000 annual fee allowing access to the radio link is only available to those who can afford it (i.e. the larger retail outlets and businesses). These differentials in financial clout also extend to the ability to contribute to CCTV. The installation of each camera is costed at £15,000 and the LCCP approached businesses to fund a camera. The funding process is made problematic by contradictions between local and national business interests. As one local business manager expresses it:

> I think there is a benefit to the city in having CCTV. If it is good for the city it is good for me as a businessman. If more people are coming into the city we all get a share of their custom. I took this point to my head office outside of Liverpool. We had already contributed to the capital funding of the system but, as far as revenue was concerned, I had to tell the LCCP 'sorry mate my boss said no'. I'm not saying this as a general point but my superiors will not go overboard in putting money into Liverpool when we pay high rates and they think the city has a history of mal-administration (representative 2, of Stores' Committee).

Other players, however, justified funding the cameras as it is a necessary feature of what they deem to be good business practice:

> We can fund cameras in our domain. Being involved in the pavement café culture means we want to be able to have tight control over anyone who gets up to mischief. So it will be very useful to us. It is a legitimate extension of our business interests and quite correctly we should pay for it and make contributions towards it (private developer 2, affiliated to LCCP).

The fractures within local capital have led to intense debates regarding responsibilities for funding. As one interviewee states, 'it seems inequitable that other people who benefit may not necessarily be paying for it' (representative of LCCP). Such comments are directed at businesses and police:

> If you think about what the CCTV system costs, the total revenue costs and you think, well, how many policemen is that? It is just a joke. The relative cost for CCTV is a lot, but it is just a drop in the ocean compared to a police car and they [the police] get more benefit from CCTV (Chairman, Stores' Committee).

The LCCP scorned the lack of financial input into the camera network because, as previously mentioned, 'realistically it is a policing tool' (ibid.) – a tool owned by the private sector but from which, as other key players observe, the police derive ideological and practical benefits.

These issues impinge upon related debates concerning the management and control of CCTV.

Management and control

> We make the point, and I think it is a very healthy one, that this is a separate and independent body. I think the worse thing is if the police had control of the system. I'm not saying anything improper would happen ... but I think public perception and credibility is everything. Whilst we've got Mr and Mrs Bloggs on board, great (City Centre Manager).

While the 'independence' of the CCTV network is stressed by the the key players, this masks deeper ambivalences around the management of CCTV both as a policing tool and as a marketable product, which needs to be sold 'properly'. For other players the positive notion of 'independence' is challenged by a concern that control of the system was unnecessarily ubiquitous and vague. The lack of 'detailed control' points to problems of ownership of the system:

> At the moment responsibility for the system lies between the City Centre Manager and the private sector; the police and the City Council. Nobody owns it and everybody owns it. Everyone wants to promote it and nobody is actually promoting it. Nobody really seems to be championing the cause of CCTV in a clear and consistent way (Economic Development Officer, Liverpool City Council).

'Championing the cause of CCTV' points to a concern that its effectiveness – though apparent and agreed by all – needs to be marketed more aggressively. Such marketing needs to be directed at potential contributors to the system:

> CCTV is doing its work. The private interests behind it are quite progressive and, on the whole, very supportive because we have a long-term interest. Many others need to be convinced that they need to invest in this, year in year out. Funding can tend to dry up because people can't see the impact that CCTV is having on promoting the product of the city centre. It's a selling job. CCTV needs to be sold (private developer 1, affiliated to LCCP).

Another player complained that CCTV has become 'a hidden element' in the management of the city centre and that 'this hybrid arrangement' regarding its oversight only contributed to downplaying its benefits (ibid.). The process of marketing CCTV and providing information as to its effectiveness is seen as a legitimate return for those contributing to the system:

> We would not expect full accountability for every camera in every street but we would legitimately expect something in relation to an investment. If the city is to make further inroads into private sector sponsorship they [LCCP] have got to show that the system is apprehending villains. We have to show what happens with CCTV, not just images of people before or after a misdemeanour has occurred (private developer 2, affiliated to LCCP).

Trumpeting the benefits of CCTV, though, is not without its detractors, particularly if this form of selling its benefits takes a more sensationalist twist in terms of publicity at national and international levels. The release and use of CCTV footage to press and broadcast media are not necessarily seen as a good thing regarding Liverpool:

> The one thing about CCTV, which is a bad thing, is the crop of TV programmes using footage. It is interesting talking to people who are involved in that because I think they miss the point. Sometime ago there was a programme with footage from Liverpool and someone said 'wasn't it good it was on TV'. It showed a man with a knife. Some of us think this is the last thing we want – portraying the image of what Liverpool is perceived to be. This kind of thing does more damage than any good that was done by CCTV. But peoples' egos get involved and they say: 'Oh aren't I clever I spotted this or I spotted that.' CCTV should never be used publicly, because it does more damage to the city (private developer 1, affiliated to LCCP).

These tensions are managerial in nature and point to problems in presenting the CCTV network to important audiences. CCTV has to be managed in such a way so that each audience received the desired message. For the public, the system must be seen as 'credible'; for local capital, it must be perceived as 'cost effective'; and for potential outside investors, it must be seen as both these things while also reinforcing the more general perception that Liverpool city centre as a whole is being managed in a manner friendly to business. The difficulties thrown up in managing the camera network highlight a key problem for its supporters regarding how much visibility the system should have, and in what circumstances high or low visibility becomes problematic. This was illustrated with the system's launch, when it was announced that the monitoring room was housed in a secret location in the city centre. The only people to know of the location were the private security monitors, the City Centre Manager and senior police officers. Security personnel could only contact the monitoring room by radio. Secrecy is thought necessary 'in order to prevent sabotage and protect personnel' (City Centre Manager). For others involved in the camera network the idea of secrecy is counterproductive:

> When the system was launched nobody was supposed to know where it was. All this 'we've got to keep it a secret' nonsense – the secret bunker! It is silly and over-protective when you think of the potential for these things to be misconceived. It's not big brother and we don't want people to think we are in a war zone here. We need a certain level of transparency about it and proper regulation, control and monitoring, none of which we really have. It's a situation where no one really knows what's going on (Economic Development Officer, Liverpool City Council).

Embracing the system

Although CCTV managers stress the independence of the camera network, this is contradicted by concerns that the police, at least initially, were not as supportive as would have been liked. Thus, although 'the credibility of the system is their [police] credibility – they take as much applause as we do', the police were again seen to be working to their own institutional agenda, which undercut the process of partnership:

> When we set the system up there were political issues around the police and their attitude to CCTV, which meant they could not pick up the initiative, nor would local government. Now that it has become accepted and proved itself – it is now the time. In fact it is long overdue for the police to actually embrace the system – adopt it, manage it and fund it alongside the LCCP (Chairman, Stores' Committee).

For the police, however, the CCTV system – though formally acknowledged and accepted – represented a shift away from one of their key institutional goals: an increase in funding and manpower. As one police officer commented:

> I will say there is the will in the police force. The police have a problem with the question of 'will the cameras replace people?' They cannot win because when we get more cameras they will be asked to save money through loss of manpower. The police on occasion have used the 'Big Brother' argument but really it's about the politics of funding. The bottom line is the police believe they may become less visible with CCTV; they will become more of a prevention force (Home Office adviser, GOM).

For these reasons, the police in Liverpool have been described as being 'at arm's length with the system' (City Centre Manager). Although the police are involved in the bidding stage and the location of the cameras they have expressed an ambivalence directed at the central policy-making process:

> In my experience of 22 years in the police you can do a far better job by being in a place than by looking at it through a camera. The deterrent effect by a physical presence is greater than that of CCTV. I'm not overtly enthusiastic about CCTV. I see it as a tool in the armoury but not the be all and end all. This is not a view shared by some ministers, unfortunately (Superintendent, Merseyside Police, GOM).

This contradiction fed directly into tensions mentioned earlier. Fears of police downsizing are purported to be at the nub of the police 'over-playing' 'serious crime' and public order problems in Liverpool. On the other hand, giving a higher profile to these policing issues undermines the regeneration process in constructing Liverpool as a 'dangerous place' and one that is under-policed. For the police, conflict arises between the instigation of a European-style café culture and what this means for 'order' in the streets. On the one hand, this culture is thought to bring economic benefits to those investors in the service sector while, on the other hand, simultaneously generating disorder in the form of, for example, drunkenness. Thus the extension of legitimate business interests central to the regeneration process is also seen to promote sites of potential street disorder. This factor is highlighted most forcefully by the police for whom 'regeneration' brought with it potentially negative scenarios. As one interviewee states:

> We've got to manage it ... We recognise that we might actually see a rise in levels of recorded crime if the renaissance is successful ... It is part of a trade off. The benefits of the vibrant twenty-four hour

economy on the one hand balanced against the downside of more crime, more drug abuse and drunkenness (ibid.).

Leadership

The tensions among the key players in the regeneration process highlight the salience of image and the promotion of a positive reputation for Liverpool. These concerns take in a wide variety of issues that dovetail with the problem of responsibility for city centre rule. In this sense, businesses and developers readily articulate a frustration aimed at the City Council who initially were perceived as being not as enthusiastic about economic development as the private sector and as failing to take a leading role:

> We have to look at the negative images of this city and ask why people do not come here and why do the big investors not come here. There are issues about what happens in this city – how it is run. There are simple things like the state of the streets, the state of the pavements. We pay the highest business rates in the country and we seem to get some of the worst services. I was in York yesterday and Leeds two days before. They pay less rates than us but have masses of investment going into the cities and most importantly these places are spotless (Regeneration Co-ordinator, Liverpool City Council).

Difficulties are expressed regarding attracting particular retailers to the city centre who feel that doing business in Liverpool would be bad for their image. The negative sense of place is not only attributed to potential retailers but also to potential theatre patrons, shoppers and tourists. The identification of a leadership vacuum has set in motion intense debates towards achieving greater clarity in managing the city centre and imbuing it with strategic direction. For the LCCP, financial maintenance of CCTV tied in with broader issues to do with general street management:

> We need a powerful body. The LCCP can remain along with the City Centre Manager but they need a more powerful body with a powerful figurehead with responsibilities for: one, raising funds for the long term along with: two, the city council, who need to think more long term than that. I know we've already got a problem with high council tax and rates, but a service charge needs to be set up where we could establish a pool in the region of £1 million per

annum. This would ensure the marketing of this city is backed, by ensuring total street management – clean streets, empty bins and secure the tenure for CCTV (representative of LCCP).

Another interviewee, who expressed the need to harness more effectively senior contact points and inter-institutional funding differences, echoes this:

It is like the City Centre Partnership. It needs to be bigger and raise its profile with someone powerful to bring that about. We all talk about under-resourcing but all these agencies have got budgets of some description but they all seem to tail off at some unknown point. It is like the spokes and the hub, only there is not really a hub in Liverpool (Chairman, Stores' Committee).

The tensions that arise from aspects of policing and sustaining revenue funding plugs directly into debates about management of the city centre. In this sense, the establishment of the City Centre Manager is perceived as a stepping-stone from which the private sector can consolidate its power in the city centre along the lines embodied with the American-style Business Improvement Districts (BIDs).

Tensions on the ground: Police and Crime Alert

Tensions between personnel directly involved in managing and staffing the camera network are a feature of the day-to-day working of the system. As with the issues identified above, these tensions provide potentially insoluble problems as much as created opportunities for the development and creative extension of the work of partnership net-works. The manifestation of these tensions is found in three main areas: police and private security relations; the problem of discipline among security personnel; and, finally, crime displacement.

As discussed earlier in this chapter, a key function of Crime Alert is to act as a pressure group upon the police to encourage them to act against problems identified by businesses. Shoplifting, *Big Issue* vendors and street traders represent the major problems in this respect. On the latter two issues, the police have felt limited in what they could do and express concern at having to listen to 'griping' about issues that they felt were outside their remit:

We understand the stores' point of view but they tend to confuse what is actionable in a criminal sense and what is, from their view, a pain in the backside. Street trading used to be a police matter before it was licensed – okay in the old days we could move them on – make it difficult for them to operate. What it boils down to is the Stores' Committee do not like street traders in the middle of Church Street, selling products cheaper than they are. We can do very little about that because they are licensed other than argue they may cause an obstruction. This is more a public image matter rather than a police or criminal matter (city centre crime prevention officer, Merseyside Police).

The police act as an organ of discipline upon Crime Alert. This involves processes towards structuring police involvement based 'not on people moaning to the police but hard, transferable information' (ibid.). The police role in Crime Alert has run along educational lines. Aspects of policing carried out by Crime Alert members are underpinned by training and advice from the police:

If Crime Alert highlights particular problems then part of my function is to go in there and say 'look do you want to discuss this, do you want a training session on the law, do you want a training session on people with aggression?' That is part of our function although some stores provide their own training. The main problem we find with Crime Alert is the paperwork side of it. Some of the statements we get are not up to what we require in court. Often we have to go down and re-interview witnesses. The evidence is there but they have not quite got the literal skills to deal with that side of it, to put it together in a statement that is acceptable in court (ibid.).

The police role in providing advice on aspects of law and training to handle aggressive situations is often seen as a frustrating task, but is also seen to be in the interests of the police as it is they who are responsible for putting files together for the Crown Prosecution Service (CPS): 'we don't want to look as though we don't know how to put a case together' (Chairman, Crime Alert). For the police, the encouragement of greater 'professionalism' within the camera network provides some frustration.

For members of Crime Alert, the evidential process causes difficulties but underlines their greater sense of frustration aimed at the police and courts for not taking a tougher stance against categories of shoplifters. These fell into three main types: the professional, the opportunist and the drug addict (the latter usually conflated with a homeless person):

Any person on a second offence caught shoplifting is then banned from a store. This is where we get into problems with the CPS because in theory a person who has been banned from a store and who comes back in to the store is trespassing. If he is trespassing and then steals he is actually committing an act of burglary, but the police or the CPS will not bring a charge of burglary because they say that tends to prove previous bad character which cannot be brought out until he is found guilty of the offence for which he is charged. It's a Catch 22 (security manager 1, Crime Alert).

The process of working in Crime Alert is described as a 'cat-and-mouse game' where 'we tiresomely see the same old faces' (ibid.). The group campaigns for stronger sentences against shoplifters in order for them to be banned from the city centre or all stores within the centre as part of their bail condition or sentencing. For one interviewee, the failure of the courts to give 'meaningful sentences' and 'the dismal showing of police manpower on the streets, has a knock-on effect on the morale of Crime Alert members' (security manager 2, Crime Alert). However, the group is not inactive in combating its problems. Of particular concern was the identification of people who are banned from shops or had been issued with trespass notices. Stills from in-store CCTV and external footage are distributed to help private security identify potential and known shoplifters thought to be in the area. In this way, Crime Alert is able to 'make it difficult for them to move, keep them twitching over their shoulders so they think "sod this I'm not staying round here"' (security manager 3, Crime Alert).

Police scepticism towards working with some elements within the private security industry is also in evidence and highlights perceptions of institutional integrity and professionalism:

They do have a fairly mixed bunch here [in Crime Alert] in terms of experience and practice in the security field. But that's the situation – some are ex-army or with no authoritative experience at all. Others are from established security firms, vetted and trained. But you know you are not talking to a uniform bunch – some are probably in it for the wrong reasons, looking like street fighters. Some are claiming benefits and working ... others are more pro-fessional. The problem is a lack of regulation in this industry – they are badly paid and some have dodgy backgrounds (city centre crime prevention officer, Merseyside Police).

Police officers express worries over the handling of intelligence by private security:

> There is one thing that has always been a contentious issue in this grey area. That is giving photographs to non-police personnel. We are the legal authority and they have more limited powers so we are working towards Crime Alert taking on the responsibility of collating and distributing photo files which we can have access to. I don't think the police should be handing out photos to God knows who. It's also like we are saying 'do our job'. Which they can't. We have to be more careful with *our* intelligence (*ibid.*, emphasis added).

Network discipline

The process of handling, swapping and collating intelligence within Crime Alert is, as part of its function, a means to engender discipline upon private security personnel regarding what their work entails on any particular day. However, keeping members of Crime Alert 'alert' as to what and whom they are meant to be targeting is not without its problems and causes frustration for security managers. For managers, this points to gaps in the system due to 'human error' which manifests itself on the airwaves of the radio link. Radios, therefore, are often used 'inappropriately' (security manager 1, Crime Alert). At a Crime Alert meeting, the chair relayed a story to those assembled to illustrate his frustration regarding the need to maintain radio discipline:

> The other day one of our number alerted the CCTV control room to a group of youths roaming in town, clearly up to no good and doing some swiping. When it was decided to call the police in we lost visual contact because of radio interference. We can't tolerate this and use of radios for personal use has to stop. It wastes police time and the time of the boys in the control room. Anyone caught blocking radio messages gets their fingers chopped off! (field notes).

'Blocking' refers to security personnel chatting over the network. This means using the radio in a distracting manner to talk about, and track, women and girls through the city centre, football and up-and-coming leisure activities. The male gaze is not problematised, as such, by security managers (only two female security officers attended Crime Alert), only in so far as it 'blocks' the 'real' tasks to hand, but it does raise questions as to the meaning of safety in the city particularly with respect to the experience of women.

Another problem is the fact that subscriptions for the 60 radios are not always paid up and some of them would go missing. Threats to confiscate radios and barring 'deviants' from the network were not uncommon at Crime Alert meetings. 'Lack of professionalism' is also a criticism from outside Crime Alert. There are some store security personnel who, though linked to the radio network, do not attend Crime Alert meetings because of what they perceive to be its unprofessional nature. Although in agreement with the necessity of information swapping and the role of Crime Alert as a useful 'early warning system', the meetings themselves have been criticised as being 'an open forum for people to get shot of frustrations':

> To work in the city you should need qualifications rather than just walk in off the street, be given a radio – which is voiced across the city – and start talking rubbish on it. Some have had no formal training; they've been thrust into it. What they do only drags us all down (security manager, non-member of Crime Alert).

Not all security managers want to associate with Crime Alert because of 'off-putting uniforms' and 'untidy guards' (ibid.). Notions pertaining to different standards of professionalism divided those on the network.

Displacement of crime and expansion of the CCTV security network

The acceptance and utilisation of CCTV within processes of order maintenance are producing a form of logic for its own expansion. Concerns about the displacement of crime and disorder also produce a source of tension among key players involved in establishing CCTV schemes in the city centre.[23] Tensions became apparent among the wider business community within two years of the establishment of CCTV in Liverpool city centre. The cameras were seen to be having a displacement effect in Allerton, an affluent suburb lying three miles south of the city centre. The Allerton Traders' Association identified the city centre camera network as the reason for increases in thefts, and argued that retailers in the area faced mounting problems in terms of finding and funding more advanced forms of security to combat these issues (*Merseymart*, 7 March 1996: 'Spy cam plea from retailers'). While displacement is a concern for many of those who comment on CCTV, there is less analysis conducted on the contradictions and tensions within and between local business coalitions in managing 'insecurity'. The displacement issue, far from challenging the efficacy of camera surveillance, is used by its proponents as evidence for more cameras!

Any implications arising from the displacement of crime for expanding surveillance and security networks receive little attention. In Liverpool the issue of displacement in the form of 'travelling shoplifters' illustrates this issue and points to how public and private policing agencies across the urban centre increasingly find ways of co-ordinating their efforts against what one interviewee describes as 'flying wrong-doers' (Chairman, Crime Alert). Thus local partnerships co-ordinate their work, which takes on an extra-local dimension:

> At a recent meting I spoke to a security manager in Birkenhead who happened to mention that a lot of Liverpool scallies were getting picked up in Birkenhead. That got us thinking and we made inquiries in North Wales and other towns and cities. It became apparent that shoplifters and even beggars were moving around – out of Liverpool – because of our CCTV and the work of Crime Alert. We helped Birkenhead set up something similar to our system because it was becoming blatantly obvious our thieves were travelling. So if our thieves were travelling to the likes of Sheffield, Leeds and Wrexham then their thieves must be going somewhere. We realised they were coming to us because our operatives and security didn't recognise them. That's how it stared. We now have regular meetings of up to 50 or 60 people from all over the region: police, private security and CCTV operators. It's a way of swapping information on who is travelling, where and with whom and finding out how we can target them. It is a way of us getting to know who is coming to our area and who we are exporting to other areas (security manager 2, Crime Alert).

Sharing information across networks included passing names, addresses and photographs of known and potential criminals, and beggars. This information is used to monitor and restrict movement between places. For example, such information on travelling groups and individuals is passed to British Transport Police in Liverpool so they can feed back to Crime Alert regarding who is entering or leaving the city. Although a source of tension, the issue of displacement does help to extend and intensify the work of camera networks within different locations.[24] The success of these initiatives is measured in terms of the greater power conferred by collaboration in information exchange and surveillance, so that those targeted 'get tired of trying to dodge us; they feel harassed and go elsewhere' (Chairman, Crime Alert). The obvious tensions between inter-local collaboration and, at the same time, the displacement of 'troublemakers' to other locations form a central contradiction in the operation of camera networks. This contradiction feeds itself:

> We are working towards an attitude of 'not on our patch' and information exchange helps in deterring troublemakers coming into the city. But if we are successful they only go to other similar patches for our colleagues to have to deal with. So we send them more information to help get rid of them and eventually they may end up back with us (city centre crime prevention officer, Merseyside Police).

Such arguments and frustrations feed into the general desire for more security and surveillance in the city centre. The 'success' of the system and the continual discovery of 'blind spots' or gaps in the network feed the call for extensions, fine-tuning and greater sophistication of the overall network. These calls from Crime Alert personnel for extending and refining the network come together with the aspirations of senior regeneration personnel for the same end. These desires for the future expansion of CCTV can be qualitatively distinguished: the former emerge from a 'hands-on' experience of working the system, while the new primary definers take their cues for network expansion from wider political and economic considerations that underpin their ideas of a 'proper' and 'orderly' regeneration. In this sense, the development of the CCTV network generates further perceptions of insecurity ('blind spots', 'escape routes'), which, in turn, fuel calls for more security that will cover more areas of the city centre and outlying space.

Conclusion

Together with the previous chapter, this chapter has traced the development of social control within the broad trajectory of an entrepreneurial urbanism and a neoliberal state form. Building on a theoretical understanding of this state form, its role in building the 'entrepreneurial city' and its development in Liverpool, the camera network in Liverpool is understood here as part of these wider processes that form the context for the definition and articulation of local social order. It is the expression of this order and its particular mode of spatialisation upon the streets of the city that calls into question the commonsense basis for camera networks outlined at the beginning of the chapter. The *proper objects of power* outlined here bear a tentative relationship, if any, to the media and official rhetoric around street surveillance. The CCTV network reflects and reinforces the wider set of social relations and circuits of political power incumbent of the new primary definers and indicates a move to a form of surveillance and social control that forges its risk categories through a set of censures that lie beyond mere legal suspicion. The street surveillance network takes the responsibilisation strategy to the streets, reinforcing its preferred meaning by communicating to its targets and the wider public the normative contours of 'responsibility' and 'responsible behaviour' as well as their opposite categories. As the regeneration strategy seeks to rehabilitate the spaces of the city, so the surveillance network represents an attempt to responsibilise behaviour in those spaces.

However, as demonstrated in this chapter, these processes are not unfolding in a seamless manner and tensions regarding the instigation of social control practices are subject to negotiation and compromise within the matrix of locally powerful decision-making. Despite this qualification the configuration of the camera network in Liverpool and the negotiation of a social ordering strategy are characteristic of the circuits of power that neoliberal rule in the city is encouraging and aiming to materialise. The camera network is underscored by a degree of ideological unity that gives the surveillance of the streets a wider political and social meaning. Identifying, in ideological terms, the problems for order is far less problematic for the proponents of the network than establishing, in a managerial sense, the means to achieve it. The drive to 'clean the streets' and instil a spirit of 'urban pride' is underlined by the wider entrepreneurial ethos and 'politics of attraction'. These political priorities have helped reinvigorate censorious discourses aimed at incongruities in the city and constitute a normal part of a post-welfare project of neoliberal rule. When interwoven with the camera network, the narratives of censure responsibilise some activities and behaviours while disabling and/or denying legitimacy to others. The struggles around who is and is not a 'responsible' city inhabitant are driven by definitions of risk that re-order spatial relations not in the interests of the imagined 'city as a whole' but in the partial and equally imaginary interests of the locally powerful. This exploration of street surveillance in Liverpool and the issues and consequences it raises for thinking about neoliberal cities are picked up in the next and final chapter.

Notes

1 Such coverage included 'Liverpool's bid to prevent new James Bulger horror' (*Today* 7 July 1994); 'Jamie Bulger city unveils spy cameras' (*Daily Express* 6 July 1994). As *The Guardian* reported 'the system is also expected to cut the risk of toddlers being lost, or abducted like James Bulger, led away to his death 18 months ago by two boys at a shopping centre in Bootle, three miles north of the area covered by the Liverpool scheme' (6 July 1994: 'Security cameras raise hopes for big cut in city crime').

2 Children are at greater risk in the private sphere from harm caused by their own parents or those acting *in loco parentis* (*The Guardian* 1 August 1995: 'Parents' protection dilemma'). Feminist research consistently shows that risk of violence towards women, and the actuality of violence, remain in the private sphere (Mooney 2000).

3 The notion of 'dangerous place' was not constructed on the basis of local crime statistics alone. On the basis of crime statistics, Liverpool city centre would have to be seen as 'less dangerous' than the immediately surrounding areas during this period. A total of 5,954 criminal offences were reported in the first 5 months of 1994 in the police division which includes the city centre compared with 7,131 in the division covering north Liverpool. Within this period the city centre showed a higher crime rate than north Liverpool in the categories of street muggings and other thefts from the person, but these only accounted for 2.9% of all city centre crime. The statistics show that shoplifting accounted for 13% of all city centre crime (*The Independent* 6 July 1994: 'Anti-crime cameras could miss the action').

4 In Liverpool, businesses that operated within the CCTV coverage area received insurance discounts of up to 40% through a scheme entitled 'Watchguard' brokered between the Liverpool Vision and a local firm of major insurers.

5 Codes of practice for CCTV schemes were drawn up on a local discretionary basis amongst the immediate interested parties (the *Observer* 10 March 1995: 'Big brother sees too much').

6 One urban manager passed on examples to the researcher of 'successful' media coverage: 'Tapped by CCTV' (*Liverpool Echo* 10 November 1995); 'This man has just knifed a stranger to death' (*Daily Mirror* 2 December 1995); 'Camera trap' (*Liverpool Echo* 5 February 1996).

7 As an example of this, during one meeting of Crime Alert the group spent 15 minutes watching CCTV footage of a woman pushing a wheelchair with three small children in tow. The woman appeared to be pregnant. The group were keen to identify her because she was 'too dirty to be your ma [mother]'. Several minutes were taken up with the question of whether she was 'really pregnant' and whether the children belonged to her. She had been 'seen around town' and several group members and the chair requested information on the woman (field notes).

8 Gold Zone was concerned with 'the protection of central pedestrian areas' from litter, fly posting and graffiti alongside the promotion of 'brightening

up' events such as street decoration, entertainments and events (Liverpool City Council 2000). Gold Zone was initiated in the more prestigious shopping areas of the city centre and developed a 'fault-finding service' in which local members reported unwanted or untoward activities which infringed the Gold Zone initiative. Along with the Gold Zone Crew, funded by Liverpool City Council, three police officers also patrol the Gold Zone areas (*Liverpool Echo* 22 November 1999).

9 The issue of homelessness and its increased visibility on the streets of Britain through the 1980s and into the 1990s received growing national attention from media commentators and policy-makers. The notion of 'professional begging' and what the then Shadow Home Secretary Jack Straw referred to as 'aggressive begging' (*The Guardian* 9 September 1995: 'Straw defiant on begging') helped to move the debate around homelessness into the domain of street disorder and public safety.

10 The motion also condemned the Conservative government of the time 'for creating a situation in which people are driven to beg because of lack of work and lack of proper benefits' (Liverpool City Council 1996).

11 Street trading derived from the secondary economy that flourished in this period and provided local people with income and shoppers with relatively cheap merchandise. Historically the street traders, as part of the secondary economy, became subject to the 'moving on' policing described by Brogden (1982) tied to a licensing system in the early twentieth century administered through the City Council.

12 Other press headlines have included 'War on street traders' (*Daily Post* 19 May 1998); 'That's your lot' (*Liverpool Echo* 21 May 1998).

13 Discretionary surveillance of the homeless and traders is not subject to any formal debate in Liverpool regarding the use of the camera network. In the absence of general statutory control over the use of CCTV systems, operations here lie to a large extent outside the law. The Data Protection Act 1998 has provided some regulation in terms of the requirement to register information kept, the purpose of its use and access to data subjects of their files. However, breaches of the Act depend on individual citizens making complaints but, as in the case of visual surveillance, 'most people [do] not know what data is kept on them by whom' (Maguire 1998: 232). Furthermore, the Act made general exemptions for the purposes of data defined as relevant to the 'detection of crime and its prevention'.

14 This came one step closer to fruition with the extension of Liverpool's CCTV scheme that started in 2001 and is discussed in the Introduction.

15 The scheme was extended in 1998 under a £315,000 government-funded initiative that involved police and other agencies in stopping and questioning suspect truants. Some 1,000 school children were stopped in 1999 and a third of these 'gave a good reason for being out of classes' (*Liverpool Echo* 19 June 2000: 'Shocking finds in truancy blitz').

16 In Liverpool, questioning the legitimacy of young people to be on the streets has been filtered through a number of schemes. The latest initiative to come out of the liaison scheme with the New York Police Department is what is

known in the local press as the 'yob tank'. This police mobile prison tours the city locking up 'anti-social youths', fully kitted with internal and external CCTV and costing £20,000 (*Liverpool Echo* 21 January 2003: 'Reclaiming our streets').

17   Indeed, the landscape of risk in Liverpool for black people has been particularly detrimental. Black people are 7.5 times more likely than whites to be stopped, searched and arrested in the city by the police. There are over 1.4 million white people compared with fewer than 10,000 black people on Merseyside. These figures from Statewatch show that 25 of every 1,000 white people were subject to stop and search compared with 189 of every 1,000 black people. Statewatch concluded that 'This differential shows clearly that there is a major problem with the way black people are treated in comparison to white people on Merseyside' (*Statewatch Bulletin* September–October 1998: Vol. 8, no. 5).

18   Parenti (1994: 47) reinforces this point with his examination of 'urban militarism', understood as a 'creeping fortress culture' concerned with 'managing social inequality'.

19   Davis argued that: 'contemporary urban theory, whether debating the role of electronic technologies in precipitating "postmodern space", or discussing the dispersion of urban functions across poly-centered metropolitan 'galaxies', has been strangely silent about the militarization of city life so grimly visible at street level' (1990: 223).

20   This included armed patrols and the use of the Operational Support Division. The latter received record complaints in 1998. The use of CS gas received more complaints in Liverpool than anywhere else in England and Wales for 1998 (*Liverpool Echo* 5 March 1999: 'Mersey force faces CS spray row').

21   The militarisation of city life and public places may bring its own con-tradictions and generate its own insecurities, which undercut and undermine any perceptions and feelings of security thought to be generated by CCTV. The essence of this contradiction was captured by the comments of a visitor to Liverpool: 'As a visitor to your city, I read with interest the article about media bias and the way Liverpool is presented as being a gun capital ... I saw two men carrying automatic weapons in the shopping precinct and went along to the police station to complain ... But these two men carrying the automatic weapons were your policemen! They were driving slowly through the crowded centre on a peaceful, sunny afternoon with their guns resting like babies on their laps. I don't know who they were trying to impress but they frightened the life of me. What an image! Would those guardians of our safety really think of using those weapons in a crowded centre of ordinary innocent people? But I'm only a tourist' (*Merseymart* 20 June 1996: 'Not just criminals carry guns in city').

22   As one interviewee stated: 'We have to draw a distinction between a government strategy and manifesto commitments. These distinctions are unsubtle. The CCTV Challenge Competition has been patchy in its application. You have places like Kendal and Wigton getting fairly

substantive chunks of funding for CCTV and no one on Merseyside getting anything. But these are Tory marginal seats' (Superintendent, Merseyside Police, GOM).

23 The problem of the displacement of crime to areas that lie outside camera coverage has been officially recognised as a potential negative impact of CCTV schemes (Home Office 1994: 9). Among critical commentators, displacement of crime to relatively 'unprotected' areas will reinforce existing social polarisation in that CCTV is 'likely to displace crime from rich to poorer parts of cities' (Graham 1998: 100).

24 This has taken place alongside concerted efforts by local business-led networks to intensify surveillance and the evidence-gathering process in order to pressure local magistrates to increase fines and sentences for those who have broken exclusion orders (*The Guardian* 19 November 1997). More recently, 'Exclusion Notice Schemes' have been developed for the greater collation of intelligence that can keep targets on file indefinitely and be used in gaining stiffer sentences in the case of thieves (Dobie 2000: 25).

Chapter 8

Conclusion: visualising the neoliberal city

Iain Bundred's whole life is a movie. Every step he takes is captured on unseen cameras as secret watchers see his life unfold. It may seem like a plot for Jim Carrey's Hollywood hit *The Truman Show*. But this is the reality in Liverpool today, not just for Iain but for all of us ... The watchers do not care how we live our lives, as long as we stay within the law. But the pickpocket, the mugger, the armed robber, or the drunken driver knows that those hidden eyes are out there. Today the Echo takes you behind the scenes to show you a day in the life of an ordinary [Liverpool] citizen, through the eyes of the closed circuit television (*Liverpool Echo* 1 September 2000: 'Big brother is watching you')

The 'story' in a local newspaper referred to above covers 'a day in the life of an ordinary [Liverpool] citizen'. It is told using CCTV stills showing Ian Bundred, smartly dressed in suit and tie, as he goes about his normal daily routine in downtown Liverpool. Iain, in his car, is captured: going to work; entering the office; at his workdesk; doing a spot of shopping on his lunch break; buying a paper in a newsagents; driving out of the city on his way home; going back into the city by train for the evening; buying a ticket at a theatre; having a drink in a café-bar; and, finally, on his way home by train at 11.15 pm. The story of Iain as told in the local newspaper evokes the 'responsibilised citizen' for its readers, as someone who has 'nothing to fear' from visual surveillance and cares not for outmoded arguments that concern 'invasions of privacy' (ibid.). Iain, a volunteer for this *Echo* 'investigation', is like the central character in *The Truman Show*, 'astounded' to learn that his every move is caught on camera. Unlike Jim Carrey's incarnation, however, he more optimistically retorts, 'it does make you feel safe' (ibid.). In Liverpool as elsewhere, the press play a central role in 'representing order' understood as a 'morality, procedural form and social hierarchy' that is both symbolically and visually persuasive (Ericson *et al.* 1991: 1). As such, the newspaper article represents camera surveillance as *enabling* and *empowering*; it visually invokes an essentialised meaning of public space and the ideal public citizen. It promotes a assured meaning of 'safety' in relation to a certain 'quality of life,' at least for those who work, consume and acceptably entertain themselves in contemporary downtown Liverpool.

In depicting an idealised city lifestyle, the narrative of Iain represents a form of urban storytelling that has more than a provincial significance. The 'responsible citizen' presented in the local newspaper mirrors a trans-local vernacular of power that, under a broadly neoliberal ethos, is helping to shape the material form and functioning of cities of the UK and North America. In focusing on the materialisation of order, this book has sought answers to the questions of *whose order*, by *what means* is it secured and under what political and ideological conditions? In situating the rise of camera surveillance networks in the flux of social relations the book has revisited questions of power, order and social control and how the inter-relationship between these categories is being redefined under a neoliberal vernacular and allied state restructuring process. This vernacular is emerging out of, and reinforcing, an uneven and contradictory process of neoliberalisation. The trajectory of neoliberal statecraft and the kinds of social control explored in this book are articulated by an increasingly powerful group of new primary definers, whose tendentious project of street reclamation is reconfiguring conceptions of citizenship and justice in the city. In 'reclaiming' city streets and promoting a larger and more substantive social ordering project neoliberal technologies of control help promote new subjectivities (for example, around the homeless, street traders, youth) that encourage a skewed, though unevenly realised, reading of urban spaces in advanced capitalist cities and how they are idealistically contemplated and experienced. In other words, at the same time as it hails 'responsible citizens' the discourse constructed around camera surveillance also *irresponsibilises* other groups and individuals in the city. What is clear from the analysis in this book is that new technologies such as CCTV are intensifying and reinforcing an unequal *power of scrutiny* over a fractured sociospatial landscape that favours the architects of an entrepreneurial urbanism.

In light of the debates around social control, and in critical response to

219

it, the book has argued its case within a series of analytical concerns outlined in Chapters 3 and 5 and illustrated in a local case study in Chapters 6 and 7. The concerns point to a process of political, cultural and economic revitalisation that has a primary focus on the control of the streets of the city. As part of the reclamation process camera surveillance has, firstly, been located within an understanding of state institutions. 'Bringing the state back in' enriches our understanding of CCTV beyond a mere crime prevention tool and places it within circuitries of power. In this way state power has been analysed *not* as monolithic entity, in isolated segments, as either 'private' or public', *but as the outcome of term-setting alliances between and across these shifting domains.* The ideological and material possibilities for order established through these alliances are promoted through the constructions of risk that emanate from these powerful alliances and underpin strategies for sovereign control over city centre space. Thus the camera network plays an important part in reasserting a sovereign territorial control that is itself the outcome of state morphology formulated within a complex institutional ensemble or state-market nexus. In this sense the neoliberal state has not simply abandoned an interventionist role but has instead demonstrated a capacity to transform into a variety of institutional forms authorised to carry out a range of governing tasks. The expansion of camera networks is paradigmatic of these developments around institutional fusion and transformation.

Secondly, as it surveys the urban scene, CCTV is part of a normative strategy of social control. In other words, it is a practice of contemporary social ordering that, through neoliberal institutions, promotes an ideologically motivated cleansing of the streets. Arguably, the significance of this refocus on street management is *trans-local* in terms of the kinds of practice being put into effect, the targets of street management practices and the 'knowledge' transfers between regulatory and policing organisations in different localities. This book contributes to an understanding of the dissemination of neoliberal control strategies and their reception in different localities (MacLeod 2002; Peck 2003). In noting these wider concerns, the book offers a correction to neo-Foucauldian approaches, which display a propensity to prioritise the technical over the normative in this field, and in their failure to link up local issues with extra-local developments.

Thirdly, and related to the above, the use and role of CCTV are understood within the material and ideological context of its emergence – namely, within the 'entrepreneurial' forms of rule identified in Chapter 4 and discussed with reference to Liverpool in Chapter 6. In positioning camera surveillance in this way the book urges a process of 'studying up' in order to identify the locally powerful, to assess the meanings they attribute to the objects of their power and to understand how a responsibilisation process is initiated in the co-ordination of a social-ordering strategy through 'partnership'.

Fourthly, camera networks do not provide evidence for a wholesale shift in strategies of social control. The normative demarcation of urban space found in the nineteenth century city has a contemporary correspondence with the processes of articulating the proper objects of partnership power discussed in Chapters 6 and 7. Discourses, 'risky' people and activities play their part in neoliberal rule and remain salient components in the moralisation of space and in reinitiating the nineteenth century bourgeois fears of contamination and contagion. This is in contrast to those perspectives that, in the scramble to identify 'new' and 'post' orientated initiatives, *overestimate* the degree of change and *underestimate* continuity in social control practice. The struggles and political manoeuvring that underpin the drive to reinvent the capitalist cityscape can develop and accommodate new technologies but the capitalist city remains organised around some relatively settled themes (as well as staid powerful actors) that have helped proliferate the under and over-policing of selective activities and events as part of the social ordering of space. The identified hindrances to neoliberal progress show remarkable similarities across national borders (MacLeod 2002) and point to a role for policing and surveillance which not only provide a means of 'social sorting' (Lyon 2003) but a means to a wider process that seeks the *social removal* of the signs of inequality both on the streets and in public and political debate. As in the nineteenth century capitalist city, the process of 'moving them on' (Brogden 1982) and defending lines of demarcation survives as a mechanism for dealing with inequality. CCTV ensures an increasingly codified set of unequal rights regarding the use of space and, as it displaces inequality, it also reinforces the development of a hidden city in which the signifiers of inequality and other 'nuisances' are forced into an underground-outsider status that, for one writer at least, ferments the possibilities for resistance against an 'exclusionary model of public life' (Ferrell 2001: 5).[1] The trajectory of the social ordering strategy described in this book signals a move away from a welfare model of urban management and its replacement with a notion of privileged revenge that is enacted at the behest of a neoliberal vision of urban sanctity (Smith 1996: 211). The original revanchists in late nineteenth century Paris sought to reclaim the streets by coercive and moral means from the perceived ungodliness of socialist ideas and practices (ibid.). To be sure, these forms of social control have a logic that is underpinned by an overt viciousness targeted at the economically marginalised as a decidedly 'high risk' group who appear – to borrow Pratt's phraseology – 'unable to learn the lesson that neo-liberalism now expects of its subjects' (Pratt 1997: 181). The techniques of social control discussed in the previous chapter have a logic that is often underpinned by an overt viciousness that targets and reinforces political and economic marginality.

In eschewing wholesale shifts in the political economy of social control the book has explored the interests behind camera networks and the nature of the social order they reproduce. In other words, what kinds of cities are surveillance networks being developed within and helping to construct? The analysis here paints a picture not so much of the 'unhealthy' society envisaged by Durkheim but of how the categories of the 'healthy' and 'unhealthy' city and the moral geographies that accompany them are shaped by powerful and tendentious discourses that, in a hegemonic sense, define these categories and render them socially credible. The findings in this book raise questions about the changing nature of city spaces – how they are defined, used and cohabited – and the central role of street surveillance within the sociospatial production of 'the city'. As pointed out in earlier chapters, the neoliberalisation of the city and the forms of social control being implemented within it point to the increasingly strategic importance of space – its production, management and rehabilitation. For it is the new primary definers of space who are shaping a landscape of risk through which hidden spaces are also being created that attempt to deny unequal social relations. Taking these lines of inquiry challenges the script of an urban postmodern playfulness and the idea that research that casts its gaze upwards into political programmes that have institutional, material and ideological currency is passé. The remainder of this chapter discusses this landscape in the making.

Cameras and the landscape of risk

As indicated in earlier parts of the book and at the beginning of this chapter, camera networks are positioned ideologically as 'techniques of freedom'. However, in delineating the parameters of risk in the city centre the locally powerful are able to direct such networks to promote a kind of 'freedom' and 'agency' *for some* urban inhabitants while delimiting the freedom of movement and quality of life for others.

Neo-Foucauldian approaches eschew a political economy of risk that translates the latter into the spatialisation strategies discussed in the book. These approaches stress the impossibility of holistic, universalising or, what such work would prefer to call, 'totalising' theoretical understandings of contemporary 'control societies' (Rose 2000: 325). These positions fail to account for the normative aspects of power and control that underpin the construction of risk categories and processes towards what previous chapters have identified as the materialisation of a neoliberal social order. Indeed, it is these normative and ideological aspects of power that inform, and often cement, the 'diffusion' of institutional power in neoliberal statecraft and underpin the 'responsibilisation' process in the task of city building. Thus changes, instigated through partnerships, in the structure and objects of city centre rule inaugurate a *refinement* and not an *overhaul* of the ideological and political centres of power. Moreover, there is 'a tendency among risk theorists to overstate the importance of cold, actuarial calculus as the determining form of responding to system [or city] breakdown' (Rigakos 1999: 145). In thinking about the normative nature of order alongside, and not as an alternative to, techniques involved in the regulation of urban landscapes, CCTV is a key vehicle for reproducing and sustaining a particular social order, one that embodies a complex nexus of commercial as well as ideological and moral imperatives.

In the construction of a local 'regime of truth' (to borrow Foucault's phrase 1985: 93) or 'a politics of truth', the locally powerful are engaged in a process of defining problems, of a normative *and* technical nature, that hinder a particular governmental programme. These powerful definitional activities drive a tendentious spatialisation of risk that reinforces particular and established definitions of crime; the privileging of 'public' discourses of risk over 'private' and the marginalisation of other dangers in the urban environment (including insecurities generated by homelessness, sexual and racial harassment, pollution in the urban realm and white-collar crime) are part of this process and can be understood as re-fashioning, in the 'public interest', a local truth-claiming strategy. The articulation of these discourses was illustrated in Chapters 6 and 7, through an examination of the ideological outlooks of the locally powerful and the camera network. The powerful linkages displayed between various local 'expert' domains within the neoliberal state (for example, the Government Office, Stores' Committee, Crime Alert) are able, albeit with a degree of internal conflict, to articulate a vision for the city that drives a spatialisation of risk in a manner that encompasses an idealised citizenry and a desired urban utility.

It is only in 'studying up' and casting a gaze upon the locally powerful that the book is able to challenge notions of the 'risk society'. The problem of risk has been dematerialised along with the definitional processes that define risk categories, 'public safety' and social order.

Indeed, these definitional processes are bound up with attempts strategically to align the players in the partnership programme itself. For example, the identification of the homeless in Liverpool as a hindrance to a politics of growth along with the surveillance and hostility directed at this group, help to *unify*, in a normative and ideological sense, and *co-ordinate*, in managerial and policy terms, the assemblage of neoliberal rule.

This highlights another gap in the literature that fails to account for what can be called the 'technologies of fear' that are a feature of urban landscapes. Camera networks and the official discourse that surrounds them provide an indication of the increasing importance of 'fear' in the governing process. Governing through 'fear of others' and the folk-devilry this generates aids the building of an unequal city through the promotion of particular political interests. This is not to deny the reality of the fear of crime, but it is to point to how 'fears' can be 'spoken to', exaggerated and articulated for particular political ends. The manner in which campaigns of censure aimed at the homeless, street traders and other low or no-income categories reminds us of the continuing importance of authoritarian populism (Hall 1988) that, when orchestrated by the agents of city renaissance, link the themes of crime, discipline and social order to produce, not always successfully, a new common sense. In the regenerating city the rise of street camera surveillance, and the fear this feeds off and reinforces in relation to certain forms of crime, instigates a process of governance through street crime as a means to manage the degenerate. As part of the drive for a civic order, local media in Liverpool tie into this governing process with campaigns to 'Shop a Yob' along with crusades with the slogan 'Justice for All' that more often than not are aimed at the poorest sections of the population. In other words, the official discourses in Liverpool around the least powerful inhabitants of the city cannot be seen as innocent discourses that unproblematically represent the reality of a given social problem. Instead they are components of a broader landscape of risk propagated and given prominence in times of social, political and economic upheaval. Some urban scholars are beginning to address these issues and examine how 'Particular rationalities ... linked to capital ... produce fears through the process of ordering and marginalizing – themselves central to landscape as both an aesthetic and material practice' (Gold and Revill 2003: 45).

Preceding chapters outlined more than a descriptive overview of some 'new penology', with its emphasis on amoral and actuarial techniques. What goes largely unacknowledged within the risk literature is the role of the supposedly instrumental/risk organs of the corporate and business sector and the manner in which they promote new technologies like CCTV with reference to highly charged and historically developed moral discourses (Coleman 2003b). Thus, defence of property and profit margins relies upon and marshals moral signifiers and discourses of 'respectability'. It is the media-savvy managers of the neoliberal cityscape – the BIDs, city partnerships and growth spokespeople – along with other established public officials who articulate contemporary urban tales of regeneration/degeneration and moral probity as well as decay. Similar aspirations, fears and anxieties existed in the nineteenth century but now they take hold within a new neoliberalised context, couched within a 'new' language and with refreshed arguments that point to a change in the balance in state forces. Now as then, profit may be the desired goal but moral propriety, family values and civic responsibility conjoin with the growth ethic and provide a means and an end in themselves. Furthermore, it is questionable that 'the mechanisms of coercion within criminal justice [will] come to be seen less as a device for inflicting pain and more as a set of resources to be considered in reducing risk' (Shearing 2001: 217). This kind of speculation only denies the millititarisation and punitive severity being brought to bear in many cities. Rather than depicting cameras as a benign alternative to coercive – 'older' – state practices, the arguments here understand the components of spatial reordering (camera surveillance, public order policing, hybrid policing) in dialectical inter-relation to each other and as belonging to a strategy of social ordering, not always uniform and coherent, but which combines a strategy that constructs the legitimate and 'safe' uses of public space. Older and newer discourses are developing and combining to construct those groups and individuals 'deserving' of exclusionary, frequently oppressive, monitor-ing in entrepreneurial landscapes. Mapping a landscape of risk in Liverpool has had a particularly detrimental impact on black people who lodge 40% of complaints against the police in relation to stop-and- search practices and who are nearly 10 times more likely than whites to be stopped and searched in the city by Merseyside Police (*Liverpool Echo* 29 March 2004: 'Police launch race inquiry').

The impact of 'traditional' methods of policing (discussed in Chapter 5) and the problems they continue to generate for the freedom of movement and sense of belonging for sections of the population cannot be pushed aside as pertaining to some 'older' and therefore less relevant penological past that has now been eclipsed by the benevolent street camera. Established as well as 'novel' techniques for demarcating space *and their inter-relationship with each other* are missing in the 'risk' literature and the literature on CCTV. More broadly, and in relation to newer

225

techniques of control, it is a notion of the state that has escaped social theorising but which must be retained and developed if we are adequately to formulate critical responses to camera surveillance, the reinvention of the city and the process of geographical demarcation:

> it is exactly through the state (*at whatever scale*) that the position and role of the citizen and his/her relationship with society is defined, institutionalized and, on occasion, contested and challenged ... If we are concerned with formulating emancipatory policies and strategies, the state and other forms of governance remain key areas for challenging processes of exclusion and disempowerment (Sywngedouw 1996: 1502, emphasis added).

If discourses of moral abjection and corrective severity still hold a pivotal position in social ordering strategies then this belies any notion of the end of class, racial, gendered, sexual and age-based oppression. Power in its normative and ideological dimensions must be acknowledged, understood and deconstructed because the processes of reclamation, denial, containment and exclusion are not free-floating signifiers but are integral to the contemporary and contingent materialisation of order that, in the contemporary setting, is aligned to a trajectory of neoliberalisation.

Cameras and the hidden landscape

> Understanding and 'exposing' the ways that things, people, and social relations are made visible or invisible to the public eye remains an important political project (Katz 2001: 96).

This book has sought to expose the roots and development of the camera network in a manner that illuminates its relationship to the power and scope of a neoliberal political project. The cameras underpin a conception of the idealised citizen-worker-socialite hailed in neoliberal vernacular as typified in the newspaper article at the beginning of the chapter. CCTV sprung from neoliberal political thinking, both in terms of the insistence by central governments that 'partnerships' should run and fund initiatives *and* in terms of the official orientation of CCTV towards aiding the process of urban consumption (Home Office 1994: 9) and the wider city economy. The ʹentrepreneurialʹ roots of mass camera surveillance provide a clue to the uses of CCTV as a social ordering tool. Despite these clues many researchers continue to mystify camera surveillance by lauding it with some simple 'crime prevention' potential. However, within neoliberal strategies for order CCTV is central to a process of mystification in the cleansed urban form. On the development of neoliberal spaces, Katz (2001) points to the ability of gleaming and spectacular architectures to hide the consequences of neoliberal rule; consequences such as the effects from welfare cutbacks, privatisation and underinvestment in various social services. Neoliberal spaces erase the 'traces' of inequality with the construction of self-congratulatory monuments that strategically remove the poor, the dirt and dilapidation resulting from 'the wholesale disinvestments in social reproduction' (ibid.: 107). Furthermore: 'The painful reminders of the unevenness and fragmentation brought about by capitalism have been pushed out of the central spaces of the city, and significant rhetorical and physical vigilance is mounted against their return' (ibid.).

Taking this argument further camera surveillance can be understood as part of a process of 'hiding' through mystification: it hides both the processes of urban rule and order, described in Liverpool in Chapter 6, and its discontents. First, through the eye of a street camera a host of urban problems, including popular protest, homelessness, street trading and petty violations to local bye-law, become detached from any social and political context, and instead defined through the lens of crime, disorder and 'the anti-social'. Secondly, what is most obvious and yet often unacknowledged is that cameras overwhelmingly focus on the street and 'street people'. This reinforces prevailing definitions of 'crime', 'risk' 'and 'harm' as emanating *solely* from powerless and 'disaffected' people. Any irresponsible actions and social harms propagated by neoliberal strategists and corporate actors[2] are thus further inoculated by the highly selective use of the camera networks that they have established. The *unequal power of scrutiny* is reinforced as the process of mystification enlarges itself in the form of footage from street cameras appearing in crime-come-entertainment TV shows. In this scenario surveillance cameras 'make visible' their intended targets by turning them into 'other', annulled subjects to be replayed on popular crime shows as the victims of Foucault's 'dividing practices' (1984: 208), whereby the camera 'objectivises' the criminal, the deviant and the wrongdoer more often than not for the titillation, fear and entertainment of the 'law abiding' audience. This media formula portrays in synoptical[3] fashion the nightmares that may follow where the forces of urban 'degeneration' are to be allowed a free reign to threaten and contaminate the urban civic aesthetic. To be sure, these forms of social control have a logic that is underpinned by a viciousness targeted at the economically marginalised as a decidedly 'high risk' group who appear incapable of heeding the 'rules' that the neoliberal city now expects of its subjects. In other words, neoliberal vernacular has *irresponsibilised* sections of the population as a forerunner to their criminalisation and/or exclusion and removal from public space. New social subjectivities cultivated around the homeless, unemployed, selected racialised minorities and those on the borders of the 'respectable' economy underpin the targeting process and further pathologise these categories as incongruous folk-devils of the neoliberal landscape; unclean, sometimes petty violators who illegitimately inhabit a sanitised urban aesthetic.

Street camera surveillance disproportionately surveys and casts suspicion on the poor in the spaces of the city. The construction of 'the theme park city' and the building of security-minded institutions to police it only reinforce these processes, so that those walking the streets who are teenagers, dressed inappropriately and without branded shopping bags (low-income groups) are likely targets of security personnel whose 'nose' for suspicion has been directed at those who appear to be 'walking or standing without due cause'. In many cities in the UK public and private police are working together in organisations such as Crime Alert where, despite organisational differences, policing agencies find common ground in constructing and sharing a commonsense morality of public space. Normative processes are manifest in the discursive exchanges between public and private police and are integral parts of the low-level social ordering activities that construct and demarcate 'responsible' and 'irresponsible' uses of city centre space. The members of Liverpool's Crime Alert characterise the objects of their powerful gaze as 'dross', 'scallies', 'knobs', 'hawkers', 'urchins' and 'fake homeless'. These constructions of city space complement and reinforce the broader visions for order in the city that emanate from the primary definers of neoliberal rule.

As surveillance cameras routinely monitor the street prohibitions of the neoliberal city, they also reinforce the moral codes, intolerances and normative prescriptions of its creators. Paradoxical as it may seem, for all the talk of cultural celebration and putting 'culture' at the centre of current urban renaissance drives, certain forms of culture are increasingly being subject to oppressive monitoring and curtailment. The title of European Capital of Culture for 2008 has taken place at the same time as the street culture of young people has come under attack as well as a range of perceived 'nuisances' that are tied to the secondary economy in the city and that, for the new primary definers, give the city the image of a 'bargain-basement economy'.

In situating the surveillance system within the wider political management of the city, the material highlighted here and in the previous two chapters points to the formation of a landscape of denial. Neoliberal visions propagate a discursive armoury that speaks to local populations with undertakings of increases in 'quality of life'; strong civic identity and pride; anti-social behaviour free zones; and an ideology of 'social inclusiveness' designed to underpin urban renaissance. With the most expensive and infinitely expandable camera surveillance network in the UK, Liverpool's 'friendly eye in the sky' plays a key role in the construction of urban order and discourses of 'safety'. Crucially, this *version* of urban reconstruction masks and denies the structured degradations being enacted in the name of urban renaissance and procures its justification through the 'value free' discourses that construct 'partnership', 'community empowerment' and 'quality of life'. As the book has demonstrated, categories such as these are not neutral or ideologically unanchored. It is these linguistic categories that social scientists have, on the whole, been reluctant to deconstruct and understand as a form of skewed 'neoliberal newspeak' (Bourdieu and Wacquant 2001). These categories assume a central position in the struggles over urban order and themselves mask the processes involved in building a landscape of denial: a denial that obscures public visibility of, and debate around, political agency and participation and socioeconomic inequality.

Cameras and the unequal landscape

The book has not placed the camera network within a process of state diminution or 'hollowing out' but instead within a trajectory of state *transformation*. As part of this process the book has explored how a desired mode of city life is summoned into being through discourses of regeneration. From the vantage point of the powerful, the 'new urban space' and the subjects that constitute it are constantly to be 'reassured' and rendered 'safe' in an age of property-led 'social' development and conspicuous consumption. However, as Chapter 6 illustrated with regard to Liverpool, the regeneration discourses privileging the new urban lifestyle often hide, rework or demote 'older' material realities and representations of the city such as indecorous and unwanted images of social fracture and local disparities of wealth and poverty. In reorganising the sociospatial landscape, the process of state trans-formation is reordering local political priorities.

In Liverpool, as elsewhere, features of a 'roll back' neoliberal state (Peck and Tickell 2002) sit alongside a 'roll-out' programme of intensified social surveillance and authoritarian statehood. The effects of 'roll-back' and neoliberalism's urge to re-prioritise 'needs' in recasting the politics of locality are evident in a number of ways. In Liverpool, social-welfarist objectives stand at odds with entrepreneurial forms of economic growth – at best welfare objectives are add-ons to be addressed *subsequent to* growth, city makeovers and private sector valorisation (see ibid.). The government's own Social Exclusion Unit found the gaps between wealth and poverty in Liverpool to be the most acute in the country. The contrast with the signs of investment in the city centre and the wealth of those who are repopulating it, the severe clusters of deprivation in areas surrounding the city centre are noted (Social Exclusion Unit 2003). Unemployment remains relatively high in Liverpool with those claiming benefits around 7% compared to a national average of 3% (*The Guardian* 19 April 2002: 'Mersey mission builds up to a grand climax'). What jobs are being created through the renaissance drive are in the service sector, particularly the low-wage sectors such as hotels and catering, and call centres where over 10,000 are employed throughout Merseyside (Industry North West 2003). Many jobs are grant subsidised via Objective One funding that aids employment in public sector areas such as the Criminal Records Bureau, the Child Support Agency, the Inland Revenue and the Passport Agency. This situation is lamented by local business commentators who want more private sector expansion (ibid.). In 2003 the Low Pay Commission received evidence from Liverpool Trades Unions showing that it was top of a 'shame league' regarding the position of working teenagers in the city who are entering work on poverty pay (below the minimum wage), with poor working conditions and minimal or no training (*Liverpool Echo* 6 November 2003: 'Teenage wages of poverty'). A mile to the east of the city centre lies Kensington that since 1998 has been recognised as a 'cluster of high social exclusion' and designated a Home office 'crime hotspot'. In attempting to 'bridge the gap' between this area and the city centre £61.9 million has been spent (£643,000 on CCTV and community wardens) under the New Deal for Communities programme since 1998.

However, these developments have been criticised in a report that attacked the Deal as 'failing' local residents in terms of low or no public consultation (*The Guardian* 29 October 2002: 'Whitehall "fails to let local people rule" ') and warned of a ten-year wait for local people before any signs of improvement may be evident in terms of employment prospects and educational improvements (*Liverpool Echo* 21 October 2003: 'New Deal is failing'). With an average household income significantly lower than the national average (*The Guardian* 19 April 2002: 'Mersey mission builds up to a grand climax') and nine of the twenty poorest postcodes in the UK located in the city (*The Observer* 7 July 2002: 'Can you hear the Mersey beat?'), Liverpool is a relatively poor place and three areas that surround the city centre are ranked in a government-sponsored survey as being in the top five most deprived areas in England and Wales as indicated through high unemployment, low income, poor health and poor access to education and services (*The Times* 6 May, 2004: 'Chorleywood is happiest place to live'). Criticisms that Neighbourhood Renewal funds are being 'misspent' on prestigious city centre projects (*Liverpool Echo* 6 May 2004: 'City 3 among worst areas') only reinforce a growing scepticism held by people in places like Kensington who are, for one community representative, 'being sold out' in favour of 'property speculators' (*Liverpool Echo* 8 March 2004: 'Cash down the drain'). A central and unapologetic feature of neoliberal city building is the focus on revitalising city centres and downtowns and the built-in assumption that a result of these investment-come-growth strategies will result in a 'trickle down' of wealth creation to replenish poorer constituencies outside the city centre. Challenges to this agenda from local grassroots organisations find little space in a renaissance-obsessed and pro-growth local media. However, definitional struggles around local political priorities do, from time to time, become visible and call into question the continuation of welfare needs and housing needs, and environmental disintegration as issues that neoliberal policies have sidetracked. While simple outer-estate maintenance for poor communities is subject to funding shortfalls and council 'red tape' the city centre in Liverpool is described and treated as 'the jewel in the crown'. In 2004 an £800 million consortia of public and private money will be spent on a 42-acre, high-status consumption zone that is the 'Bluecoat Triangle' (see below). This can be compared with the £20.03 million spent in 2003 as part of a 'pledge to help the poor' in Liverpool. Indeed nationally, 'clusters of social exclusion' received a total of £975 million in 2003 from Neighbourhood Renewal Funding (Neighbourhood Renewal Unit 2003). What these and other local dynamics of poverty and social exclusion point to is a reality of an increasingly divided city that is being socially demarcated with a renewed intensity. The city centre itself, as the previous chapter illustrated, is not simply governed through freedom but also the curtailment of freedom and quality of life for particular groups and categories. Within such a landscape it is not a question of whether CCTV 'works' but a question of *how* a fractured landscape such as this is, in part, surveilled, reproduced and hidden (through practices of criminalisation, exclusion and reclamation) by the operation of camera networks.

The marketing strategies that 'talk up' the attractiveness of places may succeed in skirting these issues. But they also attempt to de-politicise space in a way that is reflected in the ideological underpinnings of 'partnership'. From the Urban Development Corporations in the Thatcher era and the sprouting of BIDs in the Reagan/Bush years, to the 'Third Way' of the Clinton/Blair successions, 'partnerships' have assumed the guise of technical and neutral players in the urban scene: *dispensing with 'red tape'* (i.e. earlier and 'outmoded' democratic forms of decision-making and service delivery), while *delivering the goods* (the 'goods' usually being gentrified spaces and spectacular, headline-grabbing architectural gestures). Crucially, the perception of these spaces as orderly, clean and 'safe' is integral to the realisation of profits and their order maintenance using camera networks constitutes a form of statecraft that, in an era of 'roll out neoliberalism', is concerned 'with the aggressive reregulation, disciplining, and containment of those marginalized and dispossessed' (Peck and Tickell 2002: 389).

As the previous two chapters illustrate in Liverpool, space is increasingly strategic and the curtailment and policing of street demonstrations, leafleting and picketing which threatens the contrived retail carnival atmosphere is evidence of this and supports arguments made elsewhere concerning the erosion of the idea of 'public space' as an arena for collective debate and struggle for rights and entitlements (Mitchell 2003). If, in principle, aesthetics over-ride democratic considerations, then this principle will have only been furthered in Liverpool, where in June 2003 the City Council's claim to be 'the most business friendly in the UK' was reinforced as it was designated European Capital of Culture for 2008. In the wake of the announcement the city centre has been hailed as 'Boom Town' (*Liverpool Echo* 6 June 2003) and on the cusp of a 'Golden Age' (*Liverpool Echo* 28 January, 2004). 'Boom Town' like 'morphocity', described in Chapter 5, acts as a form of representation-as-spin that masks the street reclamation process described in these pages as it redefines the meaning of public space.

As the book goes to print, the visions of urban rule described here are being extended in Liverpool with a proposal to initiate Europe's biggest city centre building programme. At a cost of £800 million and developed and part-funded by Britain's richest man, the Duke of Westminster, this scheme includes super-expensive penthouse suites and high-end retailing that, it is argued, will increase city centre turnover by £540 million a year by 2011 (*Daily Post* 20 September 2002: 'City's £700 million rebirth in a big step forward'). Significantly, the development will instigate the building and development of up to 35 private streets with no public right of way in a 'new urban village' that extends the notion of 'Gold Zone' in the city discussed in Chapter 5. Although officially dubbed 'public realms', the areas under development are to be 'ring fenced' and patrolled by US-style quartermasters or 'sheriffs' whose role is described by one council official involved in the scheme as to 'control and exclude the riff-raff element' (Indymedia 2003). A spokesperson for the developers put forward the logic for this first step towards a Business Improvement District in the city: 'People tell us they don't come shopping to Liverpool because it's dirty, there is chewing gum all over the place and pavements are cracked. We are developing a series of quarters for the area which will have security staff making sure that people maintain reasonable standards of behaviour' (ibid.).

As Chapters 6 and 7 demonstrated, in setting out the meaning of terms like 'reasonableness' and 'responsibility', the new primary definers are able to articulate a version of the public interest in such a way as to disguise the rootedness of such flamboyant spaces of uninhibited spectacle within capitalist social relations; relations that, under neoliberal conditions, are diminishing the meaning and scope of 'the public' as well as the contours of 'freedom' in public space. Within all this, the camera network itself, as the previous chapter demonstrated, is described as a 'people's system' and the city centre as a 'people's place'. The privatisation of a significant area of the city centre heralds an extension of 'the visions' discussed in Chapter 6 and the further disenfranchisement of those long-standing targets of the camera network identified in Chapter 7. As this social ordering strategy unfolds the right to decide who walks through a city's streets will also impact upon the right to protest and public campaign in the city against, for example, shops dealing in sweatshop goods or those encouraging environmental destruction. In the privatised city, these forms of protest would become a matter of feudal-like trespass and subject to exclusion.

'The World in One City'?

As the slogan of Liverpool's Capital of Culture status, 'The World in One City' captures very well the tensions wrought in the process of global and local change and how these changes are interpreted in relation to particular cities in particular locations. On the one hand, with its officially endorsed assumptions of cosmopolitanism, pluralism and diversity, the slogan paints a city at ease with itself – post-conflictual, socially integrated and harmonious. On the other hand, a more critical interpretation may take such a slogan to represent another reality of urban life. 'The world' is indeed mirrored in 'one city' (or many cities) in the sense that advanced capitalist cityscapes – however much they aspire to market out social divisions – are spatially and socially *dis*integrated places and remain the sites for major political and sociocultural conflict. In charting these developments with regard to one city, the book calls attention to 'the local' in excavating a political economy of social control. However the neoliberalisation of city rule and the impact this is having on social control have a globalised dynamic and it is these dynamics that mutate and impact differentially at the local level. Although neoliberalism has in many respects gained a 'worldwide ascendancy', in terms of the rationale and institutional logic for running cities (Brenner and Theodore 2002: 367; Massey 1999; Wacqaunt 1999), this does not equate with an homogenised governing process nor symmetry regarding the meaning and form attributed to city spaces. The points raised are an attempt to map out a neoliberal 'logic' in the process of spatial ordering. Neoliberal rationales 'unfold in place-specific forms and combinations' (Brenner and Theordore 2002: 368) and engage with particular inherited institutional politics and cultural histories. However, the inducements to 'jump on the neoliberal bandwagon' in cities of the advanced capitalist world are strong and undercut alternative local visions of urban political rule (Peck and Tickell 2002: 393). The hegemony of neoliberalism has had considerable success in shifting the terrain of local social democracy over to a politics based *less* on accountability and *more* on public consultocracy (Fairclough 2000).

As Taylor (1997: 59) argues, global prescriptions of change, whether formulated in terms of a 'risk society' or 'postmodernism', have failed to connect 'global change to local expressions'. In exploring the emergence of local partnerships that have 'crime prevention' as a core concern, the book does not view what happens in Liverpool as happening in a political and economic vacuum. In noting this, it also becomes important to remain sensitive to global trends sweeping across national borders not least in terms of the discourses of 'crime and safety', and the image management they are a part of which are central to the promotion of neoliberal ideology and growth. In noting the importance of 'the local', it does not prohibit a contribution to wider empirical or theoretical debate around the nature of contemporary social control and in particular the trans-local shifts towards 'revanchist' forms of social control (Smith 1996; MacLeod 2002). Neo-Foucauldian-inspired approaches have stressed the micro-techniques of power and have been, as Chapter 3 noted, so excessively particularistic that it is difficult to know when, how and if the local connects to the global. The focus on the local can result in a losing site of a serious debate that ignores the similarities and discontinuities between cities. The debate can be broadened to explore the extent to which the surveillance practices explored in this book are seen as part of a 'transatlantic diffusion' of a 'new doxa on security' that is becoming increasingly visible at street level (Wacquant 1999: 319) in the same manner that an 'internationalisation of regeneration discourses' is filtrating at the local level (Raco 2003: 245). The technologies of neoliberal rule are important but less so than the normative visions that underpin them and drive the criminalisation of a range of urban 'nuisances' that in some instances reinforce a punitive response to the poor and poverty itself.

This is not an argument for a brushing aside of the peculiarities and contingencies involved in policing and monitoring particular places but it is to point to the interface between global discourses of 'regeneration' and their reception at, and role within, the local level and governance of place. What has also been stressed is that although the composition of state managers has shifted in the last 75 years, the ideological conditions of their work have changed little in terms of those groups and individuals targeted as problematic over the same period have remained broadly the same. Brogden (1991: 1) used the phrase 'uniformed garbage men' to describe the proper objects of police power in nineteenth century Liverpool as they swept up the poor and casualised labour as the objects of mercantile fear and discomfort in the city. It will be interesting to look at how the current reinvention and re-gentrification of the city centre of Liverpool – evidenced in the celebrated arrival of London property agents and the drive to establish the city's first £1 million city centre penthouses – will impact on the continuing class-based discourse of fear, violence and crime that underpins the camera network.

These points underpin the lack of a deeper historical narrative of social control within theorisations of risk, but also remind us that revanchist policies of reclamation will not unfold evenly between different locations. But evidence suggests they *are* unfolding across national boundaries (Wacquant 1999) and, in the UK, encouraged by the 'partnership' approach organised through the Crime and Disorder Act and Business Improvement Districts that have grown out of private sector jostling for greater power and position in the decision-making process at local and national level over the last 20 years. Information swapping between cities on 'quality of life' policing tactics (zero tolerance) does not simply mean Liverpool is like New York (which the former is twinned with and does swap security-related information with), but it does point to a recognition by local elites of similar problems and 'hindrances' that may require a policing 'option-as-solution'. In this sense, the growth machine ethic which is helping bind a new consensus across the neoliberal state also underpins a defensive and revanchist social movement that is pushing the boundaries of 'crime and safety' initiatives so that they are increasingly defined through the targeting of 'street nuisances' that mirror the urban social defence practices found in the nineteenth century city. Street camera surveillance is part of a broader movement to *re-gate* the city while at the same time adding support to a political strategy that is resulting in the intensification of social demarcation between richer and poorer sections of the population.

Challenging the politics of vision?

The application of neoliberal policies has accentuated the problem of challenging their hegemony, both within and outside academia. This is partly because the contemporary notion of 'public interest' has increasingly been aligned to, and made to work alongside, the visions of urban renaissance discussed in this book. This 'public interest' articulated by the locally powerful, as Chapter 6 illustrated, seems to be establishing itself around an evocation of 'a rhetorical appeal to an essential community of "the city" or "the people" ' (Goss 1996: 228). This has reworked the notion of 'the public' and tied it to a wider and depoliticised ideology of 'urban patriotism' (ibid.) that is articulated by growth managers, media outlets and other 'new' and 'old' primary definers. In Liverpool this patriotism attempts to build a hegemony of vision that looks 'back to the future' in selectively reworking images of an earlier period through slogans such as 'Liverpool: A Mercantile City', 'Home of the Beatles' and 'The World in One City'. These 'safe' representations hide the 'respectable' fears of returning to a past that is the antithesis of neoliberal order – 1980s left-wing politics, worker militancy, urban degeneration and disorder, and the flight of capital. Any risk of contamination to the hegemony of vision is cast as a threat and endangering a carefully marketed reinvention of the city and its inhabitants that denies aspects of the city's past and its present. These issues that fall under the politics of image predominate local political thinking and rarely include the wider public, who are themselves constructed in ideal-typical fashion as latent responsibilised city ambassadors with their own marketing potential. More generally, Fairclough (2000: 127–32) argues that 'what now passes as public debate takes place in the mass media ... and is ... constrained by market forces'. A form of 'consultation as promotion' (ibid.) permeates the institutions of neoliberal rule and CCTV in particular. Behind the glamour of city patriotic fervour and its much-vaunted promises of growth are hidden the less palpable effects of neoliberal rule. As has been argued throughout, it is these less marketable and relatively hidden aspects of city building that are often presented as 'suitable enemies' and the socially unworthy inhabitants within the contemporary city.

The nature of the neoliberal state and the forms of street surveillance that accompany it raise questions about social justice and challenges to the inequities of the surveillance society. What can be done in this landscape reinforced by surveillance technology and associated moral crusades? Many have questioned the impartiality of urban surveillance and have described contemporary cities as 'hostile to difference' (Sibley 1995) or have identified contemporary social control methods as leading to 'the exclusion of diversity … in practice' within cities (Flusty 2001: 664). Scholars around CCTV have come to similar conclusions in that contemporary surveilled cities are places where 'difference is not so much to be celebrated as segregated' (Bannister *et al.* 1998: 27). Flusty notes that the rise of 'interdictory space' may see cities develop whole areas that are 'riskless' and empty of 'those who practice other ways of being' (2001: 264). But what does it mean to say that camera networks repress difference? The language of 'difference' underlines much critical work in the area of surveillance and urban space and seems to lament the fading of a past where 'difference' and 'diversity' of conduct and identity were at least afforded a measure of recognition in 'public space'. This assumption is questionable as the historical material in Chapter 5 demonstrates; public space has since the inception of the modern capitalist city been, and continues to be, politically constructed, having 'highly scripted and delimited roles' (Ruddick 1996: 135) for women of different classes, black people and different age categories. Degrees of continuity are evident in the social assignment of risk, its relationship to fear and policing as social demarcation.

The notion of 'difference' is analytically vague and sits uncomfortably with the issues raised in this book. For some critics the language of difference has operated as an inferior replacement for a marginalised language that prioritises a focus on inequality (Malik 1996), with the former mystifying the shifting contours of unequal social relations. A more critical approach is needed in this area, in particular a focus on how adaptations of the discourse of difference (in its more celebratory incarnations) are themselves produced within the centres of power that orchestrate and market the neoliberal landscape.[4] This notion of neoliberal difference exists through marketing strategies that construct 'cosmopolitanism' and along with its postmodern, 'radical' counterpart it constructs a dematerialised notion of identity and deflects critical attention that should be focused on the dynamics of inequality within the contemporary city. The focus on difference does not apply to the issues discussed in this chapter or this book which instead have together sought to develop a political economy of surveillance – and by implication, therefore, a political economy concerning the construction of 'difference' (Harvey 1992: 596). Debates concerning the right to access, use and define the city need to take on material issues through which inequality is brought into focus as something to be challenged, not celebrated or seen as merely 'different'. Unequal relations between rich/poor, men/women, gay/straight and young/old are precisely *relations* that have been managed and negotiated through state activities via combinations of welfare, moral education, and censure and exclusion from public space. For some who inhabit our cities, their identity, through the eyes of a surveillance camera, is constructed in wholly negative terms and without the presence of negotiation and choice that middle-class consumers may enjoy. Therefore, it is not suggested in this book that the homeless should be 'returned' to the city streets and be 'celebrated', as some exotic nomadic tribe in a city built on a 'politics that celebrates marginality rather than seeking to redress it' (Mitchell 2001: 82). Besides this being unrealistic in the current climate, it is also a politically irresponsible position to adopt for those who advocate and/or identify themselves as 'progressive', theoretically or otherwise. The icy winds of neoliberalism may have frozen out the notion of universal rights and entitlements in the city, but that is no excuse for lapsing into the celebration of some bogus notion of consumption-led identity politics.

Surveillance that concerns itself with 'social sorting' does *nothing* to address, and *everything* to reproduce, boundaries of inequality. Lyon (2003), however, provides a challenge to this in the form of a post-privacy strategy. Again, though, this challenge leaves aside some thorny structural issues. According to Lyon, a problem with modern surveillance is that it lacks a 'human' touch. It is 'the face' that needs to be brought 'back' into the equation, for it is the face that forms the basis for ethically and morally regulating and humanising the surveillance society – of making it fairer. It seems that the presence of faces and bodies 'calls data users to establish trust' (ibid.: 27). But problems with this approach remain: such as how did 'the face' in historical terms make a positive impact upon the policing of black communities? As many studies demonstrate, this policing was very front line, 'in your face' and embodied from the times since plantation and slavery up until today. The black body has been, and continues to be, hugely symbolic and representative of disorder for state and corporate servants. This body continues to be a site for the enactment of brutalising violence. Sure, disembodied surveillance may make the path to social justice less likely but it will take more than the *presence* of the faces and bodies of the oppressed to transform unequal social relations. Lest we forget, the very presence of such 'dangerous' bodies has often been justified as enough to 'cause' anxiety, fear and mistrust as a basis for punitive intervention from 'data users' and powerful groups whose diminished propensity for 'understanding and tolerance' is all too evident. Rendering visible the faces of those *behind*, for example, the camera lens must also be a priority – if only in calling the powerful to account for their increasingly intrusive and unjust surveillance practices. Related to this it is important not to forget that CCTV does not operate in vacuum and, as this book has argued, sits alongside and complements other regulatory and policing initiatives that contribute to local order. Furthermore, contrary to neo-Foucauldian thinking, 'repression' and violence have not disappeared as tools of social ordering and should not be understood as *alternatives* to CCTV. Statistics for traditional surveillance methods such as police stop-and-search tactics against black people remain disproportionately high in the UK and the USA. Along with intrusive camera surveillance, these 'old' penological methods contribute to a curfew on freedom of movement in the city; of who can move where, when and how within a locality (Coleman *et al.* 2002). Sovereign control in the city maintains coercive aspects of rule as a central means to territorial control and social ordering (Stenson 1999: Coleman 2003a).[5]

It seems all the more difficult to 'humanise' surveillance practices when the nature of neoliberal rule is so obscure to the public eye and lines of accountability so blurred. In the era of the 'entrepreneurial city', which has reproduced and marketed a reinvigorated 'local elite', this observation is particularly relevant. The mushroom growth of partnerships aimed towards governing a range of local problems has highlighted the issue of locating 'the powerful' within often dense and informal alliances that are relatively closed off from public access and scrutiny. The democratic deficit within urban rule generally, and with CCTV in particular, is high, where millions are spent on glossy marketing and legitimation strategies that appeal to inclusive ideals of 'the city' or 'the people', united by a circumscribed notion of 'civic pride' and 'civic duty'.

Rethinking 'crime prevention' in the city

This book has not been led by a policy-orientated agenda nor has it been concerned with trying to find improvements in, and legitimate yet more funding of, street camera surveillance. In other words, the questions posed and formulated in the book have been constructed outside 'statist political imaginary' which has 'assisted the state in setting limits on theoretical imagination' (Neocleous 2003: 6). Furthermore, the book has explored aspects of this state imaginary and how this has inter-related with, and given meaning to, the trajectory of social control. Scrutinising the powerful, and opening up for examination 'their' visions, anxieties and meanings attributed to city space, has implicitly questioned the value of a criminology that increasingly neglects an analysis of the dynamic processes implicated in the transformation of city spaces that is occurring in accordance with a particular citified vision. With crimi-nology and criminologists increasingly pressured into accepting 'evidence-led policy' political rhetoric and its associated lavish funding regimes based in the Home Office in the UK (see Tombs and Whyte 2003: 26–8), the state has been able to close off wider theoretical research questions with a narrow re-emphasis on 'crime reduction'. In the context of over £250,000,000 of public money having been spent on CCTV between 1992 and 2002 and, at best, 'mixed' results as to its crime reduction status (McCahill and Norris 2002: 2), criminologists would do well to ask wider questions and to explore the kind of social relations and state institutions camera surveillance is reflecting and reinforcing. A consequence of being dominated by state agendas – whether couched in terms of 'regeneration' or 'crime reduction' – is that the state itself disappears off the radar of critical intellectual scrutiny. This 'disappearance' has been evident in both the meta-theorising of the 'post-' schools of thought reviewed earlier in the book (and which have mirrored the neoliberal state's own imagery) and within the empirical-administrative streams, or post-theoretical works. Criminology is weakened as an intellectual and social force for change if it cannot look into and unmask the workings and contours of state power (see the contributions in Tombs and Whyte (2003) for a contemporary excavation of these forces). In standing outside the state terrain on questions of camera surveillance and scrutinising the political and ideological motivation for surveillance of the streets, the book has presented a challenge to the 'surveillance society'. This has been done in a manner that has – at the very least – questioned the powerful development of neoliberal mentalities in constructing state power and technologies of control. Far from taking state definitions of 'the problem of crime' for granted, the book has argued instead for understanding how a 'neoliberal order' sets the context through which 'risk' categories, that include 'crime', are generated by normative and moral visions for sociospatial order. Accepting state-generated risk categories as given will not advance our understanding of *why* and under *what circumstances* behaviours and groups are singled out for attention and other harmful activities go relatively unnoticed. Thus while this book lays no claim to be policy relevant, it does make a claim for a critical understanding of 'crime prevention' projects in city centres by scrutinising the state discourses and practices that underpin them. Criminologists need to think beyond the official discourse of 'crime prevention' and see how practices subsumed under this label play a role in the symbolic and material organisation of space and how these spaces are constructed through 'crime prevention' in a manner that reveals as much as conceals their political constitution. Although this book has not dealt with resistance to the kind of cityscapes described in these pages (see Ferrell 2001) its impetus has come from a concern to re-institute the state back into criminological theorising and thinking about social control and sociospatial ordering in urban centres.

In contrast to the totalising impetus of much of the governmentality literature, this book has developed a case study to look at the politics of social ordering and the powerful agents and agencies involved. From this it has been demonstrated how visions for order neither have their roots in some generalised and decontextualised notion of 'panoptic power' nor do they exemplify some notion of 'action at a distance' – metaphorical or real (Rose 1996: 43). Instead, the vision for urban order described here has a material quality and is a highly interventionist, tendentious and political vision of social control that seeks to deny, partly through mystification but equally through coercion, the less equitable consequences of neoliberal rule. As a guarantor of the freedoms that the citizen-worker-socialite enjoys, street cameras attempt to filter out and re-represent the meanings of social inequality and social justice. Furthermore, it simply cannot be imagined in a neoliberal landscape that a CCTV-inspired narrative could appear as a press story and sympathetically relay 'a day in the life of an ordinary homeless person', a day of being threatened by local businesses, and of verbal and physical abuse from public and private police – not to mention coping with the weather. The newspaper narrative that began this chapter clarifies the position that the protection of the truly vulnerable is not the job of a contemporary urban surveillance camera. Nor indeed has public space been 'imagined' in the local media from the point of view of the potential dangers for women as they move through 'public' and 'private' space. Nobody interviewed in this study identified or addressed the safety of women as an issue in the city. The same disregard was in evidence on the subject of forms of racial violence in the city. As this book argues, the imagery of the 'friendly eye in the sky' is *construed ideologically* as 'friendly' to some beneath its gaze more than others. In building 'safer cities' for corporate growth, the poor in particular, if visible at all, have become irresponsibilised eyesores whose stake in the new-fangled neoliberal channels of citizenship and political representation is being eroded (Harvey 2001; Centre for Public Services 2002).

The main conclusions discussed here are not to be taken as a definitive excavation of neoliberalism and street camera surveillance in practice. This book raises further questions for future research. The strategies for ordering city space should not be assumed as translating smoothly into practice and creating an ideal utopia of the ever-controlling or punitive city. The study of the locally powerful presented here does not preclude – indeed it logically points to urgency of – a complementary study of the experiences of those targeted by urban surveillance networks. In this book the voices of the homeless, young people (and particularly young black people) and street traders, as subjects of a powerful and detrimental labelling process, have been left silent. Their perception of 'city life' and the world of meaning they hold represent an untapped reservoir of knowledge that, if studied, could yield a fuller and more enriched understanding of the processes described in this book, namely: the unfolding of entrepreneurial forms of rule and their impact upon 'the urban experience' of the relatively powerless. This would not preclude an analysis of the role of risk taking and other 'attractions' for those involved in the transgression of normative and/or legal orders (Hayward 2002).

More broadly, the hegemony of neoliberal rule cannot be taken as given and will therefore be incomplete and open to contestation. Thus, conflicts which arise alongside local state projects which clash with identified transgressors, local public and grassroots organisations need to be researched, particularly as these state projects often assume rather than demonstrate local community support and participation in relation to such projects. Research into the meaning and practice of contemporary local democracy – including processes of communal exclusion and oppositional appropriation by locally powerful networks – would itself further enhance our appreciation of the trajectory of neoliberal rule. Taken together, these are important issues that have been marginalised in both criminological and geographical literature and need to be incorporated into a wider understanding of neoliberal cities. These kinds of questions can aid understanding between different urban locations in order to explore similarities and differences of practice and experience regarding the social ordering strategies that partnerships seek to develop (Edwards and Hughes 2002; Stenson 2002) and how entrepreneurial or neoliberal rule operates more generally (Hall and Hubbard 1996; Peck 2003). These wider questions traverse the thorny issue of the tensions between theoretical generalisation and empirical findings from particular politico-cultural locations. The political economy of city building and the practice and uses of surveillance, as described in this book, have a complex inter-relationship that nontheless reinforce particular patterns of social ordering in the city that are not confined to 'the local'.

It is the very complexity, at times obscure nature, of neoliberal statecraft that confounds researchers. But understanding this state form is important if we are to deconstruct the kinds of social ordering strategies that are being developed and confront processes of exclusion and disempowerment that run conterminous with the surveilled city. Policies are increasingly being constructed that encourage social hostility that feeds social fracture and drives a new morality of folk-devil politics. The wider challenge lies in grasping and responding to the wider authoritarian tendencies in the neoliberal state as it skews public accountability and scrutiny under a veil of self-congratulatory promotionalism and newspeak. Identifying and unmasking these state forms will aid the challenge to a surveilled and unjust urban space. It will also render visible the processual nature of criminalisation that is fostering a class of contemporary urban outsiders, defined by their incompatibility with the hegemony of vision presently shaping the cityscape. Questioning the value of neoliberal forms of rule also means questioning the efficacy of mass camera surveillance in a way that will undermine its official status as a credible 'answer' to the continuing inequities and social divisions that are at present intensifying under the neoliberal agenda itself.

Notes

1 Jeff Ferrell documents how the 'anarchic' inhabitants of the neoliberal city, such as street musicians, skateboarders, graffiti artists and other underground groups, are at the forefront of battles to 'retake occupied territory, to construct an open city, to reassemble public space and public community as something more, and less, than death camp Disneyland' (2001: 246).

2 See Coleman *et al.* (2002) for a discussion of harmful corporate activities in and around Liverpool and ignored in mainstream 'community safety' discourses. According to Friends of the Earth it is the poorest communities around Liverpool that are bearing the brunt of pollution from the vast petro-chemical complex in the Runcorn basin (*Liverpool Echo*, 17 April 2001: 'Pollution hits region's poor').

3   We live, as Mathiesen (1997) argues, in a 'viewer society', where through the
    mass media, the 'many can see the few'. In the case of popular crime shows,
    where the images of the street contextualise 'the action' – or to paraphrase
    Michael Moore in *Bowling for Columbine* – 'the powerful white guy chases the
    powerless black guy', the synoptic principle works by 'disciplining
    consciousness' through info-tainment in a manner that legitimates the
    definitions of crime and danger most congruent with the worldviews of the
    powerful.

4   The language of difference lies at the heart of current attempts to re-image
    cities. As a trend in official discourse, 'diversity' plays an ideological role at
    the centre of a politics of growth and 'quality of life' vernacular, as
    exemplified in Liverpool's slogan for its current Capital of Culture status –
    'The World in One City'. This is not to say that such ideas must be discounted
    out of hand, rather they should be approached critically and seen as part of a
    wider politics of legitimation that contextualise the possibilities and
    limitations of the ideas of 'participation' and 'democracy' in neoliberal cities.

5   As argued elsewhere, 'modern penal severity' has been, and continues to be,
    central to 'modern states' development'. Furthermore, 'as tools of
    governance … measures of repression, containment, reclamation or
    exclusion reappear in remarkably similar forms, remarkably intact in both
    justification and procedure, when social and political change creates a space
    for their application' (Brown 2002: 32).

Appendix

Interviewees

Interviewees identified by occupational title and/or institution

Chairman, Crime Alert
Chairman, Merseyside Development Corporation
Chairman, Stores' Committee
City centre crime prevention officer, Merseyside Police
City Centre Manager, Liverpool City Centre Partnership (LCCP)
Home Office Adviser, Government Office for Merseyside (GOM)
Liverpool City Council, Economic Development Officer
Marketing Director, Mersey Partnership
Private developer 1, affiliated to LCCP
Private developer 2, affiliated to LCCP
Regeneration Co-ordinator, Liverpool City Council
Representative of LCCP
Representative 1 of Stores' Committee
Representative 2 of Stores' Committee
Security Manager 1, Crime Alert
Security Manager 2, Crime Alert
Security Manager 3, Crime Alert
Security Manager, Mersey Travel Rapid Response Unit
Security Manager, non-member of Crime Alert
Superintendent, Merseyside Police, GOM

Total of twenty

References

Adams, J. (1995) *Risk*. London: UCL Press.

Arber, S. (1993) 'Designing samples', in N. Gilbert (ed.) *Researching Social Life*. London: Sage, 68–92.

Arksey, H. and Knight, P. (1999) *Interviewing for Social Scientists: An Introductory Resource with Examples*. London: Sage.

Atkinson, R. (1999) 'Discourses of partnership and empowerment in contemporary British urban regeneration', *Urban Studies*, 36 (1): 59–72.

Audit Commission (1999) *Safety in Numbers: Promoting Community Safety National Report*. Audit Commission for Local Authorities.

Bannister, J., Fyfe, N.R. and Kearns, A. (1998) 'Closed circuit television and the city' in C. Norris, *et al.* (eds) *Surveillance, Closed Circuit Television and Social Control*. Aldershot: Ashgate, 21–39.

Barry, A. (1996) 'Lines of communication and spaces of rule', in A. Barry, *et al.* (eds) *Foucault and Political Reason: Liberalism, Neo-liberalism and Rationalities of Government*. London: UCL Press,123–42.

Barry, A., Osbourne, T. and Rose, N. (eds) (1996) *Foucault and Political Reason: Liberalism, Neo-liberalism and Rationalities of Government*. London: UCL Press.

Bassett, K. (1996) 'Partnerships, business elites and urban politics: new forms of governance in an English city?,' *Urban Studies*, 33 (3): 539–55.

Beck, A. and Willis, A. (1995) *Crime and Insecurity: Managing the Risk to Safe Shopping*. Leicester: Perpetuity Press.

Becker, H.S. (1963) *Outsiders: Studies in the Sociology of Deviance*. New York, NY: Free Press.

Belcham, J. (1992) 'Introduction: the peculiarities of Liverpool', in J. Belcham (ed.) *Popular Politics, Riot and Labour: Essays in Liverpool History, 1790–1940*. Liverpool: Liverpool University Press.

Bell, C. (1978) 'Studying the locally powerful: personal reflections on a research career', in C. Bell and S. Enal (eds) *Inside the Whale*. Oxford: Pergaman Press.

Bianchini, F. (1990) 'The crisis of urban public social life in Britain: origins of the problem and possible responses', *Planning, Policy and Research*, 5 (3): 4–8.

Bourdieu, P. and Wacquant, L. (2001) 'NewLiberalSpeak: notes on the New Planetary Vulgate', in *Radical Philosophy: A Journal of Socialist and Feminist Philosophy*, 105 (January/February): 2–5.

Brenner, T. and Theodore, N. (2002) 'Cities and geographies of "actually existing neoliberalism"', *Antipode*, 24 (3): 349–79.

British Security Industry Association (1997) *Security Direct: The Official Annual Directory of the British Security Industry Association*. Suffolk: Hour Glass Publishing.

Brogden, M. (1982) *The Police: Autonomy and Consent*. London: Academic Press.

Brogden, M. (1991) *On the Mersey Beat: Policing Liverpool between the Wars*. New York, NY: Oxford University Press.

Brown, B. (1995) *CCTV in Town Centres: Three Case Studies. Police Research Group Paper 68*. London: Home Office.

Brown, M. (2002) 'The politics of penal excess and the echo of colonial penality.' Paper presented to European Group for the Study of Deviance and Social Control, England, April.

Brown, S. (1998) 'What's the problem girls? CCTV and the gendering of public safety', in C. Norris *et al*. (eds) *Surveillance, Closed Circuit Television and Social Control*. Aldershot: Ashgate, 201–20.

Bryman, A. (1988) 'Introduction: "inside" accounts and social research in organisations', in A. Bryman (ed.) *Doing Social Research in Organisations*. London: Routledge, 1–20.

Bryman, A. (2002) 'The Disneyfication of society', in G. Ritzer (ed.) *McDonaldization: The Reader*. London: Sage, 52–9.

Centre for Public Services (2002) *Our City is Not for Sale: The Impact of National, European and Global Policies*. Newcastle upon-Tyne: Newcastle City Council Trade Unions.

Chartered Institute of Public Finance and Accountancy (1999) *Council Tax Demands and Precepts 1998/1999*. London: Institute of Public Finance.

Christopherson, S. (1994) 'The fortress city: privatised spaces, consumer citizenship', in A. Amin (ed.) *Post-Fordism: A Reader*. Oxford: Blackwell, 409–27.

Citysafe (1998) *Crime and Disorder Audit for Liverpool 1998*. Liverpool: Liverpool Community Safety Partnership.

Citysafe (2000) *CCTV in Liverpool: Briefing Paper*. Liverpool: Liverpool Community Safety Partnership.

Clarke, J. and Newman, J. (1997) *The Managerial State: Power, Politics and Ideology in the Remaking of Social Welfare*. London: Sage.

Cochrane, A. (1993) *Whatever Happened to Local Government?* Buckingham: Open University Press.

Cockburn, C. (1977) *The Local State: Management of Cities and People*. London: Pluto Press.

Cockcroft, W.R. (1991) *From Cutlasses to Computers: The Police Force in Liverpool, 1836–1989*. Shropshire: S.B. Publications.

Cohen, S. (1972) *Folk Devils and Moral Panics: The Creation of the Mods and Rockers*. London: MacGibbon & Kee.

Cohen, S. (1979) ' "The punitive city": notes on the dispersal of social control', *Contemporary Crisis*, 3 (4): 339–63.

Cohen, S. (1983) 'Social-control talk: telling stories about correctional change', in D. Garland, and P. Young (eds) *The Power to Punish: Contemporary Penality and Social Analysis*. London: Heinemann Educational Books, 101–29.

Cohen, S. (1985) *Visions of Social Control*. Cambridge: Polity Press.

Cohen, S. (1987) 'Taking decentralization seriously: values, visions and policies', in J. Lowman *et al.* (eds) *Transcarceration: Essays in the Sociology of Social Control*. Aldershot: Gower, 358–79.

Coleman, R. (2003a) 'Images from a neoliberal city: the state, surveillance and social control', *Critical Criminology: An International Journal*, 12 (1): 21–42.

Coleman, R. (2003b) 'CCTV surveillance, power and social order: the state of contemporary social control', in S. Tombs and D. Whyte (eds) *Unmasking the Crimes of the Powerful: Scrutinising States and Corporations*. New York, NY: Peter Lang, 88–104.

Coleman, R. (2004) 'Watching the degenerate: street camera surveillance and regeneration', *Local Economy* 19(3), 199–211.

Coleman, R. and Sim, J. (1998) 'From the dockyards to the Disney store: risk, surveillance and security in Liverpool city centre', *International Review of Law, Computers and Technology*, 12 (1): 27–45.

Coleman, R. and Sim, J. (2000) ' "You'll never walk alone": CCTV surveillance, order and neo-liberal rule in Liverpool city centre', *British Journal of Sociology*, 51 (4): 623–39.

Coleman, R., Sim, J. and Whyte, D. (2002) 'Power, politics and partnerships: the state of crime prevention on Merseyside', in A. Edwards and G. Hughes (eds) *Crime Control and Community: The New Politics of Public Safety*. Cullompton: Willan Publishing, 86–108.

Collinge, C. and Hall, S. (1997) 'Hegemony and regime in urban governance: towards a theory of the locally networked state', in N. Jewson and S. MacGregor (eds) *Transforming Cities: Contested Governance and New Spatial Divisions*. London: Routedge, 129–40.

Collins, N. (1994) *Politics and Elections in Nineteenth Century Liverpool*. Scolar Press.

Cotterrell, R. (1984) *The Sociology of Law: An Introduction*. London: Butterworths.

Crawford, A. (1997) *The Local Governance of Crime: Appeals to Community and Partnership*. Oxford: Clarendon Press.

Crewe, I. (1974) 'Introduction: studying elites in Britain', in I. Crewe (ed.) *Elites in Western Democracy*. London: Croom Helm, 9–52.

Crime Concern (1989) *Report on the Feasibility of CCTV in Liverpool City Centre*. Crime Concern.

Crowther, C. (2000) 'Thinking about the "underclass": towards a political economy of policing', *Theoretical Criminology*, 4 (2): 149–67.

Currie, E. (1997) 'The scalpel, not the chainsaw', *City*, 8 (December): 132–7.

Curtis, B. (1995) 'Taking the state back out: Rose and Miller on political power', *British Journal of Sociology*, 46 (4): 575–89.

Davies, S. (1996a) 'The case against: CCTV should not be introduced', *International Journal of Risk, Security and Crime Prevention*, 4 (1): 315–31.

Davies, S. (1996b) *Big Brother: Britain's Web of Surveillance and the New Technological Order*. London: Pan Books.

Davis, M. (1990) *City of Quartz: Excavating the Future in Los Angeles*. London: Verso.

Deakin, N. and Edwards, J. (1993) *The Enterprise Culture and the Inner City*. London: Routledge.

Defert, D. (1991) '"Popular life" and insurance technology', in G. Burchill *et al.* (eds) *The Foucault Effect: Studies in Governmentality*. London: Harvester Wheatsheaf, 211–50.

Department of Environment, Transport and the Regions (2000) *Local Strategic Partnerships: Consultation Document, October 2000*. London: Department of Environment, Transport and the Regions.

De Sousa Santos, B. (1992) 'State law and community in the world system: an introduction', *Social and Legal Studies*, 1 (2): 131–42.

Ditton, J. (1998) 'Public support for town centre CCTV schemes: myth or reality?', in C. Norris *et al.* (eds) *Surveillance, Closed Circuit Television and Social Control*. Aldershot: Ashgate, 221-8.

Dobbie, M. (2000) 'Exclusion orders in operation here …' *Communicate*, 8 (August): 24–7.

Donnison, D. and Soto, P. (1980) *The Good City: A Study of Urban Development and Policy in Britain*. London: Heinenmann.

Douglas, M. (1992) *Risk and Blame: Essays in Cultural Theory*. London: Routledge.

Edgar, D. (1985) 'Why aid came alive', *Marxism Today*, September: 26–30.

Edwards, A. and Hughes, G. (2002) 'Introduction: the community governance of crime control', in G. Hughes and A. Edwards (eds) *Crime Control and Community: The New Politics of Public Safety*. Collumpton: Willan Publishing, 1–19.

Edwards, J. (1997) 'Urban policy: the victory of form over substance', *Urban Studies*, 34 (5–6): 825–43.

Eisenschitz, A. and Gough, J. (1998) 'Theorising the state in local economic governance', *Regional Studies*, 32 (8): 759–68.

Elliot, L. (1996) 'Labour's mean streets', *Guardian*, 4 June.

Ericson, R. (1994) 'The division of expert knowledge in policing and security', *British Journal of Sociology*, 45 (2), June: 149–75.

Ericson, R., Baranek, P. and Chan, J. (1991) *Representing Order*. Buckingham: Open University Press.

Ewald, F. (1991) 'Insurance and risk', in G. Burchell *et al.* (eds) *The Foucault Effect: Studies in Governmentality*. London: Harvester Wheatsheaf, 197–210.

Fairclough, N. (2000) *New Labour, New Language?* London: Karia Press.

Fay, S.J. (1998) 'Tough on crime, tough on civil liberties: some negative sspects of Britain's wholesale adoption of CCTV surveillance during the 1990s', *International Review of Law, Computers and Technology*, 12 (2): 239–71.

Feeley, M. and Simon, J. (1992) 'The new penology: notes on the emerging strategy of corrections and its implications', in *Criminology*, 30 (4): 449–74.

Feeley, M. and Simon, J. (1994) 'Actuarial justice: the emerging criminal law', in D. Nelken, (ed.) *The Futures of Criminology*. London: Sage, 173–201.

Ferrell, J. (2001) *Tearing down the Streets: Adventures in Urban Anarchy*. New York, NY: Palgrave.

Fiske, J. (1993) *Power Plays, Power Works*. London: Verso.

Flusty, S. (2001) 'The banality of interdiction: surveillance and control and the displacement of diversity', *International Journal of Urban and Regional Research*, 25 (3): 658–64.

Foucault, M. (1977) *Discipline and Punish*. London: Allen Lane.

Foucault, M. (1984) 'The judicial apparatus' in W. Connolly (ed.) *Legitimacy and the State*. Oxford: Blackwell, 201–21.

Foucault, M. (1985) 'Truth, power and sexuality', in V. Beechey and J. Donald (eds) *Subjectivity and Social Relations*. Milton Keynes: Open University Press, 89–96.

Foucault, M. (1991) 'Governmentality', in G. Burchell *et al.* (eds) *The Foucault Effect: Studies in Governmentality*. London: Harvester Wheatsheaf, 87–104.

Frankel, B. (1987) *The Post-industrial Utopias*. London: Polity Press.

Fryer, P. (1984) *Staying Power: The History of Black People in Britain*. London: Pluto Press.

Furbey, R. (1999) 'Urban "regeneration": reflections on a metaphor', *Critical Social Policy*, 14 (4): 419–45.

Fyfe, N.R. (1995) 'Crime, space and society: key research themes, findings and questions in the 1990s', *Scottish Geographical Magazine*, 111 (3): 182–4.

Fyfe, N.R. and Bannister, J. (1996) 'City watching: CCTV surveillance in public spaces', *Area*, 28 (1): 37–46.

Gamble, A. (1988) *The Free Economy and the Strong State*. London: Macmillan.

Garland, D. (1990) *Punishment and Modern Society: A Study in Social Theory*. Oxford: Clarendon Press.

Garland, D. (1996) 'The limits of the sovereign state: strategies of crime control in contemporary society', *British Journal of Criminology*, 36 (4): 445–71.

Garland, D. (2000) 'The culture of high crime societies: some preconditions of recent law and order policies', *British Journal of Criminology*, 40: 347–75.

Garland, D. (2001) *The Culture of Control: Crime and Social Order in Contemporary Societies*. Oxford: Oxford University Press.

Garland, D. and Young, P. (1983) 'Towards a social analysis of penality', in D. Garland and P. Young (eds) *The Power to Punish: Contemporary Penality and Social Analysis*. London: Heinemann, 1–36.

Gifford, Lord, Brown, W. and Bundey, R. (1989) *Loosen the Shackles: The First Report of the Liverpool 8 Inquiry into Race Relations in Liverpool*. London: Karia Press.

Goffman, E. (1961) *Asylums: Essays on the Social Situation of Mental Patients and other Inmates*. Harmondsworth: Penguin Books.

Gold, J.R. and Revill, G. (2003) 'Exploring landscapes of fear: marginality, spectacle and surveillance', *Capital and Class*, 80 (Summer): 27–50.

Gold, R.L. (1969) 'Roles in sociological field observations', in G.J. McCall and J.L. Simmons (eds) *Issues in Participant Observation: A Text and Reader*. Reading, MA: Addison-Wesley, 30–9.

Gordon, G. (1991) 'Governmental rationality: an introduction', in G. Burchell *et al.* (eds) *The Foucault Effect: Studies in Governmentality*. London: Harvester Wheatsheaf, 1–51.

Gordon, P. (1987) 'Community policing: towards the local police state?', in P. Scraton (ed.) *Law, Order and the Authoritarian State*. Milton Keynes: Open University Press, 121–44.

Goss, J. (1993) 'The "magic of the mall": an analysis of form, function, and meaning in the contemporary retail built environment', *Annals of the Association of American Geographers*, 83 (1): 18–47.

Goss, J. (1996) 'Disquiet on the waterfront: reflections on nostalgia and utopia in the urban archetypes of festival market places', *Urban Geography*, 17 (3): 221–47.

Graham, S. (1998) 'Towards the fifth utility? On the extension and normalisation of CCTV', in C. Norris *et al.* (eds) *Surveillance, Closed Circuit Television and Social Control*. Aldershot: Ashgate, 89–112.

Graham, S. (2000) 'The fifth utility', *Index on Censorship*, 29 (3): 194.

Gramsci, A. (1971) *Selections from the Prison Notebooks*. London: Lawrence & Wishart.

Groombridge, N. and Murji, K. (1994) 'As easy as AB and CCTV?', *Policing*, 10 (4): 283–90.

Gusfield, J.R. (1963) *Symbolic Crusade: Status Politics and the American Temperance Movement*. Urbana, IL: University of Illinois Press.

Halcomb, B. (1993) 'Revisioning place: de- and re-constructing the image of the industrial city' in G. Kearns and C. Philo (eds) *Selling Places: The City as Cultural Capital, Past and Present*. Oxford: Pergamon Press, 133–43.

Hall, S. (1988) *The Hard Road to Renewal: Thatcherism and the Crisis of the Left*. London: Verso.

Hall, S., Critcher, C., Jefferson, C., Clarke, J. and Roberts, B. (1978) *Policing the Crisis: Mugging, the State and Law and Order*. London: Macmillan.

Hall, S. and Scraton, P. (1981) 'Law, class and control', in M. Fitzgerald *et al.* (eds) *Crime and Society: Readings in History and Theory*. London: Routledge & Kegan Paul.

Hall, T. and Hubbard, P. (1996) 'The entrepreneurial city: new urban politics, new urban geographies', *Progress in Human Geography*, 20 (2): 153–74.

Hall, T. and Hubbard, P. (1998) 'Afterword: mappings of the entrepreneurial city', in T. Hall and P. Hubbard (eds) *The Entrepreneurial City: Geographies of Politics, Regime and Representation*. Chichester: Wiley, 309–19.

Harding, A. and Garside, P. (1995) 'Urban and economic development' in J. Stewart and G. Stoker (eds) *Local Government in the 1990s*. London: Macmillan, 166–87.

Harvey, D. (1985) *The Urbanisation of Capital*. Oxford: Blackwell.

Harvey, D. (1988) *The Urban Experience*. Oxford: Blackwell.

Harvey, D. (1990) *The Condition of Postmodernity: An Inquiry into the Origins of Cultural Change*. Oxford: Blackwell.

Harvey, D. (1992) 'Social justice, postmodernism and the city', *International Journal of Urban and Regional Research*, 16 (4): 588–601.

Harvey, D. (2001) *Spaces of Hope*. Edinburgh: Edinburgh University Press.

Harvey, L. (1990) *Critical Social Research*. London: Unwin Hyman.

Hay, C. (1996) *Re-stating Social and Political Change*. Buckingham: Open University Press.

Hayward, K. (2002) 'The vilification and pleasures of youthful transgression', in J. Muncie *et al.* (eds.) *Youth Justice: Critical Readings*. London: Sage, 80–93.

Home Office (1991) *Safer Cities: Progress Report, 1990–1991*. London: Home Office Crime Prevention Unit.

Home Office (1994) *CCTV: Looking Out For You*. London: Home Office.

Home Office (1995) *CCTV Challenge Competition*. London: Home Office.

Home Office (1996) *Crime Prevention News*. London: Home Office (April–June).

Home Office (1998) *Guidance on Statutory Crime and Disorder Partnerships: Crime Disorder Act 1998*. London: Home Office.

Home Office (1999) '£170 million package for CCTV and estate regeneration'. Press release, 16 March.

Home Office (2003) 'Begging becomes a recordable offence' (http://www.homeoffice.gov.uk/n_story.asp?item_id=699).

Hough, M., Clarke, R.V.G. and Mayhew, P. (1980) 'Introduction', in R.V.G. Clarke and P. Mayhew (eds) *Designing out Crime*. London: HMSO.

Howell, S.L. (1994) 'A theoretical model for caring for women with chronic non-malignant pain', *Qualitative Health Research*, 4 (1): 94–122.

Hubbard, P. (1996) 'Urban design and city regeneration: social representations of entrepreneurial landscapes', *Urban Studies*, 33: 1441–61.

Hudson, B. (1996) *Understanding Justice: An Introduction to Ideas, Perspectives and Controversies in Modern Penal Theory*. Buckingham: Open University Press.

Hudson, B. (1997) 'Social control', in M. Maguire *et al.* (eds) *The Oxford Handbook of Criminology* (2nd edn). Oxford: Clarendon Press 451–72.

Hughes, G. (1996) 'The politics of criminological research', in R. Sapsford (ed.) *Researching Crime and Criminal Justice*. Milton Keynes: Open University Press, 58–89.

Hughes, G. (1998) *Understanding Crime Prevention: Social Control, Risk and Late Modernity*. Buckingham: Open University Press.

Humphries, J. and McDonald, R. (1995) *Morphocity: Architectural Odyssey.* Liverpool: Centre for Architecture, Liverpool John Moores University.

Hunt, A. (1996) 'Governing the city: liberalism and early modern modes of governance', in A. Barry *et al.* (eds) *Foucault and Political Reason, Liberalism, Neo-liberalism and Rationalities of Government'*. London: UCL Press, 167–88.

Hunt, A. and Wickham, G. (1994) *Foucault and Law: Towards a Sociology of Law as Governance.* London: Pluto Press.

Hunter, I. (1996) 'Assembling the school', in A. Barry *et al.* (eds) *Foucault and Political Reason, Liberalism, Neo-liberalism and Rationalities of Government.* London: UCL Press, 143–66.

Industry North West (2003) 'The Liverpool "boom" is doomed without private sector business', 2(3) March (www.industrynorthwest.co.uk/back/ v2i3march2003/steve brauner.htm).

Indymedia (2003) 'The Duke and chums turn the screws on the working class' (www.indymedia.org.uk/en/regions/liverpool/20/03/12/282695.html).

Innes, M. (2003) *Understanding Social Control: Deviance, Crime and Social Order.* Maidenhead: Open University Press.

Ivison, D. (1998) 'The technical and the political: discourses of race, reasons of state', *Social and Legal Studies*, 7 (4): 561–6.

Jessop, B. (1990) *State Theory.* Cambridge: Polity Press.

Jessop, B. (1997) 'The entrepreneurial city: re-imaging localities, redesigning economic governance, or restructuring capital?', in N. Jewson and S. MacGregor (eds) *Transforming Cities: Contested Governance and New Spatial Divisions.* London: Routledge, 28–41.

Johnson, L. (1992) *The Rebirth of Private Policing.* London: Routledge.

Judd, D. and Parkinson, M. (1990) 'Urban leadership and regeneration', in D. Judd and M. Parkinson (eds) *Leadership and Urban Regeneration: Cities in North America and Europe.* London: Sage, 13–30.

Jupp, V. (1989) *Methods of Criminological Research.* London: Allen & Unwin.

Katz, C. (2001) 'Hiding the target: social reproduction in the privatised urban environment', in C. Minca (ed.) *Postmodern Geography: Theory and Praxis.* Oxford: Blackwell, 93–110.

Kettle, M. and Hodges, L. (1982) *Uprising: The Police, the People and Riots in British Cities.* London: Pan Books.

Kinsey, R. (1985) *Merseyside Crime and Police Surveys: Final Report.* Liverpool: Merseyside County Council.

Klein, N. (2000) *No Logo.* London: Flamingo.

Koskela, H. (2003) '"Cam era" – the contemporary urban panopticon', *Surveillance and Society*, 1 (3): 292–313 (http://www.surveillance-and-society.org).

Lacey, N. (1994) 'Introduction: making sense of criminal justice', in N. Lacey (ed.) *A Reader in Criminal Justice.* Oxford: Oxford University Press.

Lacombe, D. (1996) 'Reforming Foucault: a critique of the social control thesis' in *British Journal of Sociology*, 47 (2): 332–52.

Lane, T. (1987) *Liverpool: Gateway of Empire*. London: Laurence & Wishart.

Latham, R. (2000) 'Social sovereignty', *Theory, Culture and Society*, 17 (4): 1–18.

Lea, J. and Young, J. (1984) *What is to be Done about Law and Order?* Harmondsworth: Penguin Books.

Lemert, E.M. (1967) *Human Deviance, Social Problems and Social Control*. Englewood Cliffs, NJ: Prentice Hall.

Ling, T. (1998) *The British State since 1945: An Introduction*. Cambridge: Polity Press.

Liverpool City Centre Partnership (1994) *CCTV in Liverpool City Centre: A Partnership Approach to a Safer City*. Liverpool: Liverpool City Centre Partnership.

Liverpool City Centre Partnership (1995) *Public and Private Sectors: Working Together for a Better City Centre*. Liverpool: Liverpool City Centre Partnership.

Liverpool City Council (1987) *Liverpool City Centre: Strategy Review*. Liverpool: Liverpool City Council.

Liverpool City Council (1993) *Liverpool City Centre Plan*. Liverpool: Liverpool City Council, Planning and Development Services.

Liverpool City Council (1994) *Operators Handbook: Incorporating the Code of Practice*. Liverpool: Liverpool City Council.

Liverpool City Council (1996) *Report to the Joint Homeless and Supported Housing Sub-Committee*. Liverpool: Liverpool City Council.

Liverpool City Council (1997a) *Ambitions for the City Centre: Liverpool's Draft City Centre Strategy for the Next Five Years*. Liverpool: City of Liverpool Planning and Transportation Service.

Liverpool City Council (1997b): *Action Plan – Regeneration Agenda for Liverpool: To Develop a Safer City*. Liverpool: Liverpool City Council, Officer Partnership Group.

Liverpool City Council (2000) *Gold Zone*. Liverpool: Liverpool City Council, Communication Department, March.

Liverpool City Council (2001) *Liverpool City*, 11. Liverpool: Liverpool City Council.

Liverpool Stores' Committee (1992) *Mission Statement*. Liverpool: Stores' Committee.

Loader, I. (1997) 'Policing and the social: questions of symbolic power', *British Journal of Sociology*, 48 (1): 1–18.

Logan, J.R. and Molotch, H.L. (1987) *Urban Fortunes: The Political Economy of Place*. Berkeley, CA: University of California Press.

Loveday, B. (1999) 'Tough on crime or tough on the causes of crime: an evaluation of New Labour's crime and disorder legislation', *Crime Prevention and Community Safety: An International Journal*, 1 (2): 7–24.

Lovering, J. (1997) 'Global restructuring and local impact', in M. Pacione (ed.) *Britain's Cities: Geographies of Division in Urban Britain*. London: Routledge, 63–87.

Lyon, D. (2001) *Surveillance Society: Monitoring Everyday Life*. Buckingham: Open University Press.

Lyon, D. (2003) 'Surveillance as social sorting: computer codes and mobile bodies', in D. Lyon (ed.) *Surveillance as Social Sorting: Privacy, Risk and Digital Discrimination*. London: Routledge, 13–30.

MacLeod, G. (2002) 'From urban entrepreneurialism to a "revanchist city": on the spatial injustices of Glasgow's renaissance', *Antipode*, 34 (2): 602–24.

MacLeod, G. and Goodwin, M. (1999a) 'Space, scale and state strategy: rethinking urban and regional governance', *Progress in Human Geography*, 23 (4): 503–27.

MacLeod, G. and Goodwin, M. (1999b) 'Restructuring an urban and regional political economy: on the state, politics, scale and explanation', *Political Geography*, 18: 697–731.

Madsen, H. (1992) 'Place-marketing in Liverpool: a review', *International Journal of Regional and Urban Research*, 16 (4): 633–40.

Maguire, M. (1998) 'Restraining big brother? The regulation of surveillance in England and Wales', in C. Norris *et al.* (eds.) *Surveillance, Closed Circuit Television and Social Control*. Aldershot: Ashgate, 229–40.

Malik, K. (1996) *The Meaning of Race: Race, History and Culture in Western Society*. London: Macmillan.

Marriner, S. (1982) *The Economic and Social Development of Merseyside*. London: Croom Helm.

Marriott, J. (1999) 'In darkest England: the poor, the crowd and race in the nineteenth century metropolis', in P. Cohen (ed.) *New Ethnicities, Old Racisms*. London: Zed Books, 82–100.

Massey, D. (1999) 'On space and the city', in D. Massey *et al.* (eds) *City Worlds*. London: Routledge, 157–77.

Mathiesen, T. (1997) 'The viewer society: Michael Foucault's panopticon revisited', *Theoretical Criminology*, 1 (2): 215–34.

McCahill, M. (1998) 'Beyond Foucault: towards a contemporary theory of surveillance', in C. Norris *et al.* (eds) *Surveillance, Closed Circuit Television and Social Control*. Aldershot: Ashgate, 41–65.

McCahill, M. and Norris, C. (2002) 'CCTV in Britain', *Working Paper* 3, Urban Eye (www.urbaneye.net/results/euwp3.pdf).

McLennan, G. (1996) 'Post-Marxism and the "Four sins" of Modernist theorising', *New Left Review*, 218 (July/August): 53–74.

McMahon, M. (1990) '"Net-widening": vagaries in the use of a concept', *British Journal of Criminology*, 30 (2): 121–49.

McMahon, M. (1992) *The Persistent Prison: Rethinking Decarceration and Penal Reform*. Toronto: Toronto University Press.

Meegan, R. (1989) 'Paradise postponed: the growth and decline of Merseyside's outer estates', in P. Cooke (ed.) *Localities: The Changing Face of Urban Britain*. London: Unwin Hyman, 198–234.

Mersey Partnership (1997) *Investment for the Future: Merseyside a Pool of Talent*. Liverpool: Mersey Partnership.

Merseyside Police Authority (1996) *Annual Report, 1995/1996*. Liverpool: Merseyside Police Authority.

Merseyside Police Community Strategy Safety Department (1998) *Merseyside: A Safe Place to do Business?* Liverpool: Merseyside Police, Community Strategy Safety Department.

Merseyside Socialist Research Group (1980) *Merseyside in Crisis*. Liverpool: Merseyside Socialist Research Group.

Merseyside Socialist Research Group (1992) *Genuinely Seeking Work: Mass Unemployment in Merseyside in the 1930s*. Liverpool: Liver Press.

Midwinter, E. (1971) *Old Liverpool*. Newton Abbot: David & Charles.

Miller, P. and Rose, N. (1990) 'Governing economic life', *Economy and Society*, 19 (1): 1–29.

Mills, C.W. (1970) *The Sociological Imagination*. London: Pelican Books.

Mitchell, D. (2001) 'Postmodern geographical praxis? Postmodern impulse and the war against homeless people in the "postjustice" city', in C. Minca (ed.) *Postmodern Geography: Theory and Praxis*. Oxford: Blackwell, 57–92.

Mitchell, D. (2003) *The Right to the City: Social Justice and the Fight for Public Space*. New York, NY: Guilford Press.

Molotch, H. and Logan, J. (1985) 'Urban dependencies: new forms of use and exchange in US cities', *Urban Affairs Quarterly*, 21: 143–69.

Mooney, J. (2000) *Gender, Violence and the Social Order*. London: Macmillan.

Morris, R.J. and Rodger, R. (1993) 'An introduction to British urban history, 1820–1914', in R.J. Morris and R. Rodger (eds) *The Victorian City: A Reader in British Urban History, 1820–1914*. Harlow: Addison Wesley Longman, 1–39.

Mort, F. (1987) *Dangerous Sexualities: Medico-moral Politics in England since 1830*. London: Routledge & Kegan Paul.

Muir, R. (1907) *A History of Liverpool* Liverpool: Williams & Northgate.

Murphy, A. (1995) *From the Empire to the Rialto: Racism and Reaction in Liverpool, 1918–1948*. Birkenhead: Liver Press.

Murray, C. (1990) *The Emerging Underclass*. London: Institute of Economic Affairs.

NACRO (2002) *To CCTV or not to CCTV? Current Review of Research into the Effectiveness of CCTV Systems in Reducing Crime*. London: NACRO.

Neighbourhood Renewal Unit (2003) 'Neighbourhood Renewal Fund allocations' (http://www.neighbourhood.gov.uk/88table.asp).

Neocleous, M. (2003) *Imagining the State*. Maidenhead: Open University Press.

Nerve: Liverpool's Grassroots Arts, Cultural and Social Issues Magazine (2004) Issue 2.

Norris, C. (2003) 'From personal to digital: CCTV, the panopticon, and the technical mediation of suspicion and social control', in D. Lyon (ed.) *Surveillance as Social Sorting: Privacy, Risk and Digital Discrimination*. London: Routledge, 249–81.

Norris, C. and Armstrong, G. (1998a) 'Introduction: power and vision', in C. Norris *et al.* (eds). *Surveillance, Closed Circuit Television and Social Control*. Aldershot: Ashgate: 3–18.

Norris, C. and Armstrong, G. (1998b) 'The suspicious eye', *Criminal Justice Matters*, 33 (Autumn): 10–11.

Norris, C. and Armstrong, G. (1999) *The Maximum Surveillance Society: The Rise of Closed Circuit Television*. Oxford: Berg.

Norris, C., Moran, J. and Armstrong, G. (1998) 'Algorithmic surveillance: the future of automated visual surveillance', in C. Norris *et al.* (eds) *Surveillance, Closed Circuit Television and Social Control*. Aldershot: Ashgate, 255–76.

Nott-Bower, W. (1926) *Fifty-two Years a Policeman*. London: Edward Arnold.

Oc, T. and Tiesdell, S. (1997) *Safer City Centres: Reviving the Public Realm*. London: Paul Chapman Publishing.

O'Malley, P. (1996) 'Risk and responsibility', in A. Barry *et al.* (eds) *Foucault and Political Reason: Liberalism, Neo-liberalism and Rationalities of Government*. London: UCL Press, 189–207.

O'Malley, P. (2004) 'Penal policies and contemporary politics', in C. Sumner (ed.) *The Blackwell Companion to Criminology*. Oxford: Blackwell, 184–95.

Oxford, K. (1981) *Evidence to the Scarman Inquiry, Chief Constable of Merseyside*.

Parenti, C. (1994) 'Urban militarism: "Drastic situations require drastic measures"', in *Z Magazine*, June: 47–52.

Parenti, C. (1999) *Lockdown America: Police and Prisons in the Age of Crisis*. London: Verso.

Park, R.E. (1967a) 'The city: suggestions for the investigation of human behaviour in the urban environment', in R.E. Park *et al.* (eds.) *The City*. Chicago, IL: University of Chicago Press, 1–46.

Park, R.E. (1967b) 'Community organisation and juvenile delinquency', in R.E. Park *et al.* (eds) *The City*. Chicago, IL: University of Chicago Press.

Parkinson, M. (1985) *Liverpool on the Brink: One City's Struggle against Government Cuts*. Heritage Policy Journals.

Parkinson, M. (1990) 'Leadership and regeneration in Liverpool: confusion, confrontation, or coalition?', in D. Judd and M. Parkinson (eds) *Leadership and Urban Regeneration: Cities in North America and Europe*. London: Sage, 241–307.

Parsons, T. (1951) *The Social System*. London: Routledge & Kegan Paul.

Pearce, F. and Tombs, S. (1998) 'Foucault, governmentality, Marxism', *Social and Legal Studies*, 7(4): 567–75.

Pearson, G. (1975) *The Deviant Imagination*. London: Macmillan.

Pearson, G. (1983) *Hooligan: A History of Respectable Fears*. London: Macmillan.

Peck, J. (2003) 'Geography and public policy: mapping the penal state', *Progress in Human Geography*, 27 (2): 222–32.

Peck, J. and Tickell, A. (2002) 'Neoliberalizing space', *Antipode*, 34 (3): 380–404.

Picciotto, S. (1996) 'Fragmented states and international rules of law', *Inaugural lecture, University of Lancaster*, 31 January.

Pitts, J. (1992) 'The end of an era', *Howard Journal of Criminal Justice*, 31 (2): 133–49.

Poulantzas, N. (1978) *State, Power, Socialism*. London: NLB.

Power, M.J. (1992) 'The growth of Liverpool', in J. Belcham (ed.) *Popular Politics, Riot and Labour: Essays in Liverpool History, 1790–1940*. Liverpool: Liverpool University Press.

Pratt, J. (1997) *Governing the Dangerous: Dangerousness, Law and Social Change*. Sydney: Federation Press.

Raco, M. (2003) 'New Labour, community and the future of British urban renaissance', in R. Imrie and M. Raco (eds) *Urban Renaissance? New Labour, Community and Urban Policy*. Bristol: Policy Press, 235–49.

Reeve, A. (1998) 'The panopticisation of shopping: CCTV and leisure consumption', in C. Norris *et al.* (eds) *Surveillance, Closed Circuit Television and Social Control*. Aldershot: Ashgate, 69–87.

Rigakos, G.S. (1999) 'Risk society and actuarial criminology: prospects for a critical discourse', *Canadian Journal of Criminology*, 41 (2): 137–50.

Rose, N. (1996) 'Governing "advanced" liberal democracies', in A. Barry *et al.* (eds) *Foucault and Political Reason: Liberalism, Neo-liberalism and Rationalities of Government*. London: UCL Press, 37–64.

Rose, N. (2000) 'Government and control', *British Journal of Criminology*, 40 (4): 321–39.

Rose, N. and Miller, P. (1992) 'Political power beyond the state: problematics of government', *British Journal of Sociology*, 43 (2): 173–205.

Roy, A. (1999) *The Cost of Living*. London: Flamingo.

Ruddick, S. (1996) 'Constructing difference in public spaces: race, class and gender as interlocking systems', *Urban Geography*, 17 (2): 132–51.

Rusche, G. and Kirchheimer, O. (1968) *Punishment and Social Structure*. New York, NY: Russell & Russell.

Ryan, J. (1994) 'Women, modernity and the city', *Theory, Culture and Society*, 11: 35–63.

Savage, M., Warde, A. and Ward, K. (2003) *Urban Sociology, Capitalism and Modernity*. London: Macmillan.

Schlesinger, P. and Tumber, H. (1995) *Reporting Crime: The Media Politics of Criminal Justice*. Oxford: Clarendon Press.

Schwendinger, H. and Schwendinger, J. (1975) 'Defenders of order or guardians of human rights?', in I. Taylor *et al.* (eds) *Critical Criminology*. London: Routledge & Kegan Paul, 131–6.

Scraton, P. (1985) *The State of the Police: Is Law and Order out of Control?*. London: Pluto Press.

Scraton, P. and Chadwick, K (1991) 'Theoretical and political priorities of critical criminology', in K. Stenson and D. Cowell (eds) *The Politics of Crime Control*. London: Sage, 161–85.

Scraton, P., Jemphrey, A. and Coleman, S. (1995) *No Last Rights: The Denial of Justice and the Promotion of Myth in the Aftermath of the Hillsborough Disaster*. Liverpool: Liverpool City Council.

Sharpe, J.A. (1984) *Crime in Early Modern England, 1550–1750*. London: Longman.

Shaw, C.R. and McKay, H.D. (1942) *Juvenile Delinquency and Urban Areas*. Chicago, IL: University of Chicago Press.

Shearing, C.D. (2001) 'Punishment and the changing face of governance', *Punishment and Society*, 3 (2): 203–20.

Shearing, C.D. and Stenning, P.C. (1985) 'Private Security: Implications for Social Control', Social Problems 30(5): 493–506.

Shearing, C.D. and Stenning, P.C. (1996) 'From the panopticon to Disney World: the development of discipline', in J. Muncie *et al.* (eds) *Criminological Perspectives: A Reader*. Milton Keynes: Open University Press, 413–22.

Sheptycki, J. (1997) 'Insecurity, risk suppression and segregation: some reflections on policing in the transnational age', *Theoretical Criminology*, 1 (3): 303–15.

Short, J.R. and Kim, Y.K. (1999) *Globalisation and the City*. Harlow: Longman.

Sibley, D. (1995) *Geographies of Exclusion*. London: Routledge.

Sim, J., Scraton, P. and Gordon, P. (1987) 'Introduction: crime, the state and critical analysis', in P. Scraton (ed.) *Law, Order and the Authoritarian State*. Milton Keynes: Open University Press, 1–70.

Simey, M. (1985) *Government and Consent*. London: Bedford Square Press.

Smart, C. (1984) *The Ties That Bind: Law, Marriage and the Reproduction of Patriarchal Relations*. London: Routledge & Kegan Paul.

Smith, N. (1996) *The New Urban Frontier: Gentrification and the Revanchist City*. London: Routledge.

Soja, E.W. (1995) 'Postmodern urbanization: the six Restructurings of Los Angeles', in S. Watson and K. Gibson (eds) *Postmodern Cities and Spaces*. Oxford: Blackwell, 125–37.

Soja, E.W. (1996) *Thirdspace: Journeys to Los Angeles and other Real-and-imaginary Places*. Oxford: Blackwell.

Sparks, R. (1992) *Television and the Drama of Crime: Moral Tales and the Place of Crime in Public Life*. Buckingham: Open University Press.

Social Exclusion Unit (2003) (http://www.socialexclusionunit.gov.uk/jobs_enterprise/JEconsultationPN.doc).

Sorkin, M. (1992) 'Introduction: variations on a theme park', in M. Sorkin (ed.) *Variations on a Theme Park: The New American City*. New York, NY: Hill Wang, xi–xv.

Stedman Jones, G. (1981) 'The threat of outcast London', in M. Fitzgerald *et al.* (eds) *Crime and Society: Readings in History and Theory*. London: Routledge & Kegan Paul in association with the Open University Press, 173–88.

Stenson, K. (1997) 'Rethinking liberal government – the case of crime prevention'. Paper presented to the conference *'Displacement of social policies'*, University of Jyvaskyla, Finland, 15–17 January, 1–17.

Stenson, K. (1999) 'Crime control, governmentality and sovereignty', in R. Smandych (ed.) *Governable Places: Readings on Governmentality and Crime Control*. Aldershot: Ashgate, 45–73.

Stenson, K. (2000) 'Some day our prince will come: zero tolerance policing and liberal government', in T. Hope and R. Sparks (eds) *Crime, Risk and Insecurity: Law and Order in Everyday Life and Political Discourse*. London: Routledge, 215–37.

Stenson, K. (2001) 'The new politics of crime control', in K. Stenson and R.R. Sullivan, (eds) *Crime, Risk and Justice: The politics of Crime Control in Liberal Democracies*. Cullompton: Willan Publishing, 15–28.

Stenson, K. (2002) 'Community safety in middle England – the local politics of crime control', in G. Hughes and A. Edwards (eds) *Crime Control and Community: The New Politics of Public Safety*. Cullompton: Willan Publishing, 109–39.

Sumner, C. (1994) *The Sociology of Deviance: An Obituary*. Buckingham: Open University Press.

Sumner, C. (1997) 'Social control: the history and politics of a central concept in Anglo-American sociology,' in R. Bergalli and C. Sumner (eds) *Social Control and Political Order: European Perspectives at the End of the Century*. London: Sage, 1–33.

Sumner, C. (2004) 'The social nature of crime and deviance', in C. Sumner (ed.) *The Blackwell Companion to Criminology*. Oxford: Blackwell, 3–31.

Swyngedouw, E. (1996) 'Reconstructing citizenship, the re-scaling of the state and the new authoritarianism: closing the Belgian mines', *Urban Studies*, 33 (8) 1499–521.

Taplin, E. (1994) *Near to Revolution: The Liverpool General Transport Strike of 1911*. Liverpool: Bluecoat Press.

Taylor, I. (1997) 'Crime, anxiety and locality: responding to the "condition of England" at the end of the century', *Theoretical Criminology*, 1 (1): 58–75.

Taylor, I. (1999) *Crime in Context: A Critical Criminology of Market Societies*. Oxford: Polity Press.

Taylor, I., Walton, P. and Young, J. (1973) *The New Criminology: For a Social Theory of Deviance*. London: Routledge & Kegan Paul.

Tebbit, N. (1991) *Unfinished Business*. London: Weidenfeld & Nicolson.

Thrift, N. (2000) '"Not a straight line but a curve", or, cities are not mirrors of modernity', in D. Bell and A. Haddour (eds) *City Visions*. Harlow: Prentice Hall, 233–63.

Tilley, N. (1998) 'Evaluating the effectiveness of CCTV schemes', in C. Norris *et al.* (eds) *Surveillance, Closed Circuit Television and Social Control*. Aldershot: Ashgate, 139–52.

Tombs, S. and Whyte, D. (2003) 'Scrutinising the powerful? Crime, contemporary political economy and critical social research', in S. Tombs and D. Whyte (eds) *Researching the Crimes of the Powerful: Scrutinising States and Corporations*. New York, NY: Peter Lang, 3–45.

van Swaaningen, R. (1997) *Critical Criminology: Visions from Europe*. London: Sage.

Wacquant, L. (1999) 'How penal common sense comes to Europeans: notes on the transatlantic diffusion of the neoliberal doxa', *European Societies*, 1 (3): 319–52.

Walkowitz, J. (1992) *City of Dreadful Delight: Narratives of Sexual Danger in Late Victorian London*. London: Virago Press.

Waller, P.J. (1981) *Democracy and Sectarianism: A Political and Social History of Liverpool, 1868–1939*. Liverpool: Liverpool University Press.

Ward, K.G. (2000) 'A critique in search of a corpus: re-visiting governance and re-interpreting urban politics', *Transactions, Institute of British Geographers*, 25: 169–85.

Ward, K. (2003) 'Entrepreneurial urbanism, state restructuring and civilising "new" east Manchester', *Area*, 35 (2), 116–27.

Weiss, L. (1997) 'Globalisation and the myth of the powerless state', in *New left Review*, 225 (September/October): 3–27.

Weiss, L. (1998) *The Myth of the Powerless State: Governing the Economy in a Global Era*. Oxford: Blackwell.

Williams, C.A. (2002) 'Police surveillance in historical context'. Paper given at Essex University, 7 March.

Williams, E. (1964) *Capitalism and Slavery*. London: André Deutsch.

Wilson, J.Q. (1975) *Thinking about Crime*. New York, NY: Basic Books.

Worrall, A. (1990) *Offending Women: Female Law Breakers and the Criminal Justice System*. London: Routledge.

Zukin, S. (1992) 'Postmodern urban landscapes: mapping culture and power', in S. Lash and J. Friedman (eds) *Modernity and Identity*. Oxford: Blackwell, 221–47.

Zukin, S. (1996a) 'Space and symbols in an age of decline', in A.D. King (ed.) *Representing the City: Ethnicity, Capital and Culture in the 21st Century Metropolis*. London: Macmillan, 43–59.

Zukin, S. (1996b) 'Cultural strategies of economic development and the hegemony of vision', in A. Merryfield and E. Swyngedouw (eds) *The Urbanisation of Injustice*. London: Lawrence & Wishart, 223–43.

Index

'abnormalities' 21
access in criminological research 57–80
'action at a distance' 28, 29, 35, 39, 241
Action for Cities initiative 76
Action Plan – Regeneration Agenda for Liverpool: To Develop a Safer City 145, 173–4
actuarialism 23–5, 37–8, 223, 224
'advanced liberalism' 28
Albert Dock 73, 137–8
'alcohol-free zones' 176
Allerton, displacement effect 210
Ambitions for the City Centre 138–9, 142
American cities 67
    see also Los Angeles; 'new American city'
Anti-Social Behaviour Act (2003) 111
'appeals to community' 191
'architectural policing of social boundaries' 192
armed force see militarisation
attraction, politics of see politics of attraction
authoritarian populism 224

'bargain basement economy' 147, 185
    see also secondary economy
'be-street-safe' 111–12
beggars, targeting 176–7, 179–80
BIDS (Business Improvement Districts) 69–70, 73, 175–6, 206, 233, 235
Big Issue vendors 177–9, 180
    and tensions between the police and Crime Alert 206–7
bio-power 21
Birkenhead 113, 211
black communities
    in Liverpool 99
        geographical demarcation 104, 188
        harassment 100, 103–4, 225
    policing 238
        stop-and-search practices 216n, 225, 239
    youth
        studying 242
        targeting 186
Bluecoat Triangle 138, 231, 232–3
boundaries of separation 74
'boundary erection' 74

Britain *see* UK
British Social Attitudes Survey
     (1995) 76
built environment
     boundaries of separation 74
     new urban forms 73–4
Bulger, James 106, 153
Business Improvement Districts
     (BIDS) 69–70, 73, 175–6, 206, 233,
     235
business involvement in
     partnerships 78
          effect on use of CCTV 160–1
          with the police 124–5, 166–8
by-laws 185

café bar culture 146–7, 176, 200
     and street disorder 204–5
'capitalist circuit of cultural
     knowledge' 142
capitalist power 18
capitalist state and social control 18,
     19
'carceral city' 72
carceral institutions 21
carceral punishment 20
CCTV 11, 12, 36, 39, 192–3, 240
     and crime prevention 2, 39, 153
     'democratic deficit' 3, 239
     formal regulation 153
     global use 4
     and the hidden landscape 221,
          226–9
     and 'hiding' through
          mystification 227
     and the 'human touch' 238–9
     and 'interpretive construction'
          118
     and the landscape of risk 222–6
     official discourses 2, 4–5, 13–14,
          153
     and panopticism and disciplinary
          power 21
     and partnership forms of rule 8
     political and cultural credence 3,
          35
     and the politics of risk 49
     as a practice of social ordering 3,
          30, 220, 223
          research into 50–62, 63
     and private sector expertise 6
     public credibility 163
     and the repression of differences
          237
     in the UK *see* UK
     and the unequal landscape 229–33
     see also mobile patrol CCTV
          vehicles
'CCTV Challenge Competitions' 77,
     196–9
CCTV network in Liverpool 1–2, 5,
     36, 108, 136, 213
     attitude of the police 164, 203–4
     establishment 154, 157–9
     expansion 5, 210–12
     funding 5, 158–9, 161–2
          effect of politics 196–9
          and levering local revenue
               199–201
     launch 153–4
     link up with transport network
          187
     location of cameras 163
     maintenance costs 161–2, 199–200
     management and control 162–4,
          201–3
     marketing 201–2
     'nothing to hide, nothing to fear'
          188–90
     objectives 162
     and public credibility 163
     rationalisation 159–61
     responsibility for 158–9, 201
     and school truants 187
     and 'street cleanliness' 176
     targeting the cameras 172–4,
          188–9
     and urban renaissance 155–90
     use to monitor street trading 184,
          185–6
     see also 'Operation Commando'

central government
  communication between local
    government and 123
  and crime control 39
  funding for CCTV 197–9
  see also 'joined up' government
'chains of enrolment' 33–4, 46–7
'charm school' 148
Chicago School 16, 90
children
  use of CCTV to protect 153, 154
  see also youth
Children and Young Persons Act
  (1933) 100
cities
  commodification 68–9
  and the fragmentation of morality
    and culture 16
  as 'growth machines' 67, 129,
    235–6
  information swapping 235
  marketing see marketing of cities
  neoliberal rule 117–51
  nineteenth-century see nineteenth-
    century cities
  order maintenance 3, 7
  re-marketisation 84
  and social control 6–7, 33
  see also American cities;
    'entrepreneurial cities'; 'global
    cities'; Liverpool; neoliberal
    cities
citizen-worker-socialites 226, 241
'city centre ambience' 141
city centre management agencies 140
City Centre Managers 140, 206
  attitude to street traders 181
  management of the CCTV
    network 162, 163
City Centre Strategy 142
city centres
  articulation of social order 143
  perceptions 76
  reasons for decline 79
  shift in the rule 141

City Council of Liverpool 105–6, 133,
  134, 143, 144, 205, 206
City Representatives see Town Watch
city spaces
  changing nature 222
  strategies for ordering 30, 242
  see also urban spaces
Citysafe 108–9
'Citysafe War on Crime' 111
'civic pride' 142, 149, 239
civic responsibility 81
'civil society', distinction between
  'state' and 43, 84
civility
  discourses of 81, 148
  zero tolerance culture of 147–8
'class based cues', social
  differentiation through 74
class power and social control 20
closed circuit television see CCTV
coercion 38, 225
  and neo-Marxist theories of social
    control 18–19
  popular consent for 19
Cohen's 'net-widening' thesis 25, 40
commodification of cities 68–9
'community'
  idea of 191
  as a means of government 29
  promotion 76
  support 242
  see also black communities
'community' based crime prevention
  78
'community safety' 78
conferences 123, 142
  attendance at 123
    for research purposes 61
  see also Ambitions for the City
  Centre; Merseyside: the future
consent and neo-Marxist theories of
  social control 18
Conservatives and CCTV 5, 77
'consultation as promotion' 236
'consultocracy' 192

consumerist spaces 73–4
'control culture' 18
'control societies' 223
'cosmopolitanism' 237
'creative destruction' 69
'creative management of conflict' 191
crime
    as an everyday risk 39
    displacement 210–12
    management 23
    rise in recorded 75
    as a 'soft' issue 144
    urban regeneration and 81–2
    see also 'fear of crime'
Crime Alert 54, 124, 140, 164–9
    and Big Issue vendors 178–9
    and the CCTV network in Liverpool 163
    functions 165, 168–9
    membership 165
    monthly meetings 164–5
        access to 60–1
    and normative bonding 169, 228
    about the homeless 178–9
    police role 207
    radio network problems 209–10
    and street traders 184
    tensions between the police and 167, 206–9
    unprofessional nature 210
Crime Concern 76–7
crime control
    de-politicization 24
    merging with notion of 'quality of life' 81
    and responsibilisation 38–9, 52
    and risk assessment 24
    role of CCTV 5
    sites of responsibility 24–5
Crime and Disorder Act (CDA) (1998) 5, 39, 55, 77–8, 82
Crime and Disorder Strategy for Liverpool 109
crime displacement and expansion

of the CCTV security network 210–12
Crime Hotspot fund 114
crime prevention
    and 'appeals to community' 191
    investment by the private sector 77
    merging with notion of 'quality of life' 81
    'multi-agency' and 'partnership' initiatives 31, 39
    'responsibilisation strategies' 77–8
    rethinking 239–43
    role of CCTV 2, 39, 153
    see also 'politics of prevention'; Safer Cities Projects
Crime Prevention Agency 77, 196
Crime Reduction Programme 5
Crime Reduction Unit 196
criminal element and CCTV 164
criminal justice as a social ordering practice 53–4
criminalisation, processes of 18, 19–20, 243
criminality and street trading 183–5
criminologists, and the process of city building 12
criminology 20
    access in research 57–60
    and evidence-led policy' 240
'criminology from below' 52
'critical criminology' 20, 30
'critical social research' 52
culture
    circumscribed notions 174, 228
    fragmentation 16
    see also café bar culture; 'control culture'; 'enterprise culture'; European Capital of Culture; street culture

'dangerous classes' 16, 65, 90–1
    see also black communities
Data Protection Act (1998) 215n
de-politicization of crime control 24

decentering of the state 41–2
'defining down' of deviance 40
delinquency 21, 22
'democratic deficit' 78
    in partnerships 68, 71, 123, 132
    within urban rule 239
denial, landscape of 229
deviancy 17
    'defining down' 40
    definition 151
    labelling 18, 21
    segregation and stigmatisation 25
difference, discourse of 74, 237–8
disciplinary power 20–1, 23, 24
disempowerment 226, 243
'Disneyisation' 108, 114
    see also 'theme park'
Disneyland 24
'dispersal of discipline thesis' 24–5
displacement of crime and the
    expansion of the CCTV security
    network 210–12
'dividing practices', Foucault's 227
Durkheim, Emile 13–14, 16

'economy of play' 150
'educational' approaches to the
    homeless 177–8
educational aspect of neoliberal rule
    149
'elite studies' 54
'enemies within' 19
'enterprise culture' 67–8
'entrepreneurial cities' 10, 43, 70,
    123, 129, 239
    identification of the powerful 54
    and the production of materials
        and texts 61
'entrepreneurial' forms of rule 220–1
entrepreneurial urbanism 6, 115
European Capital of Culture 138,
    150, 228, 232
'European city', Liverpool as 139,
    146–8, 181
European Market 181

evidence–led policy and criminology
    240
exclusion 226, 243
    tolerance of 81
'Exclusion Notice Schemes' 217n
'exclusionary environments' 73
'exclusionary model of public life'
    221
exclusionary-based control 25, 225

fear, discourses of 7, 84
'fear of crime' 19, 75–6, 224
    and the use of CCTV 153–4, 157
fear of the 'other' 74, 90, 224
field notes 60–1
flower sellers 100
folkdevilry 18, 40, 224, 228, 243
Foucault, Michel 14
Foucault's 'dividing practices' 227
Foucault's 'governmentality thesis'
    26–7
'freedom' 27–8, 37, 231
    in public space 233
    see also 'techniques of freedom'
functionalist theories of social
    control 15–17
funding
    the CCTV network in Liverpool 5,
        158–9, 161–2
        effect of politics 196–9
        and levering local revenue 199–
            201
    competitive bidding 68, 133, 198
    and leadership 133
    for local-level development of
        CCTV 5–6, 77
    for Merseyside Police 109–10, 127,
        161
        effect of CCTV 204
    and partnerships 134–5
    see also Objective One funding
        status

gatekeepers 57
geographical information systems

(GIS) 78, 116n
Gifford Inquiry 104
'global cities' 81
global economic restructuring 67
global prescriptions of change 4,
233–5
'globalisation' and the state 42
'Gold Zone' 175, 232
Gold Zone wardens 185
government *see* central government
Government Office for Merseyside
(GOM) 120, 122, 132–3, 134
attitude to street traders 181
role in bidding process for CCTV
198
Urban Regeneration section 109
'government through crime' 6
'government-at-a-distance' 39
governmentality 14–15, 26–9, 30, 35,
37–8
studies in 34
see also 'new governmentality'
growth, politics of 8, 67
'growth machines', cities as 67, 129,
235–6
'growth mentality' 149

hand-held video cameras 110–11
'hard' marketing issues 144
headgear, banning 187–8
'a hegemony of vision' 47
Heysel Stadium Disaster (1985) 106
hidden landscape 222
CCTV and 221, 226–9
Hillsborough Disaster (1989) 106
historical trajectory of social control
in Liverpool 87–115
A History of Liverpool 95, 104
'history of the present' group 26
'hollowed out' state 39–40, 71, 229
Home Office Crime Hotspot fund
114
homeless
study of 242
targeting 112–13, 176–80, 224

'human touch' and surveillance
238–9

idealised urban aesthetic 11
image
manipulation 69
and safety 145, 146
see also 'politics of image'; re-
imaging
'image problem' of Liverpool 11, 70,
89, 105, 106–7, 143, 160, 205
'incivilities' 79, 80
inequality 7, 18, 237–8
social removal of signs 81, 221,
227, 241
informal control 25
information gathering and sharing
by Crime Alert 166, 168–9
by the police 124–5, 168, 194, 196
information swapping between cities
235
intelligence, handling by private
security 209
'interdictory space' 237
'interpretive construction' and
CCTV 118
interventionist theories of social
control 23
interviewing the powerful 34, 61–2
interviews, responses of partnership
players 60
irresponsibilisation of groups 219,
228

'joined up' government 82
Juvenile Liaison Scheme (1949) 102

Kensington 5, 230
key players, identification 55–7

laissez-faire 84
landscape of denial 229
landscape of power 82
law, role in control strategies 18
law and order, politicisation 4, 75–6

LCCP *see* Liverpool City Centre
Partnership
leadership 68, 132–6
in the regeneration of Liverpool
205–6
liberal interventionist theories of
social control 23
liberal theories of social control 15–
17
licensing of street traders 181, 182–3
Liverpool
black communities *see* black
communities
CCTV network *see* CCTV network
in Liverpool
as a 'European city' 139, 146–8,
181
gaps between wealth and poverty
230–1
historical trajectory of social
control 10–11, 87–115
1945 to the 1980s 101–2
contemporary 107–14
from the 1980s 103–7
late eighteenth century to 1930s
94–101
'image problem' 11, 70, 89, 105,
106–7, 143, 205
leadership 132–6
marketing 137, 142–9
neoliberal state in 11, 117–51
partnership in 8, 45, 108
orchestrating 119–21
political economy from the early
nineteenth century to the 1980s
91–4
and the politics of attraction 136–
41
contextualization 141–9
population 91–2
public transport 186–7
racism 99, 104, 188
re–imaging *see* re-imaging of
Liverpool
urban regeneration *see* urban
regeneration in Liverpool

urban renaissance *see* urban
renaissance in Liverpool
Liverpool City Centre Crime
Prevention Panel 157
Liverpool City Centre Partnership
(LCCP)
funding of the CCTV network
199–201
and leadership 205–6
see also Liverpool Vision
Liverpool City Centre Plan (1993)
139
Liverpool City Council 105–6, 133,
134, 143, 144, 205, 206
Liverpool City Police 97–8, 102
Liverpool Corporation Act (1936) 93
Liverpool John Moores University
59
Liverpool Sanitary Act (1847) 96
Liverpool Vision 59, 120, 121, 133,
139–40, 141
and civic propriety 174–5
and education of service staff 148
role in funding of CCTV 161
local crime prevention 78
local government, communication
between central government and
123
local level
'making partnerships work' 122
power of the state 37
social control 31, 62–3
local populations 68
see also 'community'
local press
and the image of CCTV 163
and the image of street traders
182
and the issue of leadership 135–6
and re-imaging 129–32
'Local and Proud' initiative 175
local revenue for funding of CCTV
in Liverpool 161–2, 199–201
Local Strategic Partnerships 82
locally powerful 11, 36, 63
access to 58–9

and partnerships 119
reconfiguring 71
researching 51–3
tensions 190–2
about militarisation 193–5
and the urban fabric 146
Los Angeles 65
loss prevention strategies 24
low income in Liverpool 230
low-level social-ordering activities 228
lower-level social-ordering agents 56–7

'managerial state' 36
manpower, police see police manpower
market economies, deregulation 4
marketing
the CCTV network in Liverpool 201–2
of cities 69, 70–1, 231–2
Liverpool 137, 142–9
marketisation of security provision 65, 88
Marks & Spencer 166–7
mass private property 24
materialisation of order 6, 14, 31–2, 219
media
and the image of CCTV 163, 164
public debate in 236
use of street camera footage 227
see also press
meetings, attendance 60–1
Mersey Partnership 137, 143–4, 175
Mersey Travel 111, 186–7
Merseyside: the future 130, 142
Merseyside Development Corporation 137
Merseyside Plan (1944) 94
Merseyside Police 102
and Crime Alert
role in 207
tensions between 167, 206–9

funding 109–10, 112, 127, 161
effect of CCTV 204
and Liverpool CCTV network 158–9
attitude to 164, 203–4
effect on manpower 204
management 162
and local partnerships 109, 120, 123–7, 134
working with business 124–5, 166–8
and the private security industry 208–9
and proactive policing 113
as responsible partners 127–8
street cleansing initiatives 110–11
and Town Watch 170
Merseyside Safer Cities 109
Merseyside's Objective One funding status 138, 139
micro techniques of power 63
Militant Tendency 105–6, 133
militarisation 113, 192–6, 225
minor offenders 40
mobile patrol CCTV vehicles 112
monarchical punishment 20
moral boundaries 74
moral considerations of partnerships 46, 191
'moral environmentalism' 89–90
morality
effect of actuarialism 24
fragmentation 16
remoulding of working class 98–9
role in social control 35, 225
see also remoralisation
morality and policing social boundaries in the nineteenth-century city 89–91
contemporary correspondence 7, 221, 225, 235
morality of power 155
morphocity 87, 88
mystification, process of 227

'negative' reporting 130
Neighbourhood Renewal Funding 231
Neo-Foucauldian perspectives on social control 20–3, 220, 222–3, 234
neo-Gramscian approach 19
neo-Marxist theories of social control 14, 18–20
  and 'criminology from below' 52
neoliberal cities 231
  material contradictions 88
  and social control 65–84
  visualisation 218–43
neoliberal difference 237
neoliberal discourse and social order in British cities 75–9
neoliberal order 71–5
neoliberal rule 28, 33, 37, 66
  in cities 117–51
  co–ordination 83
  educational aspect 149
  hegemony 242
neoliberal statecraft 10, 36, 66, 71, 84, 223, 243
  development 4, 8–9
  identification of the powerful 54
neoliberal state
  approaching subjects and access 57–60
  development 83
  investigation of social control agents 50–62
  and spaces 67–71
  surveillance network 11
  tensions within 190–212
    at the highest strategic levels 190–206
    on the ground 206–12
neoliberal technologies of rule 28–9, 46
neoliberalisation 3
  as a trans-local process 4, 219
neoliberalisation of space 10
neoliberalism 62

impact on the urban spatial form 69–70
'net-widening' thesis, Cohen's 25, 40
network sampling 57
'new American city' 73
'the new criminologies of everyday life' 39
New Deal for Communities programme 230
'new governmentality' 51
New Labour and CCTV 5–6, 77
'new penology' 23, 35, 173, 224
New Police see Liverpool City Police
new primary definers 4, 8, 10, 114–15, 118, 219
  and CCTV 154, 156
  confidence of 60
  role and self-interest 43–4, 150–1
  and shifts in urban governance 70
  see also primary definers
'new right' 67
nineteenth-century cities 65
  morality and policing social boundaries 89–91
  contemporary correspondence 7, 221, 225, 235
normalisation 21
'nuisances', targeting 79

Objective One funding status 134, 138, 139, 230
offenders and CCTV 164
Officer Partnership Group 120, 144, 173
official documents, collection of 61
'Operation Change' 179
'Operation Commando' 102
'Operation Forensic Cult' 110
'Operation Goldwing' 112
'Operation Tranquility' 110
order 10
  idealogical signification and material realisation 88
  materialisation 6, 14, 31–2, 219
  meaning 8

means to achieving 191
role of the press in representation 219
see also law and order; neoliberal order; social order
order maintenance in cities 3, 7
organisations, access 57–8
'other', fear of 74, 90

panopticism 20–2, 35, 46, 241
and cities 71–2
Park, R. E. 16
Parsons, Talcott 17
'participant-as-observer' 60
partnership 55, 83
and leadership 132–6
orchestrating 119–21
and policing 121–7
partnership forms of rule 4, 45
and CCTV 8
partnership players, responses during interviews 60
partnerships 52, 66, 69, 224, 232
aspects of policing outside the control 195
between powerful local interests 47
business involvement *see* business involvement in partnerships
constitution of the state through 37
for crime prevention 39
'democratic deficit' 68, 71, 123, 132
and funding 134–5
and 'image' and 'attractiveness' 145
and the locally powerful 119
'making partnerships work' 122, 191
and neoliberal statecraft 4, 223
political and moral considerations 46, 191
tensions between the public and 191–2

and urban government 68, 83
see also public-private partnerships; responsible partners
party politics 134
persuasion, politics of 191
pitch spaces 181
violations of 184
'place attractiveness' 145
'place entrepreneurs' 70
place identity, reshaping 142–3
place management 70
'pluralisation' of government 27
police
effectiveness 75
as information brokers 124–5, 168, 194, 196
militarisation 113, 192–6, 225
relations with the press 130–1
as responsible partners 127–8
see also Liverpool City Police; Merseyside Police
Police Act (1964) 101
Police Court and Prison Gate Mission 98
Police Intelligence Unit 169
police manpower 75
effect of CCTV 204
in Merseyside 110
policing
aspects outside partnership control 195
of black communities 238
see also private policing; public order policing
policing in Liverpool
1945 to the 1980s 101–2
contemporary 107–14
from the 1980s 103–5
late eighteenth century to the 1930s 95, 97–8, 99–101
and partnership 121–7
see also Merseyside Police
policing social boundaries in the nineteenth-century city 89–91

contemporary correspondence 7,
221, 225, 235
political considerations of
partnerships 46, 191
political economy in Liverpool early
nineteenth century to the 1980s
91–4
political economy of surveillance
and risk 35, 238
political hierarchy, studying up
118–19
'political infighting' 134
'political technologies' 20
politicisation of law and order 4,
75–6
politics
effect on funding of CCTV 196–9
see also de-politicization; party
politics
politics of attraction in Liverpool
136–41
contextualization 141–9
'politics of change', central-local
tensions 198–9
politics of growth 8, 67
'politics of image' 66, 108, 196, 236
politics of persuasion 191
'politics of prevention' 83
politics of social ordering 241
'politics of truth' 223
politics of vision 118
CCTV as a tool 187
challenging 236–9
popular masses, relationship
between social control and 19
population of Liverpool 91–2, 105
education 147
see also local population
post-Fordist urban economy 72
post-Foucauldian perspectives 9, 14,
46, 47
post-Marxist theories of social
control 20
post-state understanding of social
control 9

postmodern city 72
poststructuralism 14, 20
Poulantzas, N. 18–19
power 3, 15, 226
beyond the state 26–9, 35
landscape 82
morality 155
neo-Foucauldian perspectives 20–
3, 46
normative dimensions 84, 223
spatialisation 72
see also capitalist power; proper
objects of power; state power
power of scrutiny 219
relationship of street cameras to
189
unequal 227
the powerful 3, 10, 14, 36
identification 10, 54–5, 239
interviewing 61–2
scrutinising 51–3
see also locally powerful
powerful local interests,
partnerships between 47
powerful organisations, access 57–8
press
and the image of CCTV 13, 163
role in 'representing order' 219
see also local press
press-police relations 130–1
primary definers 8, 43–4
composition of groups 55
see also new primary definers
prisons, panoptic regime 20–1
'the private, distinction between 'the
public' and 40–1
private policing 24
private property, mass 24
private sector
increased role 6, 45, 68, 140, 156
and use of CCTV 156, 159–60
investment in crime prevention 77
see also public-private
partnerships
private security industry

growth 75
and the handling of intelligence
209
police attitude 208–9
privatisation of public space 51, 73,
233
profit maximisation 24, 225
proper objects of power 8, 46, 154,
172–4, 189, 213
'pseudo-public space' 65
psychology 20
'the public'
distinction between 'the private'
and 40–1
meaning and scope 233, 236
tensions between the goals of
partnership decision-making
processes and 191–2
public anxiety 75–6
public interest 192, 223, 233, 236
CCTV as a response 13–14, 17
definition 131
public order policing 81
in the 1930s 101
militarisation of 193–6
and urban renewal and
regeneration 155
'public realm' 79
public space
destruction of accessible 65
difference and diversity in 237
erosion of idea 232, 233
meanings and uses 4, 66
privatisation 51, 73, 233
safety of women and children
153, 154
visions 3
public transport in Liverpool 186–7
public-private partnerships 4, 8, 10,
31, 67
mindset of 50–1
punishment, techniques of 20
purification of the streets 174–6

'quality of environment' and street

trading 183
'quality of life' 71, 81, 143, 219
merging of 'crime control/
prevention' with 81
'quality of life' policing 81, 114

racism in Liverpool 99, 104, 188, 241
radio network problems for Crime
Alert 209–10
Rapid Response Unit (RRU) 187
re-imaging of Liverpool 88, 137, 138,
142–9
and the press 129–32
use of CCTV 156, 160
re-marketisation of cities 84
reclamation strategies
justification 79–80
revanchist 235
regeneration see urban regeneration
'regime of truth' 223
Regional Development Agencies 68
rehabilitation 23
remoralisation of risk 30
remoralisation and street
reclamation 79–82, 83
in Liverpool 151
rescaling of the state 10, 40–4
researchers, role 60–1
resources, allocation see funding
'respectability', discourses of 225
responsibilisation
of potential victims 112
and the state 38–40
see also irresponsibilisation
responsibilisation process 127–9,
221, 223
responsibilisation strategies 38, 39,
46–7, 127, 149
for crime prevention 77–8
'responsibilised citizen' 40, 218–19
'responsibilised liberty' 27–8
responsibilised self-governance,
objects of 147–8
responsibility
for the CCTV network in

Liverpool 158–9, 201
proportioning of 23
see also civic responsibility
responsible partners and the
  responsibilisation process 127–9
retailers, working with the police
  166–8
revanchism 221, 234, 235–6
'right to the city' 189, 190
risk 14
  and CCTV 154, 222–6
  remoralisation 30
  and social control 23–6, 35, 192,
    220
  and the status of crime 39
'risk' orientated crime and safety
  initiatives 79
'risk society' 25
'risk suppression' 66

Safer Cities Projects 39, 76, 81
Safer Merseyside Partnership 109
safety 10, 66, 219
  and 'image' 145, 146
  public concern 75–6
  and the regeneration process
    173–4
  of women 241
  see also 'community safety'
sampling strategies 55–7
school truants 111, 186–7
'Scotland Division' 95–6
scrutiny, power of *see* power of
  scrutiny
secondary economy 185, 228
  Liverpool late eighteenth century
    to 1930s 97, 99
  see also 'bargain basement
    economy'
security 10, 73, 144
  and CCTV 13
  marketisation 65, 88
  public concern 75–6
self-governance, responsibilised
  147–8

senior police involvement in the
  regeneration process 126–7
  and militarisation 195–6
separation, boundaries of 74
service-based economy 148–9
Shop Lifting Squad 169
shoplifters 208
  see also 'travelling shoplifters'
shopping malls 73–4, 79
Single Regeneration Budget 39, 81,
  134
skateboarders 187
slave trade 91
'snowball' sampling 57
social boundaries
  policing 7
    in the nineteenth-century 89–91
  see also architectural policing of
    social boundaries'
social control 2
  at the local level 31, 62–3
  in cities 6–7, 33
  and class power 20
  coercive aspects 19
  constituent elements 49
  exclusionary potential 51
  historical trajectory in Liverpool
    10–11, 87–115
  interpretation of contemporary 6–
    8
  liberal and functionalist theories
    15–17
  liberal interventionist theories 23
  Neo-Foucauldian perspectives
    20–3, 220, 222–3, 234
  neo-Marxist theories 18–20
  and the neoliberal city 65–84
  new orthodoxy 4–6
  normative strategy 220, 223
  political-moral nature 3
  post-state understanding 9
  and power beyond the state 26–9
  relationship between the popular
    masses and 19
  responsibility for the enactment 40

and risk 23–6, 35, 192, 220
social reaction theory 17–18
and the state 10, 14, 18, 155,
    225–6
and state sovereignty 36–7
techniques and norms 153–213
theoretical issues 9
social control agents 50–62
social differentiation through 'class
    based cues' 74
social discipline, decline 19
'social ecology' approach 16
social exclusion see exclusion
social hierarchy, studying up 118–19
social incivilities 79, 80
social inequality see inequality
social justice 237, 241
social order 2
    articulation 143
    in contemporary British cities
        75–9
    effect of cities 16
social ordering 48–9
    CCTV and 3, 8, 154, 164, 226
        research into 50–62, 63
    and criminal justice 53–4
    politics 241
    trajectory 221–2
'social ordering practices' 47
    CCTV as 53–4
social reaction theory of social
    control 17–18
social relations, normative ordering
    44–50
social removal of signs of inequality
    81, 221, 227, 241
social sciences 21
'social sorting' 221, 238
'social sovereignty' 38
social surveillance 8
'social-control talk' 9
societal folk-devils 18, 40, 224, 228,
    243
sociospatial control and CCTV 3, 30
'soft' marketing issues 144

'soul training' 20
sovereignty and the state 36–8
    effect of large commercial
        complexes 24
space 6
    and neoliberal states 67–71
    neoliberalisation 10
    ordering 74, 82
    relationship between control
        practices and demarcation of 7
    strategic importance 222
    see also consumerist spaces; pitch
        spaces; public space; urban
        spaces
spatial reclamation 138
spatial reordering
    components 225
    see also CCTV; public order
    policing
spatialisation
    city visions and street reclamation
        141–9
    processes 62
spatialisation of power 72
spatialisation of risk 223
the state 69
    distinction between 'civil society'
        and 43, 84
    and the normative ordering of
        social relations 44–50
    power beyond 26–9, 35
    reconstitution 4
    rescaling 10, 40–4
    and 'responsibilisation' 38–40
    role 14
    and social control 10, 14, 18, 155,
        225–6
    and sovereignty 36–8
        effect of large commercial
            complexes 24
    transformation 229
    and urban centres 65–6
    see also neoliberal state
state boundaries 42
state coercion see coercion

state power 10, 14, 15, 22–3, 29, 30–1, 37, 220, 240
  distinction between 'the public' and 'the private' 40–1
  as 'sociospatial activity' 42
state surveillance 41
'state'/'market' distinctions in partnerships 4
state/society relations 43, 84
statecraft, process of 34
stop-and-search practices 104, 105
  and the black community 216n, 225, 239
Stores' Committee 120, 140–1, 165, 175
  argument for use of CCTV 160–1
  attitude to the homeless 177
  attitude to street traders 181, 182–3
  and funding of the CCTV network 200
  see also Crime Alert
street cameras see CCTV
'street cleanliness' 70, 175–6
  initiatives by Merseyside Police 110–11
  Liverpool late eighteenth century to 1930s 98
  and street trading 183
street culture 187–8, 228
street management 174–6
  trans-local 220
street reclamation and remoralisation 79–82
street surveillance see CCTV
street sweeping 148–9
street trading 166, 180–6
  study of 242
  and tensions between the police and Crime Alert 206–7
Street Trading: The Facts 182
studying up 9, 10, 51–3, 63, 118–19, 220–1, 223
'suitable enemies' 237
surveillance beyond the state 41

surveillance methods
  traditional 239
  see also CCTV; stop-and-search practices
surveillance society
  challenge to 240
  inequities 237
'surveillance studies' 35–6
'suspect communities' 89
suspicion, categories of 185
'suspiciousness', interpretive basis 118
'sustainable projects' 135

'techniques of freedom', camera networks as 222
'technologies of fear' 224
technologies of rule 27
  within neoliberal government 28–9
tensions within the neoliberal state 190–212
  between the locally powerful 190–2
territorial control and state institutions 36–8
territorial ordering 36
'theme park'
  characterization 73, 147–8, 228
  see also Disneyisation
'Third Way politics 82, 232
tourism in Liverpool 137–8
town centre management (TCM) 80
town centre managers 80
  see also City Centre Managers
Town Watch 148, 164, 170–2
'Townsafe' initiative 113
Toxteth 103–4
'Toxteth Section' 103
trans-local neoliberalisation process 4, 219
trans-local street management 220
'translation' 29
'travelling shoplifters' 211
'Travelsafe' 111

Truancy Watch 187
truants from school 111, 186–7
'turf politics' 134

UK
and CCTV 3, 7–8, 75, 77
local-level developments 5–6
effect of a neoliberal market
philosophy 45
neoliberal discourse and social
order 75–9
'partnership' approach 66, 67
and revanchist policies of
reclamation 235
undercover surveillance of the
homeless 178
unemployment in Liverpool 105, 230
history of 93–4
youth 101
unequal landscape, CCTV and
229–33
'unhealthy society' 14
unlicensed sellers 185
urban aesthetic landscape
creation 137
idealised 11
threats to 174, 182
urban centres 7
and the state 65–6
see also cities
urban degeneration 66
urban fabric
condition of 145
'situational measures' 145–6
urban governance
and partnerships 68, 83
shifts 4, 70
urban landscape, re-imaging and
marketisation 142–9
'urban patriotism' 236
urban public space see public space
urban reform programmes in the
nineteenth-century city 90
urban regeneration 49, 68
as a cause of street disorder 204–5

and 'city centre ambience' 141–9
and crime and disorder 81–2
global discourses 235
local press as agents 129–32
role of the police 125–7
frustration with 194–5
undermining by police initiatives
196
underpinning ideological
frameworks 119
'urban regeneration' initiatives 10
urban regeneration in Liverpool
141–9
key agencies 136–41
leadership 205–6
urban renaissance in Liverpool 108–
9, 114
as a cause of street disorder 205
and CCTV 155–90
and culture 228
and influencing Merseyside
Police 196
neoliberal discourses 117–18
'unwelcome' groups and
activities 173, 189
urban restructuring 2, 72, 74–5
and CCTV 36
urban rule 74
'democratic deficit' 239
urban spaces 2, 43
demarcation 221
see also city spaces
urban surveillance cameras see
CCTV
USA
'partnership' approach 66
see also American cities

Victorian morality 90–1
video cameras, hand-held 110–11
vision, politics of see politics of
vision
visual surveillance see CCTV
visualisation of the neoliberal city
218–43

Watch Committees 97, 101
welfare objectives 70, 230
'what works' 50
women
    in Liverpool
        employment 93
        harassment 100
    safety 241
    use of CCTV to protect 153, 154
Women's Shelter 98
working class morality, remoulding
    98–9
'The World in One City' 150, 233–4

'yob tank' 216n
'Yob Tzar' 111

'Your City, Your Choice' 149
youth
    banning of headgear 187–8
    in Liverpool
        in the 1930s 100–1
        1945 to the 1980s 102
    low pay 230
    policing 111, 186–8
    street culture 187–8, 228
    study of 242
    see also children

zero tolerance culture of civility 147–
    8
zero-tolerance policing 81
    in Liverpool 113–14